STUDYING WRITING

WRITTEN COMMUNICATION ANNUAL
An International Survey of Research and Theory

Series Editors
Charles R. Cooper, *University of California, San Diego*
Sidney Greenbaum, *University College, London*

Written Communication Annual provides an international forum for cross-disciplinary research on written language. The **Annual** presents the best of current research and at the same time seeks to define new research possibilities. Its purpose is to increase understanding of written language and the processes of its production and comprehension. Each volume of the **Annual** focuses on a single topic and includes specially commissioned papers from several countries.

Volumes in This Series
Volume 1   STUDYING WRITING: Linguistic Approaches
Charles R. Cooper and Sidney Greenbaum
Volume 2   DISCOURSE AND DISCRIMINATION (tent.)
Teun A. van Dijk

STUDYING WRITING:
Linguistic Approaches

edited by

CHARLES R. COOPER,
University of California, San Diego

SIDNEY GREENBAUM,
University College, London

WRITTEN COMMUNICATION ANNUAL
An International Survey of
Research and Theory

Volume 1

SAGE PUBLICATIONS
The Publishers of Professional Social Science
Beverly Hills   London   New Delhi

For information address:

SAGE Publications, Inc.
275 South Beverly Drive
Beverly Hills, California 90212

SAGE Publications India Pvt. Ltd.
M-32 Market
Greater Kailash I
New Delhi 110 048 India

SAGE Publications Ltd
28 Banner Street
London EC1Y 8QE
England

Printed in the United States of America

International Standard Book Number 0-8039-2372-4
International Standard Serial Number 0883-9298

FIRST PRINTING

Contents

Preface

This volume inaugurates the *Written Communication Annual: An International Survey of Research and Theory*. The *Annual* is part of Sage Publications' new publishing program in composition studies, a program that includes *Written Communication: A Quarterly Journal of Research, Theory, and Application. Written Communication,* now in its third year, is edited by John Daly and Stephen Witte.

In each issue, the journal publishes articles on diverse topics in composition studies. By contrast, the *Annual* focuses on a single topic, elaborating it from a number of perspectives; unlike many annuals, it does not review research from the previous year. Further, the *Annual* brings together research on a topic from scholars in several countries, in particular ensuring that North American and European scholars are represented in each volume. This international scope of the *Annual* is reflected in its Advisory Board and also in that one series editor is American, the other British.

Over the years, the *Annual* will focus on a wide range of topics within the interdisciplinary field of written communication, including topics as divergent as document design and the history of writing instruction. The editorial policy statement on page 2 suggests the range of possible topics. We have already scheduled volumes on discourse and discrimination (1986, Teun van Dijk, editor) and international studies of writing achievement (1987, Alan Purves, editor). We welcome suggestions for future volumes from our readers.

—*Charles R. Cooper and*
Sidney Greenbaum
Series Editors

Introduction

Written discourse and composition are being studied pro-
ductively these days from perspectives as different as literary theory
and computer simulation. In this volume, we collect studies from the
perspective of linguistics.

The studies presented here illustrate the importance of text linguistics and discourse analysis for research on written communication. They also illustrate the value of analyzing in depth the text
characteristics of particular genres, such as news stories, narratives,
and problem-solutions. In addition to presenting the results of
analyses of written texts from a linguistic perspective, this first volume of the *Written Communication Annual* proposes productive
methods for discourse analysis and identifies new directions for
research on written communication.

The chapters in this volume deal with a number of major topics:

- differences between speaking and writing
- thematic organization of sentences in text
- alternation of given and new information in text
- the influence of framing decisions on topical focus during composing
- the structure of news stories
- the structure of problem-solution texts
- the relation of commentary to text
- the relation of conversation to text
- the contributions of propositional and framing analysis to cognitive
  modeling

In the opening chapter, Wallace Chafe contrasts speaking and
writing, concluding that "the two modes of production almost in-

evitably lead to substantially different products." Drawing on samples of one adult's speaking and writing, Chafe surveys the major differences in these two modes. By contrasting written with spoken samples, he is able to establish many of the special constraints and possibilities of writing.

Jan Firbas provides a careful, comprehensive introduction to functional sentence perspective (FSP), a theory of "how the semantic and syntactic structures of the sentence function in fulfilling the communicative purpose" of the sentence. FSP requires that we examine a sentence both in the context of previous sentences in that text and also in the text's situational context. Firbas offers an FSP analysis of three brief texts: fictional, journalistic, and epistolary.

William Vande Kopple places FSP in historical perspective and explicates its various current formulations, noting the significance of Firbas's work on FSP. Vande Kopple chooses the *given/new* formulation for analyzing texts. He explains that, as with all FSP formulations, dividing a sentence into given and new information enables us to learn "how a text got to various points . . . where the text has been . . . what information has set the stage for other information . . . how the text hangs together." Relying in part on Chafe's early work, Vande Kopple presents careful definitions of *given, new,* and *information* and then goes on to summarize his recent research on the readability of brief texts in which given (predictable) information precedes new information in sentences. Vande Kopple concludes with a wide-ranging review of new developments in the definition and analysis of given and new information in texts. Readers will value his closing list of possibilities for needed interdisciplinary research based on the given/new distinction—research on "writers, information, texts, and responses to texts, in English and in other languages."

Vande Kopple suggests that analyzing written texts may inform us about the processes used by writers and readers. Stephen Witte and Roger Cherry make a strong case for learning about the writing process from analyzing written products. In an analysis of five essays written for the same assignment and of two reading-aloud protocols, Witte and Cherry show how linguistic notions of framing and topical focus can inform us about writers' decisions to translate their discourse purposes into readable text. Their use of the concept of framing anticipates Frederiksen's chapter at the end of this volume.

The chapters by Firbas, Vande Kopple, and Witte and Cherry illustrate particular text linguistic methodologies—FSP and

framing—for analyzing any written discourse. The next two chapters provide detailed global analyses of particular discourse types:
Teun van Dijk analyzes news reports, and Michael Hoey analyzes
problem-solution essays. From his analysis of hundreds of news
reports from many countries, van Dijk proposes a schema for news
discourse. After providing a theoretical framework for discourse
schema, he outlines in detail the categories of news discourse, drawing on four news reports of the same event as examples. He shows
how his schemata are useful for interpreting news reports—for
example, his conclusions that "news discourse is primarily about
discourse" and "most of its sources are textual"—and then proposes
several new lines of research on news discourse.

Michael Hoey begins by analyzing the familiar problem-solution
pattern in written discourse and ends by cautioning us against positing distinct patterns in written discourse. He also proposes that we
may be able to understand written discourse patterns only by studying their relation to conversation. Using several examples from
varied sources of writing—newspapers, magazines, scholarly
books—Hoey demonstrates that patterns of organization in written
discourse are nonstructural and interactive. They are nonstructural
in that we cannot fully predict a discourse pattern: Each one has too
many possible variations. They are interactive in that they can be
described and understood only by reference both to the reader and
to speech acts performed in written discourse.

Like Hoey, Chaim Rabin is interested in the relation of written
discourse to conversation. Examining the discourse status of commentary on texts, he concludes that the commentator takes the place
of conversant clarifying remarks for another conversant who invites
clarification by remarks or questions. Rabin defines a commentator
as "a person who shares the expectations and presuppositions of his
or her own society and period, and at the same time has the skill of
applying them to another way of expression through long experience with texts of that culture or period or by trained intuition."
Rabin's examples come from commentaries on Genesis and Exodus
by Rashi, a respected eleventh-century commentator on the Hebrew
Bible.

In the concluding chapter, Carl Frederiksen shows how cognitive
scientists are using discourse analysis to study text structures and
readers' understanding of texts. Frederiksen explains that current
cognitive theories distinguish between textual structures by which
meanings are encoded and communicated and conceptual struc-

tures by which knowledge from texts is represented in memory. Conceptual structures are assumed to be represented as propositions and as frames, while textual structures are evident as clause/ sentence structures and text-level structures, the text-level structures describable in part by the text features reviewed by Firbas, Vande Kopple, Witte, and Cherry in other chapters of this volume. Readers unfamiliar with recent work of cognitive scientists on discourse analysis and cognitive modeling might want to read the first two sections of Frederiksen's paper, "Cognitive Theories" and "Multilevel Models," and then skip to his final section, "Applications," to see the significance of the work he reviews in the remainder of the chapter. Frederiksen discusses semantic or conceptual models, cognitive discourse analysis, propositional analysis, and frame analysis, illustrating propositional and frame analysis on a brief text.

—*Charles R. Cooper*
La Jolla

—*Sidney Greenbaum*
London

I

Writing in the Perspective of Speaking

WALLACE CHAFE

I have spent most of my academic life looking at speaking. To say that I have "looked at" it is both paradoxical and accurate. Spoken language is produced to be listened to, not looked at, and yet our scientific tradition is such that we don't know what to do with anything unless we can put it on paper, spread it out on a desk, store it away in a drawer, cut it up and paste it together, and in all ways treat it as if it were a static thing. Working with various American Indian languages that had seldom or never been reduced to writing, I often felt pangs of discomfort. It was always clear that *reduced* was an accurate word. What ended up on paper was only a pale reflection of the rich, involving conversations, rituals, and stories that were the original experiences. It may be because of this sort of background that influential linguists earlier in this century concluded that "writing is not language, but merely a way of recording language by means of visible marks" (Bloomfield, 1933, p. 21; compare Saussure, 1960, pp. 23-24; Sapir, 1921, p. 20).

The arguments for the primacy of spoken language have often been repeated. Speaking has been with us from the very beginning of human history, whereas writing as we know it has existed for only a brief period. Even during most of that brief period there have been only a few people able to read and write, widespread literacy being a very recent phenomenon. Speaking is learned naturally and early by every normal child, whereas writing and reading are usually acquired through deliberate instruction, and the instruction depends on already acquired speaking abilities (see the discussions of these points in Hockett, 1958, p. 4). I might add that the number of individuals who ever learn to write well is impressively small. Writing does not seem to be an ability that is natural to people in the way speaking is.

It is clear now, however, that typical writing has its own properties that are different from those of typical speaking. (I use the word *typical* because it is always possible to find examples of writing that are not very different from speaking, and conversely.) Writing is ordinarily produced under circumstances that are radically different from those of speaking. It is not at all surprising that a different form (or, better, different forms) of language should have evolved as a result. Written language, one can say, has adapted to new environments of production, reception, and preservation (see Pawley and Syder, 1983).

What are these different circumstances? Speaking, of course, uses the medium of sound, writing that of sight. And speaking is typically performed in a face to face, interactive situation, writing typically in social isolation. Both the sound medium and the social interactiveness enforce a rapidity on the production of spoken language that is foreign to writing. The pace of speech is likely to be roughly in synchrony with the pace of thought, so that speaking enables language and thought to advance through time in a more or less comfortable partnership. The pace of a listener must be similar; otherwise there could be no parallel flow of ideas in two conversing minds. This pace is fostered by the interactiveness of speaking. Speakers who slow down or hesitate too long risk being interrupted or losing their audience's attention. And speakers are under constant pressure to make what they say informative and relevant; the social context imposes an on-line evaluation of their product. Furthermore, the evanescence of that product means that speakers can only modify it, once it has been produced, by saying something overtly different. That is, whatever revising takes place is laid bare before the listener.

Writing is different in all these respects. Making visible marks, whether by pen, pencil, typewriter, or word processor, is necessarily a slower process than speaking. At the same time, and for the same reason, it is a process that writers can exploit at their own leisurely pace. Although, on the one hand, writers may be hobbled by the mechanical slowness of writing, they are simultaneously freed from the insistent temporal demands of speaking. Thus they acquire the time to shape their language more finely to their ideas. They are freed as well from the need to keep their audience's immediate attention, to make what they say immediately informative and relevant. (To be sure, holding a *reader's* attention may in some ways be even more difficult, but writers can attend to that need without the same pressure of time, and the kind of skill involved is not the same.) Finally, writers have extensive power to revise what they have done, polishing it again and again if they are so inclined. And this revising process is entirely hidden from the eventual audience.

Writers, in short, have both unusual freedom and unusual opportunity in the production of language. They are free of the temporal constraints and the social pressures of face to face interaction, and they have the opportunity to change, as they will, what they have done. For these reasons writing has an extraordinary flexibility. There is a sense in which writers can produce language of any kind whatsoever, and in fact the variety of written forms they have produced is enormous, from the easy flow of Agatha Christie to the obscurity of German philosophers, from the pedantry of Ph.D. dissertations to the often sublime beauty of Shakespeare.

I certainly want to avoid suggesting that spoken language is lacking in variety of resources. Very different styles of speaking may be associated with conversing, telling stories, lecturing, orating, reciting rituals, and so on, and there may be marked individual differences among conversationalists, storytellers, lecturers, orators, and ritualists. All these different styles, however, are subject to constraints inherent in the circumstances of speaking but absent from those of writing. I will suggest below what some of these constraints are, and ways that writers may ignore them if they wish.

I am going to point out some of the ways in which written language has exploited its flexibility by comparing the spoken and written output of one articulate, and also literate, individual. I will illustrate how various features, though incipiently present in spoken language, may flourish in the hands of a writer, and in a few cases I will point to examples where other writers have exaggerated the same features for one or another literary effect.[1]

THE INTONATION UNITS OF SPEECH

There are apparently strong constraints on the amount of information that can be active in a person's mind at any one time, as well as on the length of time a particular item of information can remain active. What is "active" can be thought of as being in the focus of a person's consciousness (Chafe, 1980), or in what has traditionally been called "short-term memory." If we look at spoken language in this perspective, we find that it is produced in a series of spurts, or "intonation units," each of which typically contains about five words in English, and typically takes about two seconds to utter. Each intonation unit is uttered with a coherent intonation contour, ending usually with one of a small set of pitch patterns of the kind associated with the ends of phrases or clauses. Each typically begins with a pause. It is natural to view an intonation unit as a linguistic expression of the particular information that is active in the speaker's mind at the time it is uttered. If that is a valid interpretation, then intonation units provide us with a unique window into the nature of information flow within the minds of speakers.

It will be useful to look at a specific example of spoken language from this point of view. The following is excerpted from a transcript of a conversation during which people were talking about times in their lives when they were in grave danger. The sequences of two, three, and four dots at the beginnings of lines indicate short, medium, and long pauses. The commas and periods at the ends of lines indicate pitch patterns of the kinds perceived as signaling the ends of clauses or sentences respectively. (In a few cases, as in 2, the speaker made a false start that was broken off with no such final pitch contour.)

(1) . . . Well oddly enough it was in Japan.

(2) . . Which is not where you'd . . you know

(3) . . where most of the time I feel extreme—ly safe.

(4) . . . But . . . the first time I was in Japan,

(5) . . . in nineteen fifty . . nine,

(6) . . . I was out on the street,

(7) . . late at night,

(8) . . in downtown Kyoto,

(9) . . . wi—th

(10) . . uh in the bar district,

(11) . . . with an American man,

(12) . . . a—nd uh— . . we . . neither one of us had thought about the fact that that it was the anniversary of the bombing of Hiroshima.

(13) . . . And this was fifty nine.

(14) . . So that was . . . the fourteenth anniversary.

(15) . . It wasn't an . . . enormous long time afterwards.

(16) . . And . . a . . man who was . . . either drunk or crazy,

(17) . . . uh— came up to us on the street,

(18) . . and started speaking English.

(19) . . And saying come . . to my house.

(20) . . . Come to my house.

(21) . . . And he was . . . very peculiar.

(22) . . . A—nd uh— you know we said,

(23) . . . No.

(24) We can't.

(25) . . We're busy.

(26) . . . And so forth and so on.

(27) And then he started saying come to my house tonight you will die.

(28) . . . Tonight the bomb will fall on Hiroshima.

(29) . . . And come to my house.

(30) . . and just sort of . . repeating all of this . . over and over again.

(31) . . . a—nd . . . we—

(32) . . . well then he pulled out a knife.

(33) . . . and he started . . . after the guy I was with.

(34) . . . who sort of started circling,

(35) . . . well you know I . . . summoned a cab.

(36) . . . a—nd . . the man I was with jumped in the front seat of the cab,

(37) . . . and . . I

(38) . . oh no . . into the back seat of the cab,

(39) . . . a—nd . . . I . . got in with him,

(40) . . and the guy ran around and got in the front seat of the cab.

(41) . . . at which point we . . . started out the doors of the cab.

(42) . . . a—nd . . I said to the driver,

(43) . . that massugu.

(44) . . straight ahead.

(45) I didn't know I knew the word.

(46) . . . And the cab took off.

(47) . . . And that was the . . end of the experience.

(48) . . But . . uh . . it was

(49) . . eh it's always s—tayed with me,

(50) as how you can know words,

(51) and not know that you know them you know.

(52) . . . . Mm the intensity of it at the ti—me,

(53) was pretty awful.

(54) . . . . Mm because in . . . in good part,

(55) we were also . . . you know not only concerned about taking care
of ourselves,
(56) but also not . . . wanting . . to start . . some sort of incident.

This excerpt should provide some feeling for the general nature of
spoken intonation units. But what is their relevance for writing?

WRITTEN PUNCTUATION UNITS

The following is a piece of writing produced by the same person
who related the spoken episode above. It is taken from an academic
journal article in which the writer discussed ways in which certain
Japanese *noo* dramas were transformed into puppet plays. The
excerpt begins with a plot description, and then shifts to an expository style in the second paragraph:

Set at the isolated beach of Suma perhaps in the ninth century,
Matsukaze has as its principal characters the ghosts or spirits of two
dead fisherwomen, the sisters Matsukaze and Murasame. An itinerant
priest, seeing on the shore at Suma a curious looking pine, inquires of
a villager and learns that the tree is linked with the memory of the two
dead fisherwomen. Evening comes as the priest is reciting sutras and
invocations for the repose of the souls of the two dead women. The
spirits of the women present themselves to the priest and act out
before him the misery of their lives spent dipping salt from sea brine.
They tell of an interlude of three years when they were loved by the
courtier Ariwara no Yukihira, an exile at Suma, and speak of the
intensity of their longing after Yukihira returned to the capital. The
ghost of Matsukaze becomes convinced that Yukihira has returned.
Crying "I love him still!" she approaches a pine on the beach which, to
her deluded eyes, appears to be her lover. The chorus speaking for
Murasame and Matsukaze entreats the priest to pray for their rest.
The ghosts of the women vanish as dawn breaks. The noo ends with
lines of intentionally ambiguous beauty which play on the meaning of
the women's names: *autumn rain* (Murasame) and *pine wind* (Matsukaze). The spirits have vanished with the chorus's repeated final
line, "Only the wind in the pines remains."

Matsukaze is of the relatively familiar noo type in which a priest
encounters the spirit of a dead person, the spirit tells of its attachment

to the past, and then vanishes, imploring the priest to pray for its repose. In *Semimaru,* on the other hand, the *tsure* Semimaru and the *shite* Sakagami are both creatures of the ordinary phenomenological world, and they are equally important and interesting. In fact, the play was originally titled *Sakagami.* There is no hint of final priestly intercession leading to salvation; rather, *Semimaru* concludes without resolution as brother and sister part to meet unknown futures.

Is there anything here that corresponds to the intonation units of speaking? Since intonation units are identified in the first instance by prosodic criteria (pitch contours and hesitations), and since written language is notoriously impoverished so far as its representation of prosody is concerned, we might wonder how anything analogous could appear in writing. Behind that question lies another that is more interesting: Do writers (and readers) have intonation in mind at all, or is written language a kind from which all prosodic features have been removed?

When writing is read aloud, of course, it does have intonation, though the reader may use pitch contours quite different from the spoken norm. The very fact that people assign various kinds of peculiar prosody in reading aloud might suggest that such prosody is invented solely for that purpose, and that written language is, in itself, devoid of intonation, stress, and pauses. But introspection suggests that as both writers and readers we do assign such features to whatever we are writing or reading. For example, when I wrote the last sentence I had in mind a high pitch and strong stress on the word "do." You, as reader, may or may not have read it that way, but in either case you are likely to know what you did. I am going to assume that writers and readers assign intonation, stress, and pauses to written language, though the writing itself provides less than optimal representations of them.

Intonation *is,* of course, indicated to *some* extent—often with punctuation, less often with italics. Again I invite you to consider how you read the last sentence. Such introspection suggests that periods, commas, and other less frequent punctuation marks signal the boundaries of stretches of language to which we tacitly assign coherent intonation contours, as well as following hesitations. If that is true, then punctuation marks are at least rough delimiters of units that are analogous to intonation units. The correspondence between these "punctuation units," as I will call them, and intonation units is less than perfect, and there are individual styles and fashions in punctuating that complicate the picture. With much writing, nevertheless, and to a greater extent with the writing of experienced authors, punctuation provides a basis for segmenting written language into units that are much like the intonation units of speech. The reason is probably not so much that writers write in information spurts of that kind, but that they grasp their readers' need to process information in such chunks. Readers resemble listeners in their capacities for assimilating information. Good writers, who, as they revise, act as their own readers, may be intuitively aware of this.

If we divide the written excerpt above into punctuation units, we arrive at the following:

(57) Set at the isolated beach of Suma perhaps in the ninth century,

(58) *Matsukaze* has as its principal characters the ghosts or spirits of two dead fisherwomen,

(59) the sisters Matsukaze and Murasame.

(60a) An itinerant priest,

(61) seeing on the shore at Suma a curious looking pine,

(60b) inquires of a villager and learns that the tree is linked with the memory of the two dead fisherwomen.

(62) Evening comes as the priest is reciting sutras and invocations for the repose of the souls of the two dead women.

(63) The spirits of the women present themselves to the priest and act out before him the misery of their lives spent dipping salt from sea brine.

(64) They tell of an interlude of three years when they were loved by the courtier Ariwara no Yukihira,

(65) an exile at Suma,

(66) and speak of the intensity of their longing after Yukihira returned to the capital.

(67) The ghost of Matsukaze becomes convinced that Yukihira has returned.

(68) Crying "I love him still!"

(69a) she approaches a pine on the beach which,

(70) to her deluded eyes,

(69b) appears to be her lover.

(71) The chorus speaking for Murasame and Matsukaze entreats the priest to pray for their rest.

(72) The ghosts of the women vanish as dawn breaks.

(73) The noo ends with lines of intentionally ambiguous beauty which play on the meaning of the women's names:

(74) *autumn rain*
(75) (Murasame)
(76) and *pine wind*
(77) (Matsukaze).
(78) The spirits have vanished with the chorus's repeated final line,
(79) "Only the wind in the pines remains."

(Paragraph boundary)

(80) *Matsukaze* is of the relatively familiar noo type in which a priest encounters the spirit of a dead person,
(81) the spirit tells of its attachment to the past,
(82) and then vanishes,
(83) imploring the priest to pray for its repose.
(84) In *Semimaru,*
(85) on the other hand,
(86) the *tsure* Semimaru and the *shite* Sakagami are both creatures of the ordinary phenomenological world,
(87) and they are equally important and interesting.
(88) In fact,
(89) the play was originally titled *Sakagami.*
(90) There is no hint of final priestly intercession leading to salvation;
(91) rather,
(92) *Semimaru* concludes without resolution as brother and sister part to meet unknown futures.

We can observe immediately in passing that punctuation units 60 and 69 are discontinuous, interrupted by the material in 61 and 70, respectively. While rare in speaking, discontinuous punctuation units are fairly common in written language. The deliberateness and revisability of writing makes them easy to produce, and perhaps the fact that readers are able to scan them and, when necessary, reread them makes them more tolerable from the reading side. Note the following selection from Henry James (1903, pp. 42-43), who was particularly fond of discontinuous punctuation units:

(93) There was much the same difference in his impression of the noticed state of his companion,
(94a) whose dress was "cut down,"
(95) as he believed the term to be,
(94b) in respect to shoulders and bosom,
(96) in a manner quite other than Mrs. Newsome's,

(97a) and who wore round her throat a broad red velvet band with an antique jewel—
 (98) he was rather complacently sure it was antique—
(97b) attached to it in front.
 (99) Mrs. Newsome's dress was never in any degree "cut down,"
(100) and she never wore round her throat a broad red velvet band;
(101) if she had,
(102) moreover,
(103a) would it ever have served so to carry on and complicate,
(104) as he now almost felt,
(103b) his vision?

Discontinuous punctuation units thus present us with our first example of a feature that the circumstances of writing make easier to produce and interpret.

We noticed that spoken intonation units have a modal length of five words. What can be said of the length of punctuation units? It is perhaps surprising that many punctuation units are one and two words long. Lines 88 and 91 illustrate this type:

(88) In fact,
(91) rather,

Words and phrases like these help the reader appreciate the flow of information from one intonation unit to the next by making explicit the temporal, spatial, or logical relations that, in speaking, might be signaled by the context, if not by prosody and gesture. The prevalence of these very brief punctuation units in writing are thus a form of compensation for its contextual and prosodic impoverishment.

Except for these frequent one and two word types, punctuation units are typically somewhat longer than the intonation units of speech. How much longer they are depends on the writer and the genre; writing is highly flexible in this regard. But writers do have the time and revising power to sculpt their punctuation units into longer, more complex creations. Examples like the following are rarely found in speech:

(63) The spirits of the women present themselves to the priest and act out before him the misery of their lives spent dipping salt from sea brine.

(64) They tell of an interlude of three years when they were loved by
      the courtier Ariwara no Yukihira,

Many academic writers are especially fond of punctuation units that
far exceed the length of those in speech:

(105) Whatever their original intended purposes,
(106) they effectively discriminate against certain forms of contribu-
       tion and restrictively constrain not only the competition for a
       role in science education but also the nature of the knowledge
       examined and taught by academic scientists.

WAYS OF EXPANDING PUNCTUATION UNITS

Writers surpass speakers in their use of many specific devices the
effect of which is to create these longer and more complex punctuation units. The favorite device of all is the prepositional phrase, with
attributive adjectives, nominalizations, conjoining, and clause embedding also contributing significantly, in approximately that de-
creasing order.

The large number of prepositional phrases in the written example above is quite apparent:

(57) Set *at* the isolated beach *of* Suma perhaps *in* the ninth century,
(63) The spirits *of* the women present themselves *to* the priest and act
      out *before* him the misery *of* their lives spent dipping salt *from* sea
      brine.
(73) The noo ends *with* lines *of* intentionally ambiguous beauty which
      play *on* the meaning *of* the women's names:

and so on. This exuberant use of prepositional phrases, so typical of
written language, contrasts with the spoken pattern, where a single
intonation unit seldom tolerates more than one:

(4) . . . But . . . the first time I was *in* Japan,
(5) . . . *in* nineteen fifty . . nine,
(6) . . . I was out *on* the street,
(7) . . late *at* night,
(8) . . *in* downtown Kyoto,

Although not as numerous as prepositional phrases, either in the above example or in writing in general, attributive adjectives are also conspicuous:

(57) the *isolated* beach
(58) its *principal* characters
       two *dead* fisherwomen
(60) an *itinerant* priest
(61) a *curious looking* pine
(70) her *deluded* eyes
(73) intentionally *ambiguous* beauty

Adjectives used attributively are by no means absent from spoken language, which nevertheless has a tendency to prefer the predicate use, where the properties conveyed by adjectives are parceled out in separate assertions:

(21) . . . And he was . . . very peculiar.
(25) . . We're busy.
(52-53) . . . . Mm the intensity of it at the ti—me, was pretty awful

A third feature that has the effect of increasing the length of punctuation units is nominalization. Good examples appear in lines 66 and 90.

(66) and speak of the *intensity* of their *longing* after Yukihara returned to the capital.
(90) There is no *hint* of final priestly *intercession* leading to *salvation;*

"Intensity" is a noun formed from the adjective "intense"; "longing," from the verb "to long." Spoken language would probably say all of this rather differently, but if it did use this kind of language the tendency of a speaker would be to say something like "they *longed* for him" and "it *was intense.*" In the second example, "hint" is a noun based on the verb "to hint," "intercession" on "to intercede," and "salvation" (less directly) on "to save." If we found anything comparable in spoken language, we might expect something like, "Nobody *hints* that a priest will *intercede* to *save* people."

A fourth frequent way in which punctuation units are expanded is through the use of conjoined phrases, usually with the conjunction "and," occasionally with "or." In our sample we find the following:

(58) ghosts or spirits
(59) Matsukaze and Murasame
(62) sutras and invocations
(71) Murasame and Matsukaze
(86) the *tsure* Semimaru and the *shite* Sakagami
(87) important and interesting
(92) brother and sister

Such conjoined items are surprisingly uncommon in speaking, where the preference is to place each item in a separate intonation unit: "He was reciting sutras. Invocations too."

The majority of spoken intonation units have the syntactic form of single clauses. Most of the intonation units in the spoken example above are relatively simple clauses, as is typically the case:

(6) . . . I was out on the street,
(13) . . . And this was fifty nine.
(14) . . So that was . . . the fourteenth anniversary.
(15) . . It wasn't an . . . enormous long time afterwards.

and so on. Most of the remaining intonation units are clause fragments. Some of those are prepositional phrases, as noted earlier. Others may divide the subject and predicate of a clause into two intonation units:

(16) . . And . . a . . man who was . . . either drunk or crazy,
(17) . . . uh— came up to us on the street,

or:

(52) . . . . Mm the intensity of it at the ti—me,
(53) was pretty awful.

While speakers thus appear to be under some constraint to produce no more than "one clause at a time" (Pawley & Syder, 1983), writers have the leisure and editing ability which allows them to produce multiclause punctuation units. Those found in our written example are of several types. Some contain clauses introduced by *that* or *to* which function as complements of certain kinds of verbs:

(60ab) An itinerant priest . . . inquires of a villager and learns *that* the tree is linked with the memory of the two dead fisherwomen.

(67) The ghost of Matsukaze becomes convinced *that* Yukihira has returned.

(71) The chorus speaking for Murasame and Matsukaze entreats the priest *to* pray for their rest.

Others contain restrictive relative clauses:

(69) she approaches a pine on the beach *which* . . . appears to be her lover.

(73) The noo ends with lines of intentionally ambiguous beauty *which* play on the meaning of the women's names:

(80) *Matsukaze* is of the relatively familiar noo type *in which* a priest encounters the spirit of a dead person,

Still others contain adverbial clauses, most often of the temporal variety, with one instance in this excerpt of a purpose clause:

(62) Evening comes *as* the priest is reciting sutras and invocations for the repose of the souls of the two dead women.

(64) They tell of an interlude of three years *when* they were loved by the courtier Ariwara no Yukihira,

(66) and speak of the intensity of their longing *after* Yukihira returned to the capital.

(72) The ghosts of the women vanish *as* dawn breaks.

(92) *Semimaru* concludes without resolution *as* brother and sister part *to* meet unknown futures.

Although these clause-embedding devices are not entirely lacking in speech, writing provides an environment which fosters them, with significantly longer and more complex punctuation units as the result.

THE ONE NEW CONCEPT AT A TIME CONSTRAINT

There is a relatively strong constraint on spoken language to the effect that each intonation unit can express no more than one concept that is brand new to the discourse (Chafe, in press a). We can call this the "one new concept at a time" constraint. By *brand new* I mean a concept newly activated in the speaker's consciousness, and thus newly activated in the hearer's consciousness as well by the utterance of the intonation unit in question. By *concept* I mean a referent, such as was expressed, for example, by "an American man" in 11 or "a man who was either drunk or crazy" in 16; an event, such as was expressed by "came up to us on the street" in 17 or "started speaking English" in 18; or a state, such as was expressed by "late at night" in 7 or "in downtown Kyoto" in 8.

Because of this constraint, this speaker found it necessary to express 16-18 as three intonation units rather than one, with the brand new subject in the first, and the two events divided among the two others:

> (16) . . And . . a . . man who was . . . either drunk or crazy,
> (17) . . . uh— came up to us on the street,
> (18) . . and started speaking English.

A speaker could not normally have said all this in a single intonation unit.

The deliberateness and revisability of writing, as well as a writer's independence of the audience, both foster the bypassing of the one new concept at a time constraint. Thus our writer was able to produce:

> (57) Set at the isolated beach of Suma perhaps in the ninth century,

in which there were two new concepts expressed by "at the isolated beach of Suma" and "in the ninth century." In another punctuation unit:

> (62) Evening comes as the priest is reciting sutras and invocations for the repose of the souls of the two dead women.

the new concepts included at least "evening comes," "reciting sutras and invocations," and "for the repose of."

THE LIGHT SUBJECT CONSTRAINT

A related constraint on spoken language, which I have called the "light subject constraint" (Chafe, in press a) dictates that the subjects of clauses usually express given information, in the sense of information that is already active in the mind of the speaker and assumed to be active in the mind of the hearer as well. Such information is usually pronominalized and weakly stressed:

(6) . . . *I* was out on the street,
(21) . . . And *he* was . . . very peculiar.

Only rarely does the subject of a clause express brand new or previously inactive information. The only circumstance under which such a subject is likely to be found is that in which the clause begins a new paragraph-like section of the discourse. We do find such a subject in intonation unit 16:

(16) . . And . . a . . man who was . . . either drunk or crazy,

This was the initial intonation unit in the description of the events of the story, immediately following the setting that was presented in 1-15. (It should be noted that this subject was expressed in a separate intonation unit of its own because of the one new concept at a time constraint.) We find a parallel occurrence in 52 (where again the new subject appeared in its own separate intonation unit):

(52) . . . . Mm the intensity of it at the ti—me,
(53) was pretty awful.

52 also represents the beginning of a new paragraph-like unit, as is confirmed in this case by the extra long (four dot) pause (see Chafe, 1980, pp. 43-47).

Writers have the freedom to violate the light subject constraint as well. In our written example there are at least three such violations, the subjects in 60ab, 62, and 71,

(60ab) *An itinerant priest* . . . inquires of a villager . . .
(62) *Evening* comes . . .
(71) *The chorus* . . . entreats the priest . . .

where each of the italicized phrases conveys new information. Whereas speakers are strongly constrained to create subjects that express given information, writers find it easier to introduce new information in this role.

THE COMBINING OF UNITS

Intonation units, most often in the form of single clauses, function as the basic units of speaking, as opposed to sentences, which are often put together on the run, without conviction as to their boundaries, and with frequent changes in midcourse:

(31) . . . a—nd . . . we—
(32) . . . well then he pulled out a knife.
(33) . . . and he started . . . after the guy I was with.
(34) . . . who sort of started circling,
(35) . . . well you know I . . . summoned a cab.
(36) . . . a—nd . . the man I was with jumped in the front seat of the cab,
(37) . . . and . . I
(38) . . oh no . . into the back seat of the cab,
(39) . . . a—nd . . . I . . got in with him,
(40) . . and the guy ran around and got in the front seat of the cab.
(41) . . . at which point we . . . started out the doors of the cab.
(42) . . . a—nd . . I said to the driver,
(43) . . that massugu.
(44) . . straight ahead.

Some of these sentences seem to have ended before they should have, with afterthoughts that only partially set things right. Others seem not to have ended when they should have; in speaking, "run-on sentences" are common enough (Danielewicz & Chafe, in press; see also Crystal, 1980, pp. 155-157).

In general we can say that spoken language tends to be "fragmented" (Chafe, 1982), in the sense that it is typically constructed of a series of relatively independent clauses and clause fragments. Often the clauses are linked by "and": twenty-one of the intonation units in our spoken excerpt began with that conjunction, a typical proportion. There is little of what we might consider the "subordination" of one intonation unit to another. In this example there were only two intonation units that look like subordinate clauses:

(3) . . Where most of the time I feel extreme—ly safe.
(34) . . . Who sort of started circling,

a locative adverbial clause and a relative clause respectively. However, although both these clauses were syntactically dependent on what preceded, in both cases the preceding clause (ignoring the false start in 2) ended with a sentence-final falling pitch, the "subordinate" clause forming an intonationally separate statement.

Writing lacks the fragmented quality of speaking, making greater use of punctuation units that are syntactically and intonationally (through punctuation) dependent on other punctuation units. The dependence may be of several types. Sometimes a punctuation unit contains a participle that subordinates it to whatever follows (or precedes):

(57) *Set* at the isolated beach of Suma perhaps in the ninth century,
(61) *seeing* on the shore at Suma a curious looking pine,
(68) *Crying* "I love him still!"
(83) *imploring* the priest to pray for its repose.

Sometimes there is apposition:

(59) (two dead fisherwomen,) the sisters Matsukaze and Murasame.
(65) (the courtier Ariwara no Yukihira,) an exile at Suma,
(74, 76) (the meaning of the women's names:) *autumn rain* . . . and *pine wind* . . .

Sometimes there are several punctuation units in a series:

(80) *Matsukaze* is of the relatively familiar noo type in which a priest encounters the spirit of a dead person,
(81) the spirit tells of its attachment to the past,
(82) and then vanishes,

These and other devices are used by writers to create elaborate, integrated sentences of a sort that is rare in speech. Whereas speakers perforce construct sentences on the run, writers can linger over them, fashioning them into objects of a complexity that can sometimes be overwhelming, as in the creations of Walter Pater (1910, p. 105) and other authors around the turn of the century:

Those English critics who at the beginning of the present century introduced from Germany, together with some other subtleties of thought transplanted hither not without advantage, the distinction between the *Fancy* and the *Imagination,* made much also of the cognate distinction between *Wit* and *Humour,* between the unreal and transitory mirth, which is as the crackling of thorns under the pot, and the laughter which blends with tears and even with the sublimities of the imagination, and which, in its most exquisite motives, is one with pity—the laughter of the comedies of Shakespeare, hardly less expressive than his moods of seriousness or solemnity, of that deeply stirred soul of sympathy in him, as flowing from which both tears and laughter are alike genuine and contagious.

VOCABULARY CHOICE

Speakers must choose vocabulary on the run; they can hardly linger long over the choice of a word or phrase. Writers have time to select words and phrases that, in the best of cases, are finely tuned to express what they had in mind. A result is that written vocabulary tends to be more varied than spoken. The excerpts we have been looking at provide several illustrations of this variety.

Student writers are sometimes instructed to write dialogues without using the verb "say." We can see how our speaker relied on that one verb:

> (19) . . And *saying* come . . to my house.
> (22) . . . A—nd uh— you know we *said,*
> (27) And then he started *saying* come to my house tonight you will die.
> (42) . . . a—nd . . I *said* to the driver,

As a more leisurely writer she came up with many finer distinctions:

> (60b) *inquires* of a villager and learns that the tree is linked with the memory of the two dead fisherwomen.
> (62) Evening comes as the priest is *reciting* sutras and invocations for the repose of the souls of the two dead women.
> (64) They *tell* of an interlude of three years when they were loved by the courtier Ariwara no Yukihira,
> (66) and *speak* of the intensity of their longing after Yukihira returned to the capital.
> (68) *Crying* "I love him still!"
> (71) The chorus *speaking* for Murasame and Mtasukaze *entreats* the priest to pray for their rest.

(81) the spirit *tells* of its attachment to the past,

(83) *imploring* the priest to pray for its repose.

We can note also how the single word *cab* was used again and again in the spoken excerpt:

(35) . . . well you know I . . . summoned a *cab*.

(36) . . . a—nd . . the man I was with jumped in the front seat of the *cab*,

(37) . . . and . . I

(38) . . oh no . . into the back seat of the *cab*,

(39) . . . a—nd . . . I . . got in with him,

(40) . . and the guy ran around and got in the front seat of the *cab*.

(41) . . . at which point we . . . started out the doors of the *cab*.

(42) . . . a—nd . . I said to the driver,

(43) . . that massugu.

(44) . . straight ahead.

(45) I didn't know I knew the word.

(46) . . . And the *cab* took off.

In contrast we can note the varied reference to the pine tree in the written example:

(60a) An itinerant priest,

(61) seeing on the shore at Suma *a curious looking pine*,

(60b) inquires of a villager and learns that *the tree* is linked with the memory of the two dead fisherwomen.

or the seemingly deliberate setting up of alternative ways to refer to the two apparitions:

(58) *Matsukaze* has as its principal characters the *ghosts or spirits* of two dead fisherwomen,

(63) The *spirits of the women* . . .

(72) The *ghosts of the women* . . .

(78) The *spirits* . . .

Speakers' lack of leisure to choose words carefully appears also in their use of inexplicit pronouns, usually "it," "this," and "that," referring not to a specific referent but to a vague complex of ideas:

(1) . . . Well oddly enough *it* was in Japan.
(13) . . . And *this* was fifty nine.
(14) . . So *that* was . . . the fourteenth anniversary.
(15) . . *It* wasn't an . . . enormous long time afterwards.

There is no single, clear answer to the questions, *"What* was in Japan?" *"What* was fifty-nine?" and so on. Lexical tentativeness is also evident in a speaker's frequent use of hedges like "sort of":

(30) . . And just *sort of* . . repeating all of this . . over and over again.
(34) . . . Who *sort of* started circling,

Both inexplicit pronominal reference and hedges of this kind are largely foreign to writing. There are certainly many expressions of uncertainty in expository writing; however, they are not of this lexical nature, but reside more in statistical hedges such as "normally," "primarily," and "for the most part," and in epistemic qualifiers such as "perhaps" and "it seems" (Chafe, in press b).

To a certain extent, spoken language and written language have their own vocabularies. Most words are neutral between the two, but some that are natural to speaking are out of place in writing, whereas for others the reverse is true. The reason is not that speakers must choose words more quickly than writers, but that each kind of language has its own divergent history. In general, too, writing tends to be more conservative, simply because it is there to be looked at and kept in place. New words, or new uses of old words, typically enter the spoken language first, sometimes to be assimilated later by writers, sometimes not. In our spoken sample we have usages such as:

(33) . . . And he started . . . after the *guy* I was with.
(36) . . . a—nd . . the man I was with *jumped in* the front seat of the cab.
(46) . . . And the cab *took off.*
(49) . . eh it's always *s–tayed with* me,
(53) was *pretty* awful.

The separate history of English writing has created a partially different vocabulary, largely restricted to that medium:

(57) Set at the isolated beach of Suma *perhaps* in the ninth century,

(62) Evening comes as the priest is reciting sutras and invocations for the *repose* of the souls of the two dead women. (See also 83.)

(72) The ghosts of the women *vanish* as dawn breaks. (See also 82.)

(80) *Matsukaze* is of the relatively familiar noo type in which a priest *encounters* the spirit of a dead person,

(92) *Semimaru concludes* without resolution as brother and sister part to meet unknown futures.

Speakers would be more apt to use "maybe" for "perhaps," "rest" for "repose," "disappear" for "vanish," "meet" for "encounter," and "end" for "conclude."

INVOLVEMENT

This specialization of vocabulary impinges on a larger area of differentiation that can be associated with the "involvement" of speaking versus the "detachment" of writing (Chafe, 1982). Earlier I alluded to the fact that speaking typically takes place in an interactive environment, where the speaker is face to face with the audience, and where in fact the role of speaker typically alternates between one conversational participant and another. Writing, in contrast, typically takes place in social isolation, and in many cases the writer does not even know who the audience will be or when the work will be read. It is hardly surprising that this difference between the situations of speaking and writing should produce differences in the amount of personal involvement expressed in the resulting language.

It is often the case, as in the two examples before us, that a speaker will relate events in which he or she participated, whereas a writer will focus on events experienced by third parties. That is by no means necessarily true, for we need not look far to find first-person writing in autobiographies, personal letters, and journals. And conversations can of course be about third parties. Even so, the typical uses of speaking and writing lead to a greater frequency of first person in the former, of third person in the latter.

More unambiguously associated with speaking, and not with writing, is the use of various markers of personal interaction. The obvious marker of this sort in our present example is "you know":

(2) . . Which is not where you'd . . *you know*
(22) . . . A—nd uh— *you know* we said,
(35) . . . well *you know* I summoned a cab.
(51) and not know that you know them *you know*.
(55) we were also . . . *you know* not only concerned about taking care
of ourselves,

Speakers use this expression to reassure themselves that they are communicating adequately with their audience (see Ostman, 1981). As a clear marker of spoken involvement, "you know" is quite foreign to almost any sort of writing.

Speakers are also under constant if subtle pressure to impress their audiences with the importance of what they are saying. Labov (1972) has characterized this need in terms of a speaker's ever-present desire to avoid the response, "So what?" One manifestation of this desire is the frequent use in speaking of universal quantifiers like "all" and "never" where they obviously cannot be taken literally (Labov, in press). But there are many other forms of hyperbole. In our present example we find such words as "extremely" (with expressive lengthening of the second syllable), "enormous," "very," and "pretty awful," as well as specific reference to the "intensity" of the experience:

(3) . . Where most of the time I feel *extreme–ly* safe.
(15) . . It wasn't an . . . *enormous* long time afterwards.
(21) . . . And he was . . . *very* peculiar.
(52-53) . . . . Mm the *intensity of it* at the ti—me, was *pretty awful*.

The experience was of course intense, but my point is that this speaker was effective in communicating how intense it was.

Because speakers aim to achieve vividness, they may go out of their way to specify the places and times where events took place, in an effort to create involvement by communicating as much as possible about the concrete setting:

(1) . . . Well oddly enough it was in Japan.
(4) . . . But . . . the first time I was in Japan,
(5) . . . in nineteen fifty . . nine,
(6) . . . I was out on the street,
(7) . . late at night,
(8) . . in downtown Kyoto,

(10) . . uh in the bar district,

(12) . . . a—nd uh— . . we . . neither one of us had thought about the
fact that it was the anniversary of the bombing of Hiroshima.

(13) . . . And this was fifty nine.

(14) . . So that was . . . the fourteenth anniversary.

(15) . . It wasn't an . . . enormous long time afterwards.

Direct quotations are still another involvement device. Ten of the
intonation units in our spoken example contained such quotations:

(19) . . And saying come . . to my house.

(20) . . . Come to my house.

(23) . . . No.

(24) We can't.

(25) . . We're busy.

(27) And then he started saying come to my house tonight you will
die.

(28) . . . Tonight the bomb will fall on Hiroshima.

(29) . . . And come to my house.

(43) . . that massugu.

(44) . . straight ahead.

The written example contains two:

(68) Crying "I love him still!"

(79) "Only the wind in the pines remains."

On the other side of the coin, the quality I have been calling *detach-ment,* especially typical of expository prose, may show up in the kind
of reification accomplished through nominalization, as already de-
scribed, where events are transformed into objects:

(90) There is no *hint* of priestly *intercession* leading to *salvation;*

Abstract, inanimate subjects have a similar effect of distancing the
discourse from the typical involved situation, in which live persons
perform live acts:

(73) *The noo* ends . . .

(80) *Matsukaze* is of the relatively familiar noo type . . .

(89) *the play* was originally titled *Sakagami.*

Passives belong in the same repertoire of detachment:

> (64) They tell of an interlude of three years when they *were loved* by
>   the courtier Ariwara no Yukihira,
> (67) The ghost of Matsukaze *becomes convinced* that Yukihira has
>   returned.

Although writing may allow and even foster "detached" language, Tannen (1982) has usefully emphasized that the involvement characteristic of speaking may characterize some kinds of writing too, particularly some kinds of fiction. To round off this discussion, it may be instructive to compare two samples of language that are both highly "involved," though one has been subjected to little of the writing process while the other has undergone much. First I will present the spoken excerpt quoted above in a written format, with editing that amounts only to deleting the clear disfluencies. Writers seldom have the ear for spoken language that would allow them to produce something of this kind; if they did, we might well congratulate them on possessing such a talent:

> Well, oddly enough it was in Japan, where most of the time I feel extremely safe. But the first time I was in Japan, in 1959, I was out on the street, late at night, in downtown Kyoto, in the bar district, with an American man, and neither one of us had thought about the fact that it was the anniversary of the bombing of Hiroshima. And this was '59. So that was the fourteenth anniversary. It wasn't an enormous long time afterwards.
>
> And a man who was either drunk or crazy came up to us on the street, and started speaking English, and saying, "Come to my house. Come to my house." And he was very peculiar. And, you know, we said, "No. We can't. We're busy." And so forth and so on. And then he started saying, "Come to my house, tonight you will die. Tonight the bomb will fall on Hiroshima." And, "Come to my house." And just sort of repeating all of this over and over again.
>
> Well, then he pulled out a knife, and he started after the guy I was with, who sort of started circling. Well, you know, I summoned a cab. And the man I was with jumped in the back seat of the cab, and I got in with him, and the guy ran around and got in the front seat of the cab. At which point we started out the door of the cab. And I said to the driver, "Massugu. Straight ahead." I didn't know I knew the word. And the cab took off. And that was the end of the experience.

But it's always stayed with me, as how you can know words and not
know that you know them, you know. The intensity of it at the time
was pretty awful. Because in good part, we were also, you know, not
only concerned about taking care of ourselves, but also not wanting to
start some sort of incident.

Hemingway was a fiction writer who knew how to make the most
of his freedom from temporal and interactional constraints, and of
his ability to revise. The excerpt below, despite its vividness, shows a
number of the properties of written language that we have discussed: expansion of punctuation units through prepositional
phrases, through attributive adjectives, through conjoining, and
through both relative and adverbial clauses; elaborated sentences;
and violations of the one new concept at a time constraint. The
passage makes no obvious use of colloquial vocabulary, and the
curiously unspokenlike quotations betray the planning that went
into them. The involvement conveyed in this passage stems in part,
nevertheless, from the number of these quotations, though also
from the imagery, and from the numerous clauses that describe
someone actively doing something.

My point is that, despite the involvement it may share with spoken
language, the passage to follow could hardly have been said by a
speaker, just as the preceding passage is not something that a writer
would be likely to have written. The two modes of production almost
inevitably lead to substantially different products:

> He lay flat on the brown, pine-needled floor of the forest, his chin
> on his folded arms, and high overhead the wind blew in the tops of the
> pine trees. The mountainside sloped gently where he lay; but below it
> was steep and he could see the dark of the oiled road winding through
> the pass. There was a stream alongside the road and far down the pass
> he saw a mill beside the stream and the falling water of the dam, white
> in the summer sunlight.
> "Is that the mill?" he asked.
> "Yes."
> "I do not remember it."
> "It was built since you were here. The old mill is farther down;
> much below the pass."
> He spread the photostated military map out on the forest floor and
> looked at it carefully. The old man looked over his shoulder. He was a
> short and solid old man in a black peasant's smock and gray iron-stiff

trousers and he wore rope-soled shoes. He was breathing heavily from the climb and his hand rested on one of the two heavy packs they had been carrying.

"Then you cannot see the bridge from here."

"No," the old man said. "This is the easy country of the pass where the stream flows gently. Below, where the road turns out of sight in the trees, it drops suddenly and there is a steep gorge—"

"I remember."

"Across the gorge is the bridge."

"And where are their posts?"

"There is a post at the mill that you see there."

The young man, who was studying the country, took his glasses from the pocket of his faded, khaki flannel shirt, wiped the lenses with a handkerchief, screwed the eyepieces around until the boards of the mill showed suddenly clearly and he saw the wooden bench beside the door; the huge pile of sawdust that rose behind the open shed where the circular saw was, and a stretch of the flume that brought the logs down from the mountainside on the other bank of the stream. The stream showed clear and smooth-looking in the glasses and, below the curl of the falling water, the spray from the dam was blowing in the wind. (Hemingway, 1940, pp. 1-2)

NOTE

1. The data presented here, and the general findings mentioned throughout this chapter, come from a study sponsored by Grant NIE-G-80-0125 from the National Institute of Education. For more quantitative information see Chafe and Danielewicz (in press). The spoken data were transcribed from a narrative told by one of the participants in a tape-recorded informal dinner conversation. The written data were taken from a published article by the same individual.

REFERENCES

Bloomfield, L. (1933). *Language*. New York: Henry Holt.

Chafe, W. (1980). The deployment of consciousness in the production of a narrative. In W. Chafe (Ed.), *The pear stories: Cognitive, cultural, and linguistic aspects of narrative production*. Norwood, NJ: Ablex.

Chafe, W. (1982). Integration and involvement in speaking, writing, and oral litera- ture. In D. Tannen (Ed.), *Spoken and written language: Exploring orality and literacy*. Norwood, NJ: Ablex.

Chafe, W. (in press a). Cognitive constraints on information flow. In R. Tomlin (Ed.), *Coherence and grounding in discourse.* Amsterdam: John Benjamins.

Chafe, W. (in press b). Evidentiality in English conversation and academic writing. In W. Chafe & J. Nichols (Eds.), *Evidentiality: The linguistic coding of epistemology.* Norwood, NJ: Ablex.

Chafe, W., & Danielewicz, J. (in press). Properties of spoken and written language. In R. Horowitz & S. J. Samuels (Eds.), *Comprehending oral and written language.* New York: Academic Press.

Crystal, D. (1980). Neglected grammatical factors in conversational English. In S. Greenbaum, G. Leech, & J. Svartvik (Eds.), *Studies in English linguistics.* London: Longman.

Danielewicz, J., & Chafe, W. (in press). How "normal" speaking leads to "erroneous" punctuating. In S. Freedman (Ed.), *Evaluation, response, and revision.* Norwood, NJ: Ablex.

Hemingway, E. (1940). *For whom the bell tolls.* New York: Scribner's.

Hockett, C. F. (1958). *A course in modern linguistics.* New York: Macmillan.

James, H. (1903). *The ambassadors.* Boston: Houghton Mifflin.

Labov, W. (1972). The transformation of experience in narrative syntax. In W. Labov, *Language in the inner city: Studies in the black English vernacular.* Philadelphia: University of Pennsylvania Press.

Labov, W. (in press). The several logics of quantification. In *Proceedings of the Eleventh Annual Meeting of the Berkeley Linguistics Society.*

Ostman, J. (1981). *You know: A discourse-functional approach.* Amsterdam: John Benjamins.

Pater, W. (1910). *Appreciations: With an essay on style.* London: Macmillan.

Pawley, A., & Syder, F. (1983). Natural selection in syntax: Notes on adaptive variation and change in vernacular and literary grammar. *Journal of Pragmatics, 7,* 551-579.

Sapir, E. (1921). *Language: An introduction to the study of speech.* New York: Harcourt Brace Jovanovich.

Saussure, F. (1960). *Cours de linguistique générale* (5th ed.). [Course in general linguistics]. Paris: Payot.

Tannen, D. (1982). Oral and literate strategies in spoken and written narratives. *Language, 58,* 1-21.

2

On the Dynamics of Written Communication in the Light of the Theory of Functional Sentence Perspective

JAN FIRBAS

The theory of functional sentence perspective (FSP) deals with how the semantic and syntactic structures of the sentence function in fulfilling the communicative purpose intended for the sentence.

For instance, outside a verbal and/or situational context the words *John has been taken ill* constitute a sentence structure, but it does not serve a particular communicative purpose, which may be, for example, to state a person's health condition (*John has been taken **ill***), to specify the person affected (***John** has been taken ill*), or to affirm that the information conveyed is really valid (*John **has** been taken ill*). In other words, different communicative purposes cause the sentence structure to function in different kinds of perspective. A change in communicative purpose affects the extent to which a linguistic element contributes toward the fulfillment of a given purpose. One of the concerns of the theory of FSP is therefore to identify the role a linguistic element plays in the dynamics of communication.

Various terms have been used in discussions of this area of linguistic studies. Apart from "functional sentence perspective,"[1] let me mention at least "contextual segmentation of the sentence," "the thematic organization of the utterance," "information structure," "theme-rheme structure," "topic-comment structure," and "topic-

Author's Note: I dedicate this essay to the memories of Professor Ivan Poldauf and Professor Bohumil Trnka.

focus structure." The literature on the subject has grown greatly in recent years. *A tentative bibliography of studies in functional sentence perspective* (Tyl et al., 1970), covering the years 1900-1970, lists 663 items, and *An analytical bibliography of Czechoslovak studies in functional sentence perspective* (Firbas & Golková, 1975), covering the years 1900-1972, has 302 items. The former bibliography is composed of studies irrespective of their provenance; the latter offers brief summaries of studies written by Czechoslovak linguists only, the figures testifying to a particularly intensive interest in problems of FSP in Czechoslovakia. Since the publication of the two bibliographies numerous studies have been published, particularly outside Czechoslovakia. Regardless of the terminology employed, FSP currently attracts the attention of a great number of scholars in all parts of the world.

Influenced by V. Mathesius, J. Vachek and F. Daneš,[2] I started my work on FSP in the mid-1950s and was later joined in my investigations by a number of colleagues attached to the Brno Department of English (A. Svoboda, E. Golková, E. Horová, J. Hruška, H. Chládková, J. Chamonikolasová, and L. Urbanová).[3]

Our work is now well known and has already come in both for praise and for criticism.[4] But perhaps because the results of our research have usually appeared in publications that are not always accessible, our work has been overlooked by some researchers in this field. Gratefully accepting the invitation of the editors to contribute to the present volume,[5] I therefore propose to present some of the key issues of my approach and conclude with analyses of several brief texts.

The recent considerably increased interest in phenomena and problems of FSP has not surprisingly led to an abundance of terms and varying expositions. Before turning to the analyses of texts, I shall therefore devote some space to a theoretical discussion. As FSP is a contextual phenomenon, the contextual conditions stipulated for the examples constitute an essential part of the argument. Ample context is provided by the texts presented for analysis in the second part of the paper.

As the present volume is devoted to written communication, my contribution is restricted to the written language, and only occasionally touches on the relationship between the spoken and the written language.

THE INTERPLAY OF FACTORS DETERMINING
THE DEGREES OF COMMUNICATIVE DYNAMISM

Degree of Communicative Dynamism

Communication is a dynamic phenomenon. One of the basic concepts of the theory of FSP is communicative dynamism (CD), which refers to a quality displayed by the development of information toward a particular communicative goal. The degree of CD carried by a linguistic element is the relative extent to which this element contributes toward the further development of the communication.

In reply to *What about Peter?*, the elements of the structure *He has flown to Paris* differ in the extent to which they contribute toward the attainment of the communicative goal. *He* contributes least and *to Paris* most; *has flown* ranks between the two, its notional component, *flow-,* being more dynamic than its temporal and modal exponents, the auxiliary *has* and the suffix *−n*. The communicative goal (or communicative purpose) is to state the destination of Peter's flight.

In the above formulations, "information" covers not only purely factual content, but also attitudes, feelings, and emotions. The degrees of CD are "relative" in that the degree of CD carried by an element within a sentence is always determined in relation to the contributions that the other elements within the sentence make to the further development of the communication. As I shall later explain, "development" is not to be understood as a purely linear notion.

Any linguistic element—a clause, a phrase, a word, a morpheme, or just a vowel alternation (e.g., *sing, sang, sung)*—can become a carrier of CD as long as it conveys some meaning and in consequence participates in the development of the communication (see Firbas, in press a). In fact, even a semantic feature without a formal implementation of its own is a "linguistic element" and is therefore to be regarded as a carrier of CD; for example, the contrast implicit in *Peter stayed in London, and Paul decided to go to Edinburgh.* In the written language, the contrast between *Peter* and *Paul* and the contrast between *London* and *Edinburgh* raise the degrees of CD carried by them, but do not affect their written form. Within the language system, the carriers of CD are hierarchically organized (see Firbas, in press b). In this chapter, I shall keep to the level of sentence and clause constituents (subject, object, etc.) and deal with them as carriers of CD (but see below, for the role of the temporal and modal exponents of the finite verb).

Within written language, the distribution of degrees of CD is effected by an interplay of three factors: "linear modification," "context," and "semantic structure."

Linear Modification

"Linear modification" is a term coined by D. L. Bolinger (1952). He has appositely summed up the operation of linear modification as follows: The "gradation of position creates gradation of meaning when there are no interfering factors" (1952, p. 1125). This means that, provided there are no interfering factors, the communicative importance of the sentence elements gradually increases with movement toward the end of the sentence, the final element becoming the most important because it completes the communicative purpose of the sentence. Communicative importance determines the degree of CD: An element with a higher degree of communicative importance contributes more to the further development of the communication than an element with a lower degree of communicative importance.

Let us examine a few semantic and grammatical sentence structures, paying particular attention to the constituents in final position.

(1) He could not attend the lecture because he was ill.
(2) Because he was ill, he could not attend the lecture.
(3) He went to London in order to meet a friend.
(4) In order to meet a friend, he went to London.

In their most frequent use, the pronominal subjects convey known information. The final constituents express the communicative purpose to be fulfilled by the structures: 1 states the cause of the man's absence from the lecture, and 2 the fact of his absence; 3 states the purpose of the man's journey, and 4 the journey's destination.

Bolinger closes with the reservation "when there are no interfering factors." The interfering factors are the context and the semantic structure, which under certain conditions are capable of working counter to linear modification.

Context

An element expressing known information—information retrievable from the immediate context (the immediately relevant preceding verbal context and/or the immediately relevant situational context)—is communicatively less important. Because it contributes less to the further development of the communication, it carries a lower degree of CD than an element conveying a piece of irretrievable, new, unknown information, which brings the communication closer to the fulfillment of the communicative purpose. The following structures illustrate the point:

(5) *I* used to know *him.*
(6) *Ich* habe *ihn* gekannt.
(7) *Ich* kannte *ihn.*
(8) *Je l'*ai connu.
(9) Zna*l* jse*m ho.* "Known [past participle active] I-am him."

In the most natural use of these structures, the pronouns *(I/ich/je, him/ihn/le/ho),* as well as the formal exponents of person and number carried by the verbal form, convey retrievable information. Irrespective of position they carry low degrees of CD, operating either in the same direction as linear modification or counter to it. It follows that the contextual factor is hierarchically superior to linear modification.

Information retrievable from the immediate context and the elements expressing such information are termed "context-dependent." Such information is not only conveyed by pronouns and the verbal exponents of person and number. For instance, if merely expressing a piece of retrievable information, the noun phrase *the book* in the following sentence structure is context-dependent:

(10) Yes, I have bought *the book.*

The same applies to the equivalent phrases in 11-14.

(11) Ich kaufte mir *das Buch.*
(12) *Das Buch* habe ich mir gekauft.
(13) *(Tu) knihu* jsem si koupil.
(14) Koupil jsem si *(tu) knihu.*

Irrespective of sentence position, *the book, das Buch, (tu) knihu* carry the lowest degrees of CD, together with *I* (or *ich*) and the verbal exponent(s) of person and number. They do so irrespective of their meaning and the semantic relations into which they enter. It follows that in the interplay of factors signaling degrees of CD, context proves to be hierarchically superior not only to linear modification, but also to semantic structure.

Semantic Structure

Provided that they are context-independent, some types of semantic content and some types of semantic relation are capable of working counter to linear modification.

(15) A boy came into the room.
(16) New housing estates have mushroomed on the outskirts of our town.
(17) Grobe Fehler kommen in seinem Aufsatz vor.
(18) In seinem Aufsatz kommen grobe Fehler vor.
(19) He has composed a number of powerful symphonies.
(20) Er komponierte wunderschöne Opern.
(21) Er hat wunderschöne Opern komponiert.
(22) Wunderschöne Opern hat er komponiert.

Each of the verbs in 15-18 denotes appearance or existence on the scene, each subject a phenomenon appearing or existing on the scene, and each adverbial element a local setting. If the subject is context-independent, it carries the most important piece of information. If the verb is context-independent as well, with the adverbial element being either context-independent or context-dependent, the relative degrees of communicative importance are distributed as follows: The least important element is the adverbial (setting the scene), the most important element is the subject, and the verb ranks between the two. Under these conditions, this interpretation is certainly the most natural, the scene providing the starting point of the development of the communication and the phenomenon providing the goal. The interpretation holds good irrespective of the positions the elements occupy in the sentence.

Each verb-object combination occurring in 19-22 expresses an action and the goal of the action; the subject (which happens to be a pronoun) refers to the agent of the action. In its most natural use, the pronominal subject is context-dependent, whereas the verb and the object are context-independent. The context-independent object, which expresses the result of the action, is communicatively more important than the verb, which merely expresses the action leading to and bringing about the result. The subject provides the starting point for the development of the communication, whereas the object provides the goal reached by this development. In consequence, the element referring to the agent carries the lowest degree of CD, and the element expressing the result of the agent's action carries the highest degree. This interpretation holds good irrespective of the positions the elements occupy in the sentence.[6]

The Interplay of Linear Modification, Context and Semantic Structure

Context and semantic structure are then capable of working counter to linear modification under certain conditions and in doing so replace linear modification in signaling degrees of CD. They cannot be regarded as *interfering* factors; rather, with linear modification, they enter into an *interplay* that determines the distribution of CD over sentence elements. It is not linear modification but the context that plays the dominant role within this interplay of factors.

As linear modification is only a contributory factor, the development of the communication realized within a sentence cannot be looked upon as a merely linear phenomenon. The sentence is a field of semantic and syntactic relations that in its turn provides a distributional field of degrees of CD. This view of the sentence accords with a felicitous wording employed in the *Duden Grammar of German* (Duden, 1959, p. 599), which makes the point that a sentence does not solely operate as a "Nacheinander," but always also as a "Miteinander"; in other words, both "one-after-the-otherness" and "to-getherness" characterize the sentence. The sentence elements oper-ate within a "together" that may counteract the linearity of the "one-after-the-other."

The fact that a gradual increase in CD within a sentence need not be implemented linearly makes it necessary to draw a distinction between the linear arrangement of sentence elements and their interpretative arrangement. The latter is the arrangement of the sentence elements according to the gradual rise in CD irrespective of the positions they occupy within the sentence. Sentences with dif-ferent linear arrangements of corresponding elements may, nevertheless, have the same interpretative arrangement. Under the contextual conditions I have stipulated above, the interpretative arrangements of the elements in 5-9 are the following:

	Interpretative Arrangement	Linear Arrangement
(5)	"I him used to know."	I used to know him.
(6)	"Ich ihn habe gekannt."	Ich habe ihn gekannt.
(7)	"Ich ihn kannte.," or rather "Ich ihn -te kann-."	Ich kannte ihn.
(8)	"Je l'ai connu."	Je l'ai connu.
(9)	"Jsem ho znal.," or rather "-m ho jse- -l zna-."	Znal jsem ho.

If we compare the linear arrangements and the corresponding interpretative arrangements, we see that the two arrangements may coincide (8), or they may differ to a greater or lesser extent (the other examples) as determined by the system of word order of the language.

STATIC SEMANTICS AND DYNAMIC SEMANTICS
AND THE SCALES OF DYNAMIC SEMANTIC FUNCTIONS

A functional theory requires a distinction between two angles from which a semantic and grammatical sentence structure may be viewed: the static and the dynamic. From the static angle, the struc-ture is viewed as unrelated to any particular context; in other words, as not operating in any actual flow of communication. From the dynamic angle, it is viewed as linked with some definite contextual conditions.

From the static point of view, verbs and adjectives express characteristics, the former tending to express transient, the latter permanent characteristics. Of particular relevance to our discussion is the characteristic that may be described as "existence or appearance on the scene." There are verbs or verbal phrases that express it with unmistakable clarity (*come into view, come on the scene, come in, come up, appear, loom up, occur, present oneself, take place, turn up*) and verbs or verbal phrases that do so implicitly (as in *A wave of the azalea scent drifted into her face; A goldfinch flew over his head; Big spots gleamed in the mist; A haze hovered over the prospect; A fly settled on his hair;* see Firbas, 1975a, p. 54).

From the dynamic point of view, if a verb of appearance/existence occurs in a sentence together with a context-independent subject and an adverbial of place and/or an adverbial of time, it introduces the phenomenon expressed by the subject into the flow of communication. The verb then performs the dynamic function of expressing appearance/existence (App/Ex), and the adverbial elements perform the dynamic function of expressing the setting (Set). The subject, on the other hand, performs the dynamic function of expressing a phenomenon that appears or exists on the scene (Ph). The functions constitute a scale that reflects rising degrees of communicative importance, and hence a gradual rise in CD. The scale constituted by these dynamic functions is the Existential Scale: Set-App/Ex-Ph. This formula reflects an interpretative arrangement, not necessarily corresponding to the linear arrangement.

Under different contextual conditions, the verb of appearance/existence need not perform the dynamic function App/Ex. The semantic and syntactic framework may be the same, but if the subject is context-dependent and the adverbial element is context-independent (*The boy/He came into the room*), the communicative situation is different. The notion expressed by the subject has already emerged in the course of the development of the communication and has therefore already been introduced onto the scene. The sentence is not Ph-oriented. The subject and in consequence also the verb and the adverbial element perform different dynamic functions. The verb ascribes a characteristic to a notion that has already been introduced into the flow of communication; it performs the dynamic function of expressing a quality (Q). Consequently, the subject performs the dynamic function of expressing a quality bearer (B), and the adverbial element performs the dynamic function of expressing a specification (Sp); in the absence of a further specification (see below) the adverbial element completes the development of the communication within the sentence. It follows that in the act of communication, the sentence is Sp-oriented. The dynamic functions constitute a scale reflecting a gradual rise in CD, the Quality Scale: B = Q = Sp. Again, the formula displays an interpretative arrangement, not necessarily corresponding to the actual linear arrangement.

On the other hand, a verb that from the static point of view is not one of appearance/existence can perform the App/Ex function. For instance, if in a sentence consisting of a subject and a verb, the subject conveys information irretrievable from the immediately relevant context, it will show a strong tendency to become the goal of the message and to perform the Ph-function. The verb then recedes into the background, performing the App/Ex-function. (Compare *President Kennedy has been assassinated; Präsident Kennedy ist ermordet worden; London has been bombed; Die Schule brennt.*) Under these circumstances, the sentence becomes Ph-oriented, and the intonation center would fall not on the verb, but on the subject.

Like the Existential Scale, the Quality Scale can open with a setting. Provided that the sentence structure *Years ago a young king waged hazardous wars* is entirely context-independent, it implements the Quality Scale opening with a temporal setting: *Years ago* (Set) *a young king* (B) *waged* (Q) *hazardous wars* (Sp). The setting need not be temporal or local, although these represent the two most frequent types (the temporal setting being the more frequent of the two; see Uhlířová, 1978; Horová, 1976). Under these contextual conditions, the sentence structures of 2 and 4 open with settings respectively expressing a concomitant cause and a concomitant purpose.[7] The Quality Scale can also be expanded by one or more further specifications (FSp): *Years ago* (Set) *a young king* (B) *ruled* (Q) *his country* (Sp) *capriciously and despotically* (FSp).

A point worth considering is the relationship between the Ph-function and the B-function. It may be argued that in this sentence *a king* performs a Ph-function, because the sentence could be interpreted as corresponding to *Years ago there was a young king, who ruled his country capriciously and despotically.* The two versions indeed correspond to each other, but they are not functionally equivalent.

Whereas the amended version implements the Ph-function and the B-function (in that order) separately, the original version telescopes them into one sentence constituent *a king*, thereby implementing the two functions simultaneously. Whereas the amended version consists of a principle clause and a subordinate clause, the original version consists of one sentence, which is Sp-oriented and implements the Quality Scale.

It would be odd to open a story with *He ruled his country capriciously and despotically. Years ago there was a young king.* If the narrator does so, he or she would have to explain: "Oh, I mean a young king. There was a young king, you know."

On the other hand, the narrator may open the story (though not a fairy-tale) with the sentence *He ruled* . . . , adding no apologetic explanation and treating the character as known from the very beginning. He leads the listener/reader into the middle of the story *("in medias res")*, using this type of opening as a stylistic device.

The telescoped opening, the odd opening, and the stylistically colored opening indicate that the Ph-function can be implemented simultaneously with the B-function or remain unimplemented (becoming conspicuous by its absence), but cannot be implemented *after* the B-function: A quality bearer presupposes a phenomenon appearing/existing on the scene.

Since both scales can open with settings and since a quality bearer presupposes a phenomenon appearing/existing on the scene, the two scales can be combined into one scale that reflects a gradual rise in CD: Set = App/Ex = Ph = B = Q = Sp = FSp(s).

The scales reflect the dynamic functions of context-independent elements.

As has been shown, a context-dependent element recedes into the background and irrespective of the character of its semantic content carries a low degree of CD. Context-dependence, then, tends to neutralize the dynamic semantic function of an element; it tends to bring it down to the level of a setting. In association with clues provided by context-independent elements, a context-dependent element may still suggest a distinctly dynamic function. But being context-dependent, it cannot exceed in CD any context-independent element. For instance, in the presence of context-independent elements, *He* still suggests the B-function in *He used to go for walks* and participates in implementing the Quality Scale. But it will not exceed in CD a context-independent setting in *In the late fifties, he used to go for long walks.* I shall indicate the context dependence of an element by adding a superscripted ^{d} to the symbol representing the dynamic function: *He* (B^d) *used to go* (Q) *for long walks* (Sp); *In the late fifties* (Set) *he* (B^d) *used to go* (Q) *for long walks* (Sp). The problems of the neutralization and distinctiveness of the dynamic semantic functions await further investigation, but the scales reflect a central phenomenon in the system of language, as will be demonstrated by the text analyses offered in the final section of this chapter.

THE FOUNDATION-LAYING PROCESS AND THE CORE-CONSTITUTING PROCESS

Theme, Transition, and Rheme

The dynamics of the communication can be further illustrated by two important processes: the foundation-laying and the core-constituting processes.

Some sentence elements provide a foundation upon which the remaining elements complete the information and fulfill the communicative purpose. The elements completing the information constitute the core of the information.

All elements that are retrievable from the immediately relevant context—all context-dependent elements—are foundation-laying. As for the context-independent elements, those performing the Set-function and the B-function are also foundation-laying. Under the special conditions stated below, even an App/Ex-element can become foundation-laying.

A special part is played by the verb in the act of communication. Unless context dependent (which rarely happens), it performs the App/Ex-function (see, for instance, ex. 15-18) or, more frequently, the Q-function (see, for instance, ex. 1-14 and 19-22). When performing the Q-function, it can express the very core of the information and can consequently carry the highest degree of CD, but only if no element performing an Sp-function is present in the sentence (for example, *On the following day he died*). When performing the App/Ex-function, it can become the carrier of the lowest degree of CD and hence a foundation-laying element, but only if there is no Set-element present (for example, *[It was dark] and rain was falling*).

It follows that the semantic content of the verb and the semantic relations into which it enters play an important role in determining the functional perspective of the sentence. The verb shows an un-mistakable tendency to carry the intermediate degrees of CD within a sentence. When it does so, it begins to build the core of the "message" upon the information conveyed by the foundation-laying elements. Strictly speaking, however, it is the temporal and modal exponents of the finite verb (TMEs) that start the core-constituting process.

The TMEs are the formal means used by the finite verb to signal the basic predicative categories of tense and mood; for instance, the verbal auxiliaries (e.g., *has been* in *has been written*), the verbal suffixes (e.g., *-en* in *has been written* or *-s* in *writes*), or the vowel alternation (for example, *write, wrote, written*). The TMEs establish a link between the grammatical subject and the grammatical predicate. Their gram-matical meaning, however, is rooted in their semantic content. By indicating a temporal relation and an attitude of the speaker, they provide a link between the semantic content of the sentence and the extralinguistic reality. By starting the core-constituting process, they provide a link, and at the same time a boundary, between the foun-dation and the core. (As the start of the core-constituting process, they actually belong to the core. They do not, however, perform the function ascribable to the verb, the Q-function or the App/Ex-function, a function performed by the notional component of the verb.) The congruence of all these important linking functions places the TMEs in a central position within the language system.

In the development of the communication, the TMEs fulfill their linking functions irrespective of the dynamic functions performed by the other elements in the sentence.[8] Examples 23-32 illustrate this.

(23) His father was the famous musician Johann Strauss.
(24) The famous musician Johann Strauss was his father.
(25) The lion has killed the hunter.
(26) The hunter has been killed by the lion.
(27) Peter adores Eve.
(28) Eve adores Peter.
(29) Der Lehrer wird den Schüler preisen.
(30) Der Schüler wird von dem Lehrer gepriesen werden.
(31) A strange figure appeared in the doorway.
(32) Schwere Wolken waren auf dem Himmel erschienen.

Provided the subjects of 23-30 are the only context-dependent elements within their sentence structures and the subjects of 31-32 are context independent, the interpretative arrangements of the elements are the following. (The TMEs are represented by the TME symbol, and in addition given in full in square brackets behind it. The notional component of the verb is represented by the bare present infinitive stem. The abbreviations f and c stand for "foundation" and "core," respectively.)

(23) His father (f) TME [was] be the famous musician Johann Strauss (c).
(24) The famous musician Johann Strauss (f) TME [was] be his father (c).
(25) The lion (f) TME [has -ed] kill the hunter (c).
(26) The hunter (f) TME [has been -ed] kill by the lion (c).
(27) Peter (f) TME [-s] adore Eve (c)
(28) Eve (f) TME [-s] adore Peter (c).
(29) Der Lehrer (f) TME [wird -en] preis den Schüler (c).
(30) Der Schüler (f) TME [wird ge- -ie- -en] werden preis von dem Lehrer (c).
(31) In the doorway (f) TME [-ed] appear a strange figure (c).
(32) Auf dem Himmel (f) TME [waren, -ie- -en] erschein Schwere Wolken (c).

In all the arrangements, the TMEs occur after the foundation and introduce the core, simultaneously acting as a boundary and as a link. They fulfill this function conspicuously if the finite verb serves as a copula and its notional component merely ascribes a quality. They fulfill this function whatever the contextual conditions (but see Note 8), even if the notional component of the finite verb, which shows a strong tendency to participate in the linking function, is foundation-laying or conveys the very core of the message; for example, see the interpretative arrangements as shown by 33-38.

(33) Fall (f) TME [was ing] rain (c).
(34) Expect (f) TME [is -ed] a thaw (c).
(35) Brew (f) TME [was -ing] trouble (c).
(36) He (f) TME [-ed] die (c).
(37) The rain (f) TME [has -ed] cease (c).
(38) They (f) TME [-ed] disagree (c).

In its linking function, the notional component of the finite verb may be replaced by, for instance, an adjective:

(39) She (f) TME [was] be reluctant to admit any mistake (c).
(40) He (f) TME [is] be hesitant about trusting strangers (c).
(41) They (f) TME [are] be likely to make a mess of everything (c).

The foundation-laying elements form the *theme*. The core-constituting elements form the *non-theme*. The non-theme comprises the *transition* and the *rheme*. The transition consists of elements performing the linking function. The TMEs are the transitional element par excellence: They carry the lowest degree of CD within the non-theme and are the *transition proper*. The highest degree of CD, on the other hand, is carried by the *rheme proper*.

The theme expresses what the sentence is about and constitutes the point of departure in the development of the communication. The element or elements in the theme carry the lowest degrees of CD.[9]

THE IMMEDIATELY RELEVANT CONTEXT
AND THE TERM "CONTEXT-DEPENDENT"

In a paper published in 1957 (Firbas, 1957a, pp. 36-37; see also Firbas, 1966, pp. 30-31), I emphasized that, roughly speaking, there are two types of known information conveyed by the sentence in the act of communication: (1) information that, though forming part of knowledge shared by the writer/speaker and the reader/listener, must be regarded as unknown for the immediate communicative purpose and in this sense irretrievable from the context; and (2) information that not only forms part of common knowledge shared by the writer and the reader[10] but is for the immediate communicative purpose fully retrievable from the context.

The distinction may be illustrated from a passage in J. Harris's philosophical inquiry into language and universal grammar (1751), quoted in Brown and Yule (1983, p. 170).

'Tis here we shall discover the use of the two Articles (A) and (THE). (A) respects our *primary* Perception, and denotes Individuals as *unknown;* (THE) respects our *secondary* Perception, and denotes Individuals as *known*. To explain by an example. I see an object pass by, which I never saw till then. What do I say? *There goes A Beggar, with A long Beard.* The Man departs, and returns after a week. What do I say then? *There goes THE Beggar with THE long Beard.* The article only is changed, the rest remains unaltered.

What Harris regards as primary perception of course conveys unknown information. His example of secondary perception conveys known information of type 1, but not of type 2. The beggar with the long beard may be well known to the speaker and the listener, but it is the appearance of the beggar that the speaker wishes to announce. Various other persons known to the speaker and to the listener could have appeared on the scene. In the development of the communication "the beggar with the long beard" conveys unknown information irretrievable from the immediately relevant context.

Any kind of information irretrievable from the preceding verbal context or the situational context is to be regarded as unknown. But even if conveying retrievable information, an element may simultaneously convey a piece of information that is irretrievable. For instance, in *At first, I was at a loss whether I should ask Peter or Paul, but eventually I turned to Peter,* the element *Peter* of the *but*-clause conveys retrievable information, but at the same time it conveys the speaker's choice, which is irretrievable information. There is a wide range of types of irretrievable information expressed by elements that in other respects are carriers of retrievable information.

The identification of irretrievable information does not seem to pose a particularly difficult problem, but further investigation is needed to establish the retrievability span—the stretch of the preceding verbal context within which an element remains retrievable after its last occurrence in the verbal context. Analyzing one of Aelfric's homilies, Svoboda (1981) came to the conclusion that an element remains retrievable for a stretch of context covering seven clauses. This finding may not have general validity, but it offers an indication of the shortness of the retrievability span.

Similarly, the situational context is highly restricted. It is constituted only by those objects of the situational contexts, or their parts or features, that have become a matter of immediate attention or concern for both the speaker and the listener. For instance, two friends see a ferocious dog, which naturally becomes the object of their immediate concern. "I do hope he won't bite us," one friend says to the other, making the pronoun *he* express a referent that is retrievable from the situational context.

There are also some referents that are permanently present in the situational context: the speaker/writer, the reader/listener, human beings in general, nature in general (see Svoboda, 1983, p. 55). But even these can occasionally be referred to so as to convey some additional irretrievable information; for example, contrast *(You knew about it, but I didn't)*.

Context is, of course, a complex phenomenon and comprises a number of spheres. The immediately relevant context is one of them and is embedded in the sphere formed by the entire preceding verbal context and the entire situational context accompanying it. This sphere is then embedded within one constituted by the knowledge and experience shared by the interlocutors, which in turn forms part of the general context of human knowledge and experience.

The complexity of context is increased by possible borderline areas between the spheres. There is certainly a borderline area between the immediately relevant and the immediately non-relevant verbal and situational context. For instance, in a story about Peter and Paul, both characters can become items of permanent attention and concern for the text in question. They then behave as context dependent even though not occurring within the retrievability span (compare Svoboda's "long-lived" themes; Svoboda, 1981, p. 176).

A linguistic element can be regarded as more or less dependent on all the spheres of context. The unqualified term "context dependent," however, has to be understood as referring to the immediately relevant context.

COMMUNICATIVE PURPOSE, MULTIFUNCTIONALITY, AND POTENTIALITY

The notion of "communicative purpose" plays an important role in the dynamics of the communication, for it determines the goal toward which the information is to develop within a sentence, and also the distribution of degrees of CD over the sentence elements. Communicative purpose is multifaceted, because it can be viewed from at least three angles: the communicative purpose of the speaker/writer, the interpretation of the speaker/writer's communicative purpose by the listener/reader (which may or may not be in agreement with the speaker/writer's intention), and the communicative purpose actually implied by the sentence structure.

The distribution of degrees of CD is determined by an interplay of factors. The laws of this interplay have to be observed both by the sender and the receiver of the message; otherwise, communication would break down, sender and receiver failing to understand each other, and the sender would not be able to take over the role of the receiver and vice versa. Naturally, considering the complexity of the situation in which a semantic and grammatical sentence structure operates in the act of communication, the result of the interplay of factors may be equivocal, or the interplay may be abused by the sender, or mistakenly interpreted by the receiver, or wrongly analyzed by the linguistic investigator.

From the point of view of the user the sentence structure normally performs one function at the very moment of utterance, the one that the user intends to impose upon it. Similarly, only one function is normally performed by the sentence structure from the point of view of the receiver, the one imposed upon it by his interpretation. From each point of view, the sentence structure is monofunctional. From the point of view of the communicative act, however, the sentence structure may of course become bifunctional if each of the two imposes a different interpretation on it. It is the investigator's task to determine under which conditions a sentence structure will unequivocally perform only one function and under which conditions it will permit of more than one interpretation.

The following pair of sentence structures illustrates the distinction, the analysis assuming that *you* and *I* are context dependent and the rest context independent.

(42) While I am away, you can go on working at your paper.
(43) You can go on working at your paper while I am away.

The adverbial clause of time unmistakably functions as a setting in 42, its initial position ruling out another interpretation. In 43, on the other hand, it may serve either as a setting or as a specification. This potentiality, however, can be removed by intonation, which in the spoken language operates as an additional factor.

ANALYSIS OF TEXT 1

(1) A heavy dew had fallen. (2) The grass was blue. (3) Big drops hung on the bushes (4) and just did not fall; (5) the silvery fluffy toi-toi was limp on its long stalks, (6) and all the marigolds and the pinks in the bungalow gardens were bowed to the earth with wetness. (7) Drenched were the cold fuchsias, (8) round pearls of dew lay on the flat nasturtium leaves. (Collected Stories of Katherine Mansfield, London, Constable, 1945, p. 205)[11]

Let me first establish the dynamic semantic functions performed by the sentence elements and determine whether these functions render the sentence elements thematic, transitional, or rhematic. The abbreviation "TME" has been used throughout for all the possible formal implementations of the temporal and modal exponents, which invariably constitute the transition proper. The rest of the transition has been indicated simply by "Tr." In addition, the following abbreviations have been used: Th(eme), Rh(eme), Set(ting), App(earance)/Ex(istence), Ph(enomenon appearing/existing on the scene), B(earer of quality), Q(uality), Sp(ecification), F(urther)Sp(ecification). The rhematic elements have been italicized.

(1) *A heavy dew* (Ph, Rh) had (TME) fallen (App/Ex, Th; TME).
(2) The grass (B, Th) was (TME; Tr) *blue* (Q, Rh).
(3) *Big drops* (Ph, Rh) hung (TME; Tr) on the bushes (Set, Th)
(4) and *just* (rhematic intensifier) did (TME) *not* (negation focus anticipator) *fall* (RME; Rh);
(5) the silvery fluffy toi-toi (B, Th) was (TME; Tr) *limp* (Q, Rh) on its long stalks (Set, Th),
(6) and all the marigolds and the pinks in the bungalow gardens (B, Th) were (TME) bowed (Q, Tr) *to the earth* (Sp, Rh) *with wetness* (FSp,Rh).
(7) *Drenched* (Q, Rh) were (TME) the cold fuchsias (B, Th),
(8) *round pearls of dew* (Ph, Rh) lay (TME; Tr) on the flat nasturtium leaves (Set, Th).

Of the two rhematic elements in 6, *with wetness* carries the highest degree of CD in the whole sentence, and it is to be regarded as rheme proper. *Just* and *not* in 4 are rhematic elements. They do not normally assume the function of rheme proper, for they merely tend to accompany the rheme proper and in terms of interpretative arrangement point to it and anticipate it.

Table 2.1 presents the elements of the sentences in the interpretative arrangement. The thematic, transitional and rhematic elements are placed in separate columns. In the right margin, the designations "Existential" and "Quality" stand for the Existential Scale and the Quality Scale.

The TMEs occupy a central position within the interpretative arrangement, which coincides with their central function in the syntactic structure of the sentence. With the exception of 1 and 4, the TMEs are joined in their mediatory role by the notional component of the finite verb. (In 1 the notional component is thematic, in 4 rhematic.) The notional component predominantly serves to introduce a Ph-element into the development of the communication. The TMEs, together with the transitional components of the finite verbs, form a string separating the thematic and the rhematic layer within the paragraph.[12] These roles of the TMEs and the notional component of the finite verb emerge also from the analyses of Texts 2 and 3.

The thematic elements mostly perform the B-function and the Set-function. Only one thematic element is verbal (in 1); as the only other element present is a Ph-element, it performs the App/Ex-function. The thematic layer does not contain any context-dependent elements, though these are normally frequent in thematic layers. With the exception of the verb *fall*, all the elements constituting the thematic layer refer to parts of the bay, the place the story is about.

Even the rhematic layer shows a high degree of semantic homogeneity. The first rhematic element, performing a Ph-function, introduces the notion of "a heavy dew" into the narration, and all the remaining rhematic elements express the various forms of wetness and the effects it has produced.

In this way, the two layers form two semantically homogeneous complexes: one—the thematic complex—presenting the bay; the other—the rhematic complex—depicting the wetness affecting it. The tabular arrangement makes this particularly clear. The thematic layer presents the bay as the subject of the description offered by the rhematic layer; the rhemes express some information about the parts of the bay. This establishes and characterizes the "aboutness" feature of the thematic layer in general and the "aboutness"

TABLE 2.1

THEME	NON-THEME		SCALE
	TRANSITION	RHEME	
(1) fall Ap/Ex	TME	a heavy dew Ph	Existential
(2) the grass B	TME was	blue Q	Quality
(3) on the bushes Set	TME hung Ap/Ex	big drops Ph	Existential
(4) [ellipted]	TME	not fall Q	Quality
(5) the silvery fluffy toi-toi B on its stalks Set	TME was	limp Q	Quality
(6) all the marigolds and the pinks in the bungalow gardens B	TME bowed Q	to the earth Sp with wetness FSp	Quality
(7) the cold fuchsias B	TME were	drenched Q	Quality
(8) on the flat nasturtium leaves Set	TME lay Ap/Ex	round pearls of dew Ph	Existential

features of the individual themes in particular.[13] The degree of semantic homogeneity of a thematic or a rhematic layer within a paragraph may vary; but as the analyses of Texts 2 and 3 will also show, semantic homogeneity can play an important role in the semantic structure of a paragraph and heighten the effectiveness of the message.

All the articles occurring in the thematic layer are definite; the rhematic layer, on the other hand, contains only one definite article, all the other articles used in it being nongeneric indefinite articles or their zero plural variants. This distribution of articles is not the only one possible. As has been shown elsewhere, the definite article is not excluded from the rheme, nor is the indefinite article excluded from the theme (Firbas, 1966). Nevertheless, under favorable contextual conditions they can appear in opposition and efficiently cooperate in signaling the theme and the rheme within the sentence and the thematic and the rhematic layers within the paragraph.

The extract contains three implementations of the Existential Scale and five implementations of the Quality Scale. This reflects a predominance of the Quality Scale, testified to by other analyses even more conspicuously (Firbas, 1975b, pp. 322-331; 1981, pp. 55-66; see also the analyses of the other texts). Some readers may regard 3 and 8 as implementations of the Quality Scale. If they do so,

they will place the elements *big drops* and *round pearls,* which participate in expressing various forms of wetness, in the thematic layer,
which otherwise enumerates the parts of the scene, and the elements
on the bushes and *on the flat nasturtium leaves,* which participate in
enumerating the parts of the scene, in the rhematic layer, which
otherwise expresses various forms of wetness. They will then reduce
the high degrees of homogeneity which the thematic and the rhematic layers display.

I do not intend to deal here with the relationship between FSP
and intonation, but I note that if attentive readers place the intonation center on the elements expressing the various forms of wetness
(i.e., on the rhemes proper, according to the interpretation in the
table) they will throw into relief the core of the information.

My analysis undoubtedly bears out what Katherine Mansfield
herself has said about her own way of writing, as well as what Ian
A. Gordon, the editor of a collection of her New Zealand stories
(Mansfield, 1974), has said about her art,

> I have a passion for technique. I have a passion for making the thing
> into a *whole* if you know what I mean. Out of technique is born real
> style, I believe. There are no short cuts. (Mansfield, 1928, Vol. 2, p. 92;
> quoted after Gordon in Mansfield, 1974, p. xviii)

> I choose not only the length of every sentence, but even the sound of
> every sentence. I choose the rise and fall of every paragraph to fit her,
> and to fit her on that day and at that very moment. After I'd written it I
> read it aloud—numbers of times—just as one would *play over* a musical
> composition—trying to get it nearer and nearer to the expression—
> until it fitted her. (Mansfield, ibid, p. 88; quoted after Gordon, in
> Mansfield, 1974, pp. xviii-xix)

> There is nothing in the best writing of Katherine Mansfield that is not
> planned and executed with consummate skill. She is one of the most
> professional writers in the language and her writing can stand up to
> the most rigorous analysis (Gordon, in Mansfield, 1974, p. xxi)

The extract from Katherine Mansfield's short story did not contain subordinate clauses or semiclauses (consisting of a non-finite
verb form and an element or elements expanding it). The remaining
texts contain both types of structure.

Irrespective of its place within the network of subordination, a
subordinate clause or semiclause serves as a unit within its superor-

dinate structure, at the same time providing a distributional subfield of CD. All subordinate clauses and semiclauses that serve as units within a principal clause as well as relative clauses qualifying a headword embedded in the principal clause will be examined for the distribution of CD over their elements.[14] To simplify the analysis all such structures will be dealt with separately.

ANALYSIS OF TEXT 2

Gandhi Promises Punjab Solution but Refuses to Bow to "Cult of Violence"

From Kuldip Nayear

(1) India will solve the Punjub problem without yielding to "separatist ideologies and to the cult of violence," Mr. Rajiv Gandhi, the Prime Minister, has told the nation.
(2) Outlining Government policy on Saturday in his first television and radio broadcast since last month's victory, Mr. Gandhi promised to give priority to resolving the problem, caused by Sikh extremist demands for a separate state.
(3) The recently appointed Cabinet committee would study various aspects of the issue and suggest a solution within a specified time-frame, he said.
(4) Despite a tough attitude to the extremists, Mr. Gandhi held an olive branch to the Sikh community.
(5) He said: "In ending the sad chapter of discord, all should cooperate. The Sikhs are as much part of India as any other community." (The Times, Monday, January 27, 185, p. 7)

(1) *India will solve the Punjab problem without yielding to "separatist ideologies and to the cult of violence"* (FSp, Rh)[i], Mr Rajiv Gandhi, the Prime Minister (B, Th) has (TME) told (TME; Q. Tr) *the nation* (Sp, Rh).
(2) Outlining Government policy on Saturday in his first television and radio broadcast since last month's victory (Set., Th)[i], Mr Gandhi (B^d, Th) promised (TME; Q, Tr) *to give priority to resolve the problem, caused by Sikh extremist demands for a separate state* (Sp, Rh)[ii].

(3) *The recently appointed Cabinet committee would study various aspects of the issue and suggest a solution within a specified time-frame* (Sp, Rh)[i], he (B[d], Th) said (TME; Q, Tr).

(4) Despite a tough attitude to the extremists (Set, Th), Mr Gandhi (B[d], Th) held (TME; Q, Tr) *an olive branch* (Sp, Rh) to the Sikh community (Set[d], Th).

(5) He (B[d], Th) said (TME; Q, Tr): *"In ending the sad chapter of discord, all should cooperate. The Sikhs are as much part of India as any other community"* (Q, Rh)[i, ii].

(1[1]) India (B, Th) will (TME) solve (Q, Tr) *the Punjab problem* (Sp,Rh) *without yielding to "separatist ideologies and to the cult of violence"* (FSp, Rh).

(2[1]) Outlining (tme; Q, Tr)[15] *Government policy* (Sp, Rh) on Saturday (Set, Tr) in his first television and radio broadcast since last month's victory (Set, Tr),

(2[ii]) to give (tme; Q, Tr) *priority* (Sp, Rh) *to resolving the problem caused by Sikh extremist demands for a separate state* (FSp, Rh).

(3[1]) The recently appointed Cabinet committee (B, Th) would (TME) study (Q, Tr) *various aspects of this issue* (Sp, Rh) and suggest (Q, Tr) *a solution* (Sp, Rh) *within a specified time-frame* (FSp, Rh).

(5[1]) In ending the sad chapter of discord (Set, Th), all (B, Th) should (TME) *cooperate* (Q, Rh).

(5[ii]) The Sikhs (B[d], Th) are (TME; ascription of Q) *as much part of India as any other community* (Q, Rh).[16]

In contrast with the extract from Mansfield's short story, the newspaper report consistently retains one and the same referent throughout the thematic elements of the principal clauses: *Mr Rajiv Gandhi, the Prime Minister; Mr Gandhi; he; Mr Gandhi; He.* Each expression of the referent carries the lowest degree of CD within its thematic section, and in consequence within the entire sentence. This accounts for a very high degree of semantic homogeneity within the thematic layer of the passage. The expressions referring to Mr Gandhi constitute a *hypertheme*,[17] conveying what the entire passage is about.

If present, other thematic elements serve as points of departure as well, but only in regard to the distributional fields in which they occur. This role raises their CD within the theme. They express various aspects of the content of Mr. Gandhi's speech (see Svoboda, 1981, 1983).

The gist of the speech is presented within the rhematic layer of the passage, culminating in the rhemes proper of the two final complex distributional fields: *an olive branch* and *as much part of India as any other community*. Only in one case does the notional component of the finite verb appear within the rhematic layer (*cooperate* in the direct speech in 5[i]).

An interesting problem is posed by the relationship between the headline—Gandhi (B, Th) promises (TME; Q, Tr) solution (Sp,Rh), but refuses (TME; Q, Tr) to bow to 'cult of violence' (Sp, Rh)—and the text of the report. It could be argued that the notions occurring in the headline are repeated in the text and should therefore be interpreted as context dependent. However, the notions presented as rhematic in the headline are presented as the most important (i.e., they are rhematic) also within the direct speech contained in the opening sentence of the text, and *Gandhi* appears in that sentence with the title *Mr.*, the first name, and the designation of office. Hence, the reporter indicates that he is making a fresh start, so that in this news report (though not necessarily always) the headline and the body of the text fulfill two different communicative purposes. The headline summarizes the most important point, and the report independently gives the information in full detail.

ANALYSIS OF TEXT 3

Dear Resident,

(1) We have a major problem at International Students House of residents removing items of furniture and equipment from the public areas of the House ([1a] and I include Mary Trevelyan Hall as well as Great Portland Street house) for use in their own rooms.

(2) I write to inform you that this practice must cease (3) and as from the 5th November I will instruct the Housekeeper at GPS and the Domestic Bursar at MTH to remove any such items of furniture, etc. from residents' rooms, and to inform me of which items come from which rooms. (4) If a resident persists in misappropriating such items, then a charge will have to be made to the resident for replacing such items in their proper places.

(5) I appreciate that some residents will require extra pieces of furniture in their rooms and (6) have no objection to them purchasing such

pieces and bringing them to their rooms, provided that they do not impede the cleaning staff or, in shared rooms, other occupants.

Yours sincerely,
[signature]
Director

(1) We (B^d, Th) have (TME; Q, Tr) *a major problem* (Sp, Rh)^i at International Students House (Set, Th) *of residents removing items of furniture and equipment from the public areas of the House* (Sp, Rh)^i ([Ia] and I [B^d, Th] include [TME; Q, Tr] *Mary Trevelyan Hall as well as the Great Portland Street house* [Sp, Rh]) for use in *their own rooms* (Sp, Rh)^i.

(2) I (B^d, Th) write (TME; Q, Tr) *to inform you that this practice must cease* (Sp, Rh)^i

(3) and as from the 5th November (Set, Th) I (B^d, Th) will (TME) instruct (Q,Tr) *the Housekeeper at GPS and the Domestic Bursar at MTH* (Sp, Rh) *to remove any such items of furniture, etc. from residents' rooms* (FSp, Rh)^i *and to inform me of which items come from which rooms* (FSp, Rh)^{ii}.

(4) If a resident persists in misappropriating such items (Set, Th)^i, then (Set, Th) *a charge* (Ph, Rh)^{ii} will have to be (TME) made (TME; App/Ex, Tr) to the resident (Set^d, Th) *for replacing such items in their proper places* (Ph, Rh)^{ii}.

(5) I (B^d, Th) appreciate (TME; Q, Tr) *that some residents will require extra pieces of furniture in their rooms* (Sp, Rh)^i and have (TME; Q, Tr) *no objection* (Sp, Rh) *to them purchasing such pieces and bringing them to their rooms* (FSp, Rh)^{ii} *provided that they do not impede the cleaning staff or, in shared rooms, other occupants* (FFSp, Rh)^{iii}.

(1^1) of residents (B, Th) removing (tme; Q, Tr) *items of furniture and equipment* (Sp, Rh) *from the public areas of the House* (FSp, Rh) . . . *for use in their own rooms* (FFSp, Rh).

(2^1) to inform (tme; Q, Tr) you (Set^d, Th) *that this practice must cease* (Sp, Rh)

(3^1) to remove (tme; Q, Tr) *any such items of furniture, etc.* (Sp, Rh) *from residents' rooms* (FSp, Rh).

(3^{ii}) to inform (tme; Q, Tr) me (Set^d, Th) *of which items come from which rooms* (Sp, Rh).

(4^1) If (Tr) a resident (B^d, Th) persists (TME; Q, Tr) *in misappropriating such items* (Sp, Rh),

(4^{ii}) for replacing (tme; Q, Tr) such items (Set^d, Th) *in their proper places* (Sp, Rh).

(5^i) that some residents (B, Th) will (TME) require (Q, Tr) *extra pieces of furniture* (Sp, Rh) in their rooms (Set^d, Th)

(5^{ii}) to them (B^d, Th) purchasing (tme; Q, Tr) such pieces (Set^d, Th) and bringing (tme; Q, Tr) them (Set^d, Th) *to their rooms* (Sp, Rh)

(5^{iii}) provided (Tr) that they (B^d, Th) do (TME) *not* (neg, foc. ant., Rh) impede (Q, Tr) *the cleaning staff* (Sp, Rh) or, in shared rooms (Set, Th) *other occupants* (Sp, Rh).

A comparatively small number of items are thematic. They refer to the Director (the writer of the letter), the resident or residents, the International Students House itself, the residents' rooms, pieces of furniture; they also refer to the practice of removing pieces of furniture from their proper places, two points of time and a concomitant condition. The items of the thematic layer have a common denominator—the director of and the residents in a hall of residence, and the placing of the furniture there—and provide an appropriate foundation for the message.

The nonthematic elements are far more numerous and syntactically more complex than the thematic, as would be expected from the greater amount of CD that they carry. Furthermore, the syntactic structure of the nonthematic layer provides a strikingly greater number of distributional subfields of CD (eleven) than the thematic layer (one).

Six of the distributional subfields are provided by semiclauses. Not having a finite verb, a semiclause reduces the number of genuine TMEs within a sentence, resulting in condensation,[18] as we can see by comparing the condensed form of the first sentence of the circular with its uncondensed counterpart, see Vachek, 1955. (The interpretations in parentheses relate to the superordinate sentence level, those in brackets to the subordinate clause level.)

We (Th) have (TME; Tr) a major problem (Rh) at International Students House (Th) of residents removing items of furniture and equipment from the public areas of the House for use in their own rooms (Rh).

We (Th) have (TME; Tr) a major problem (Rh) at International Students House (Th) in that residents [Th] remove [TME; Tr] items of furniture and equipment from the public areas of the House [Rh] (Rh) so that they [Th] may [TME] make [Tr] use [Rh] of them [Th] in their own rooms [Rh] (Rh).

The TMEs occur only once in the first sentence, but three times in the second. While operating only at the superordinate sentence level in the first, they serve both at the superordinate sentence level and at the subordinate clause level in the second. Employing the TMEs only once, the first sentence makes its nonthematic section more compact and makes the linking and delimiting functions of the TMEs at the superordinate sentence level more prominent. The Director's letter shows the role that complex condensation (the use of semiclausal and nonclausal structures instead of subordinate clauses) can play in the dynamics of the communication.

The analyses of texts demonstrate the significance of the theory of FSP for composition research, even though the theory seems to be preoccupied with sentences. In fact, the theory of FSP is context oriented, paying constant regard to the way in which every sentence element is related to and eventually integrated into the context. The theory examines the context immediately relevant to the sentence and therefore explores the communicative structure of the paragraph. Analysis of the thematic and the rhematic layers of the paragraph and of the progression of communication within them leads in turn to the study of this progression beyond the paragraph to the text as a whole. Whereas the theory of FSP begins with the sentence and moves on to larger units, composition research may well choose to move in the opposite direction, taking the entire text as its starting point.[19]

NOTES

1. The English term "functional sentence perspective" is modelled on Mathesius's German term "Satz-perspective" (Mathesius, 1929a). I believe that I was the first to use it (Firbas, 1957a, pp. 171-173; 1957b), but I hasten to add that it had been suggested to me by Josef Vachek in a private communication in 1956.

2. Compare, for example, Mathesius (1929a, 1929b, 1932, 1936, 1975), Vachek (1964, 1966, 1976), and Daneš (1964, 1984). I do not refer to these scholars' earlier relevant essays, because they were written in Czech.

3. The results of our investigations have been published particularly in *Brno Studies in English* (see the bibliographies in Tyl et al., 1970; Firbas & Golková, 1975; and *Brno Studies in English 14*, pp. 15-22).

4. It is praised, for example, by Lyons (1974, p. 1006): "Current Prague school work is still characteristically functional in the sense in which this term was interpreted in the pre-World War II period. The most valuable contribution by the

postwar Prague school is probably the distinction of theme and rheme and the notion of 'functional sentence perspective' or 'communicative dynamism.'" Perhaps the severest criticism has come from Szwedek in his contribution prepared for the Conference on Contrastive Projects, Charzykowy, December 1980, which I have seen only in a preprint. The relevant part is discussed in Firbas (1983, pp. 9-36).

In addition to the Brno group there are other Czech scholars working in the field of FSP, notably the teams of Daneš and that of Sgall and Hajičová.

5. My grateful thanks are due to Sidney Greenbaum for his editorial work on my contribution as well as for his valuable comments on its preliminary version. I also wish to thank Charles R. Cooper, Tom P. Lavelle, and Cezar Ornatowski for their most welcome comments.

6. The semantic content of an object is an essential amplification of the semantic content of a transitive verb. If context independent, the amplifying content contributes more to the development of the communication than the content to be amplified (see Firbas, 1959). A context-independent object implemented by a noun conveying entirely irretrievable information cannot be replaced by a pronoun; for instance, by *him* in *You want to know what happened last Sunday. Well, I met an old friend of mine* (or: *good old Jack*, or *the man with the long beard who lives in your street*). In the spoken language, the context-independent nominal object shows a strong tendency to bear a prosodically weightier feature than the finite verb (see Firbas, 1968). This is particularly striking in German where it will do so even if preceding the finite verb *(Er hat eine hohe Auszeichnung bekommen;* see Bierwisch, 1952; Firbas, 1979, p. 37). In standard Czech, in which nonemotive word order shows a clear tendency toward a gradual rise in CD, a context-independent nominal object follows the finite verb *(Brutus zabil Cezara,* "Brutus killed Caesar"), whereas a context-dependent nominal object generally precedes it *(Cezara zabil Brutus,* "Caesar was killed by Brutus").

The same applies to the high degree of CD carried by a context-independent subject conveying a phenomenon appearing/existing on the scene. Under the contextual conditions stipulated earlier, such a subject will carry the most conspicuous prosodic feature (the intonation center) in an English, German or Czech sentence (see, for example, Schubiger, 1964, pp. 259, 264).

7. Some further examples of settings: *If she comes, she will have to help us; We can always lend you the book if you wish; Although he is not very rich, he is sure to help you and lend you some money; It will be a surprise for him when he learns about it.* Provided only the pronouns and *the book* are context independent, the *if*-clauses convey concomitant conditions, the *although*-clause a concomitant concession, and the *when*-clause a temporal setting.

8. This does not apply to "second instance" sentences, see Firbas, 1968. By a second instance sentence I mean a semantic and grammatical sentence structure that is repeated or creates the impression of being repeated in order to convey a sharp contrast for only one of its semantic contents or only one of the features of such a content. For instance, *HAS* in the structure *Father HAS explained it to him,* with a heavy contrastive intonation center on *HAS,* may indicate (among other possibilities) a contrast in time. "Second instance" sentences are a comparatively rare phenomenon. Only "first instance" sentences occur in the texts analyzed in the final section of this chapter.

9. Even the theme can be subdivided. In fact, its subdivision plays an important role in the theory of FSP. For the purpose of this essay, however, I shall not use special

terms for the subcomponents of the theme. For a discussion of the function of thematic elements, see Svoboda (1983).

10. To avoid the cumbersome repetition of the double designations of "writer/ speaker" and "reader/listener" I often use simple designations instead: occasionally "sender" and "receiver," or merely "interlocutor(s)."

11. The extract is taken from Katherine Mansfield's story "At the Bay." I have previously analyzed it to compare the FSP function of its grammatical subjects with those in the Czech translation, particularly for causes of potentiality in the Czech version (Firbas, 1966, pp. 35-36).

12. Instead of speaking of a string constituted by the transitional TMEs and the transitional components of the finite verbs, we could equally well speak of a transitional layer.

13. The terms "topic" and "comment" have not been used in my writings, but the general theme of the passage and the individual themes of its sentences indeed serve as "topics" in the ordinary meaning of the word, i.e. "subject for conversation, talk, writing, and so on." On the other hand, the ordinary meaning of "comment" needs to be somewhat extended for the contrasting term.

14. For instance, the relative subordinate clause in *you shall not fear . . . the arrow that flies by day*. Even an attributive structure consisting of a headword and a nonclausal attribute provides a distributional subfield of CD (e.g., *separatist ideologies;* see Svoboda, 1968). If it is context independent, an attribute (clausal or nonclausal) carries a higher degree of CD than its headword, irrespective of sentence position. A consistent analysis of all the subordinate structures would give an even more detailed picture of the way the various linguistic elements participate in the development of communication. As the analysis shows, syntactic subordination does not necessarily entail a fall in CD. On the contrary, it is frequently linked with a rise in CD.

15. If expanded by a context-independent element performing the Q-function, the non-finite verb performs the Q-function and is transitional. Tense and mood depend on its superordinate finite verb. In this sense, its formal exponents function as transition proper, a function analogous to that of the TMEs of the superordinate finite, but they do not express the temporal and modal indications independently. The symbol "tme" has been used to represent this function, the small letters indicating that they are not the "genuine" TMEs.

16. Within this subject complement, *as any other community* is the carrier of a higher degree of CD, at the same time carrying the highest degree of CD within the entire sentence.

17. Hypertheme is a thematic element occurring in more than one of (frequently successive) thematic sections within the thematic layer; see Daneš (1974).

18. The interpretation refers to the entire semiclause, which of course provides a subfield of its own: *in misappropriating* (tme; Q, Rh) *such items* (Set[d], Th).

19. For the wider theoretical framework in which the theory is set, the reader may find it useful to consult Mathesius (1975) and Daneš (1984). For a further study of thematic progression, see Daneš (1974) and Svoboda (1981). Of special interest are the relationship between FSP and word order and the relationship between FSP and intonation. For a discussion of the former, see Firbas (1964) and for a discussion of the latter, see Firbas (in press b).

REFERENCES

Bierwisch, M. (1952). Two critical problems in accent rules. *Journal of linguistics, 4,* 173-178.

Bolinger, D. L. (1952). Linear modification. *Publications of the Modern Language Association of America, 67,* 1117-1144.

Brown, G., & Yule, G. (1983). *Discourse analysis.* Cambridge: Cambridge University Press.

Daneš, F. (1964). A three-level approach to syntax. *Travaux linguistiques de Prague, 1,* 225-240.

Daneš, F. (1966). The relation of centre and periphery as a language universal. *Travaux linguistiques de Prague, 2,* 9-21.

Daneš, F. (1974). Functional sentence perspective and the organization of the text. In F. Daneš (Ed.) *Papers on functional sentence perspective* (pp. 106-128). Prague: Academia.

Daneš, F. (1984). *On Prague school functionalism in linguistics.* Trier: Linguistic Agency, University of Trier.

Duden Grammatik. (1959). Mannheim: Bibliographisches Institut.

Firbas, J. (1957a). K otázce nezákladových podmětů v současné angličtině [On the problem of non-thematic subjects in contemporary English). *Časopis pro moderní filologii 39:* 22-42, 165-173.

Firbas, J. (1957b). Some thoughts of the function of word order in Old English and Modern English. *Sborník prací filozofické fakulty brněnské univerzity* A5: 72-100.

Firbas, J. (1959). Thoughts on the communicative function of the verb in English, German and Czech. *Brno Studies in English, 1,* 39-68.

Firbas, J. (1964). From comparative word-order studies (Thoughts on V. Mathesius' conception of the word-order system). *Brno Studies in Engish 4,* 111-128.

Firbas, J. (1966). Non-thematic subjects in contemporary English. *Travaux linguistiques de Prague, 2,* 239-256.

Firbas, J. (1968). On the prosodic features of the modern English finite verb as means of functional sentence perspective (More thoughts on transition proper). *Brno Studies in English, 7,* 12-47.

Firbas, J. (1975a). On existence/appearance on the scene in functional sentence perspective. *Prague studies in English, 16,* 47-70.

Firbas, J. (1975b). On the thematic and the non-thematic section of the sentence. In *Style and text (Studies presented to Nils Erik Enkvist)* (pp. 317-334). Stockholm: Skriptor.

Firbas, J. (1979). A functional view of 'ordo naturalis.' *Brno Studies in English, 13,* 29-59.

Firbas, J. (1980). Post-intonation-centre prosodic shade in the modern English clause. In S. Greenbaum, G. Leech, & J. Svartik (Eds.), *Studies in English linguistics for Randolph Quirk* (pp. 125-133). London: Longman.

Firbas, J. (1981). Scene and perspective. *Brno Studies in English, 14,* 37-79.

Firbas, J. (1983). On some basic issues of the theory of functional sentence perspective (Comments on Alexander Szwedek's critique). *Brno Studies in English, 15,* 9-36.

Firbas, J. (in press a). Carriers of communicative dynamism. *Prague Studies in English, 18.*

Firbas, J. (in press b). Thoughts on functional sentence perspective, intonation and emotiveness. *Brno Studies in English, 16.*

Firbas, J., & Golková, E. (1975). *An analytical bibliography of Czechoslovak studies in functional sentence perspective.* Brno: Brno University.

Gordon, I. A. (Ed). (1974). *The New Zealand stories of Katherine Mansfield.* London: Longman.

Greenbaum, S. (1984). Three English versions of Psalm 23. *Journal of English linguistics, 17,* 1-23.

Greenbaum, S., Leech, G., & Svartvik, J. (Eds.). (1980). *Studies in English linguistics for Randolph Quirk.* London: Longman.

Horová, E. (1976). On position and function of English local and temporal adverbials. *Brno Studies in English, 12,* 93-123.

Lyons, J. (1974). Linguistics. In *The New Encyclopedia Britannica in 30 volumes, Macropaedia* (Vol. 10, pp. 992-1013).

Mathesius, V. (1929a). Zur Satzperspektive im modernen Englisch. *Archiv für das Studium der neueren Sprachen und Literaturen, 155,* 202-210.

Mathesius, V. (1929b). On linguistic characterology with illustrations from modern English. In *Actes du Premier Congrès International de linguistes à la Haye du 10-15 avril 1928.* Leiden.

Mathesius, V. (1932). La place de la linguistique functionnelle et structurelle dans le développment général des études linguistiques. *Časopis pro moderní filologii, 18,* 1-7.

Mathesius, V. (1936). On some problems of the systematic analysis of grammar. *Travaux du Circle Linguistique de Prague, 6,* 95-107.

Mathesius, V. (1975). *A functional analysis of present-day English on a general linguistic basis.* L. Dušková (Trans.), J. Vachek (Ed.). Prague: Academia.

Mansfield, K. (1945). *Collected stories of Katherine Mansfield.* London: Constable.

Mansfield, K. (1974). *The New Zealand stories of Katherine Mansfield.* I. A. Gordon (Ed.). London: Longman.

Schubiger, M. (1964). The interplay and co-operation of word-order and intonation in English. *In honour of Daniel Jones* (pp. 255-265). London: Longman.

Sgall, P., Hajičová, E., and Benešová, E. (1973). *Topic, focus, semantics.* Kronberg/Ts.: Scriptor.

Svoboda, A. (1968). The hierarchy of communicative units and fields as illustrated by English attributive constructions. *Brno Studies in English, 7,* 49-101.

Svoboda, A. (1981). *Diatheme.* Brno: Brno University.

Svoboda, A. (1983). Thematic elements. *Brno Studies in English, 15,* 49-85.

Tyl, Z., et al. (1970). *A tentative bibliography of studies in functional sentence perspective.* Prague: Institute for Czech language, Czechoslovak Academy of Sciences.

Uhlířová, L. (1978). On the statistical distribution of adverbials. *Prague studies in mathematical linguistics, 6,* 59-72.

Vachek, J. (1955). Some thoughts on the so-called complex condensation in modern English. *Sborník prací filozofické fakulty brněnské univerzity.* A4, 63-77.

Vachek, J. (Ed.). (1964). *A Prague School reader in linguistics.* Bloomington, IN: Indiana University Press.

Vachek, J. (1966). *The linguistic school of Prague.* Bloomington, IN: Indiana University Press.

Vachek, J. (1976). *Selected writings in English and general linguistics.* Prague: Academia.

3

Given and New Information and Some Aspects of the Structures, Semantics, and Pragmatics of Written Texts

WILLIAM J. VANDE KOPPLE

In recent years several closely related terms have become increasingly prominent in many different academic fields. Among these terms are *communicative dynamism, topical sentence articulation, contextual sentence organization, informational structure of the sentence, actual division of sentences, psychological subject and predicate, topic* and *comment, given* and *new, presupposition* and *focus,* and *theme, transition,* and *rheme.* The concepts signified by these terms have begun to play important roles in linguistics, psycholinguistics, information science, language acquisition, English as a second language, and translation, reading, and composition theory.

As Givón (1983a) notes, it is difficult to settle on a single source for these concepts. They have figured prominently in the work of Bolinger, of Firth and some of his coworkers, and of several linguists associated with the Prague linguistic circle. Many linguists, however, agree that Weil's *De L'Ordre des mots dans les langues anciennes comparees aux langues modernes* (1844; translated into English in 1887 with the title *The Order of Words in the Ancient Languages Compared with That of the Modern Languages)* is the ultimate source for many of these ideas. And many linguists would agree that these concepts were subsequently refined and extended most fully by Mathesius and his associates in the Prague linguistic circle as they developed the theory of Functional Sentence Perspective (FSP).

As their name indicates, Functional Sentence Perspectivists take a functional approach to language, an approach that should appeal to composition specialists in several ways. Among other things, linguistic functionalists believe that they should investigate what language does, how people use it in various ways to achieve various purposes. Thus their focus is primarily on connected texts, not on isolated or randomly connected sentences, since people rarely use the latter for communicative purposes. And in much of their work they proceed by examining the relationships between the structure and meaning of a text, the extralinguistic situation the text exists in and for, the communicative function the text apparently has, and the writer's or speaker's apparent assumptions about the state of his or her addressee's motivation, knowledge, and consciousness.

It is not surprising, therefore, that Functional Sentence Perspectivists believe that "the structure of utterances is determined by the use to which they are put and the communicative context in which they occur" (Lyons, 1981, p. 227). As a result, they begin much of their work by analyzing "the sentence [by which they generally mean an independent clause] into parts having a function in the total communication process" (Halliday, 1974, p. 43). We must realize, however, that not all FSP linguists agree on the number of parts into which a sentence should be analyzed; how the parts are to be distinguished from one another, especially in complex sentences; what the parts should be called; and what functions they have. In fact, some Functional Sentence Perspectivists have achieved a degree of notoriety for having the same view of and name for different linguistic elements or for having different views of and names for the same linguistic elements. Moreover, some of their arguments are tarnished by a lack of explicitness and by internal contradictions.

Yet we probably can say with justification that there are three dominant formulations of FSP, one of which (that based on the distinction between given and new information) is the primary concern of this chapter. These formulations correspond to each other in some details and often share terms. In fact, it is often the case that these formulations differ more in orientation and emphasis than in essence.

THREE DOMINANT FORMULATIONS OF FSP

According to one of these views, we should analyze a sentence in a text into two parts. These are most commonly named the *theme* and the *rheme,* but sometimes they are called the *topic* and the *comment* (see Kirkwood, 1969). Mathesius was one of the first to describe this distinction, and his words probably still capture what most theorists mean by *theme:* It is the segment "that is being spoken about in the sentence" (cited in Daneš, 1974, p. 106). Halliday (1967) notes that in neutral forms of sentences the element or constituent appearing first is the natural theme. Mathesius also delineates what most theorists still take the *rheme* to be: It is "what the speaker says about . . . [the] theme" (cited in Daneš, 1974, p. 106). In effect, Mathesius is saying that declarative sentences in many languages function to express something *(b)* about something else *(a)* with the preferred order of *a* before *b.* Obviously, this is a distinction very close to that between subject and predicate in philosophy and logic.

For example, consider the following sentence: "Barb runs sixteen miles a day." In it, the theme is *Barb* and the rheme is *runs sixteen miles a day.* In this and many other sentences, the theme often corresponds to the syntactic subject, and the rheme often corresponds to the complete syntactic predicate.

The second formulation of FSP, one that Daneš (1974) views as a refinement of the first, has been developed primarily by Jan Firbas (1974, 1982, this volume). He has probably been more explicit about and consistent with the definitions of terms he uses and has employed his analysis with more precision than nearly any other writer associated with FSP. Firbas writes that we can, if we wish, view each word in a sentence of a text as carrying some degree of communicative dynamism. To the best of my knowledge, he does not give these degrees absolute and numerical values; they are relative values within a sentence. That is, one segment carries the least communicative dynamism, another carries the most communicative dynamism, and each of the other segments carries a degree of communicative dynamism that is somewhere between these two extremes.

To learn how much relative dynamism a particular word carries, one must determine "the extent to which . . . [it] contributes towards the development of the communication" (Firbas, 1974, p. 19). And to do this, Firbas notes, one must bear in mind that words that can be derived from the verbal or situational context and that lead to no elaboration in subsequent sentences carry the least communicative dynamism. Further, words that cannot be derived from the verbal or situational context and that lead to the most elaboration in subsequent sentences carry the most communicative dynamism. These criteria begin to reveal why FSP is relevant to the analysis of texts. Parts of a particular sentence are distinguished on the basis of how they relate to material expressed before and after that sentence. Although admitting that a gradual increase in communicative dynamism need not be implemented in a linear fashion, Firbas hypothesizes that for many languages the "basic distribution of . . . [communicative dynamism] is implemented by a series of elements opening with the element carrying the very lowest and gradually passing on to the element carrying the very highest degree of . . . [communicative dynamism]" (Firbas, 1974, p. 22).

As I noted earlier, Firbas writes that we can assign each word in a sentence some degree of communicative dynamism. In fact, sometimes he assigns even morphemes and submorphemic units a degree of communicative dynamism. For example, he writes (1974) that in the sentence *He has fallen ill, He* carries the least communicative dynamism, *has* and *-en* have slightly more communicative dynamism, *fall-* has yet a degree more, and *ill* carries the most communicative dynamism.

But Firbas stresses that the delicacy with which we segment a sentence "depends on the purpose of the investigation" (1974, p. 25). And in most cases he would probably say that it is sufficient to divide sentences into three parts. One, called the theme, carries the least communicative dynamism; another, called the transition, carries an intermediate amount of communicative dynamism; and another, called the rheme, carries the most communicative dynamism. Thus for most purposes he would divide the example sentence into *He, has fallen,* and *ill.*

As I read more and more of Firbas's work, I increasingly suspect that in it there are emphases regarding writers, readers, and texts that should interest composition and reading specialists. Firbas focuses on how a text develops, on how it is pushed forward, on what will be written, on the introduction of contextually independent information into a text. And these foci are closely allied with a concern for the writer's perspective, for the writer's task of expanding information. At a particular point in the analysis of a text, Firbas is looking ahead, is concentrating on how the text will develop.

The third formulation of FSP, the primary concern of this chapter, is similar to the second. However, it usually analyzes sentences in texts into only two parts, develops ideas associated with contextual dependence somewhat differently than Firbas does, and has a slightly different set of emphases.

One of the segments into which theorists associated with this formulation analyze sentences is defined as the segment that bears given information. This is information that is very roughly equivalent to all that is found in or derivable from earlier portions of the text. Occasionally I will use the term *topic* for this segment, for convenience and because many other writers define *topic* in this way. The other segment of the sentence is that which expresses new information, information that is very roughly equivalent to that which is not found in or derivable from earlier portions of a text. Here again it is easy to see that FSP analyses are inherently text based, for one cannot decide what is given or new in a sentence without considering the context of that sentence.

For example, consider the following two sentences, the first of which serves to provide some context for the second:

Mr. Bosch is one of my better friends.

He happens to fear cross-country skiing.

In the second sentence *He* bears given information, and *happens to fear cross-country skiing* bears new information.

In the work on given and new information, there are emphases regarding writers, readers, and texts that differ somewhat from those of Firbas but that should also interest writing and reading specialists. That is, those working on given and new information concentrate on how a text got to various points, on where the text has been, on what information has set the stage for other information, and on how the text hangs together. These concerns are closely associated with emphases on the reader's perspective, on the reader's assimilating and connecting information (compare Halliday, 1977, on some of these points). At a particular point in a text, writers on given and new information look backwards, concentrating on how a text developed to a certain point.

In the light of the foregoing discussion, we can see that several Functional Sentence Perspectivists could examine a segment of the same sentence and posit several different communicative functions for it. Some could claim that it expresses what the sentence is about, others could claim that it carries the least communicative dynamism, and others could claim that it is the bearer of given information. All could be correct in terms of their principles of analysis and their purposes. But such correspondences do not always occur (see

Daneš, 1974; Kuno, 1977). The fact that they do not is a principal reason for the existence of three different formulations of FSP.

In the remainder of this chapter, I shall proceed primarily on the assumption that a sentence (treated primarily as if it were one main clause) in a text can be analyzed into two segments, one expressing given information and the other expressing new information.

REFINED DEFINITIONS
OF GIVEN AND NEW INFORMATION

To this point, some of the definitions that I have given have been insufficiently precise. As Dahl (1976) stresses, we must be as precise as possible about the meaning of *information* and about the meaning of *given* and *new*. For, as he shows, many different definitions of these terms occur in the work on these and related subjects.

For example, Dahl (1976) delineates several ways in which *information* is defined. Some writers define *information* in terms of all the knowledge and beliefs that a person has about the world. In these terms, given information is equivalent to a person's model or picture of the world, the person's organized set of beliefs and bits of knowledge. New information includes the knowledge and beliefs that can be added to that model or that can modify that model in some way. These distinctions will not be pursued here, since they are more relevant to the analysis of particular readers than of written texts. The information in one text might be all given to one reader and all new to another. These are indeed important distinctions, but they go beyond the scope of this chapter.

Other writers define *information* in terms more suitable for our purposes. For example, some define it in terms of generic or individual concepts, in terms of all that is associated with a particular word. Dahl (1976) refers to what we would most commonly associate with the word *books* as illustrative of a generic concept (compare Chafe, 1974). He also mentions that what we would most commonly associate with a specific person we know illustrates an individual concept.

Still other writers treat *information* in terms of linguistic elements (primarily words and phrases) and in terms of the referents of linguistic elements. Dahl shows that it is necessary to distinguish linguistic elements from their referents since different linguistic elements (for example, a proper noun *[Bob]*, a pronoun *[he]*, and identifying descriptions *[my brother]*) can all have the same referent. Treating linguistic elements and their referents as if they were identical can therefore be misleading.

In the remainder of this chapter, I will treat *information* as embracing concepts, linguistic elements, and their referents. But once we have defined information in this manner, we still must clearly distinguish given from new information. And as Prince (1981) shows, there are several views that could be taken of the distinction between given and new information.

One of these, most closely associated with Chafe (1974, 1976, 1979), is based on speakers' and writers' assumptions about the consciousness of addressees. Chafe (1976, p. 30) defines given information as "that knowledge which the speaker assumes to be in the consciousness of the addressee at the time of the utterance." And new information "is what the speaker assumes he is introducing into the addressee's consciousness" (p. 30).

Another view centers on shared knowledge. That is, given information is that which a speaker or writer assumes that the addressee knows, assumes, or can infer. New information is that which a speaker or writer assumes that the addressee does not know, does not assume, or cannot infer.

Finally, Prince (1981) mentions a perspective that is actually a conflation of two distinct views. One of these, closely associated with Kuno (1972, 1977, 1980), is based on the notion of predictability. In Kuno's terms, linguistic elements are given if they are predictable, if an addressee could predict them if they were deleted. New elements are unpredictable. The second view, most often associated with Halliday (1967, 1974, 1977, 1981), is based on the notion of recoverability. According to Halliday, a linguistic element is given if it is recoverable, if its meaning and the meaning of the structure it occurs in is reconstructable even if that element were to be omitted. Prior mention of an element is often one of the conditions of its recoverability. New elements are those that are not recoverable.

As Dahl (1976) makes clear, some recoverable elements are not predictable. To make this point, he cites the following two sentences:

A: Peter went to see Bill, but Bill was not at home.

B: Peter went to see Bill, but Peter had to return.

The subject of the second clause in each sentence cannot be predicted since one could not guess that each will appear until each actually does. However, each is recoverable; we could substitute a pronoun (*he*) for each subject and have no difficulty interpreting the full sentence.

All of these views on given and new information are obviously very closely related. For many purposes, there might not be good reasons to distinguish them so finely. In this chapter, I will adopt the view of given information which centers on elements that have been mentioned prior to a particular point in a text or that are recoverable from the text or the extralinguistic situation. New information includes the elements not meeting these criteria. These definitions seem to be the most amenable to the kind of practical analysis that writing researchers are likely to carry out.

As Chafe (1976, p. 31) reveals, "The principal linguistic effects of the given-new distinction, in English and perhaps all languages, reduce to the fact that given information is conveyed in a weaker and more attenuated manner than new information." To this Halliday (1967) adds that often this manner represents itself anaphorically, so that given information appears through reference (pronominals and demonstratives), substitutes (words like *one* and *do*), and ellipsis (no realization in the text).

In a broader linguistic context, elements marked as given or new participate in a very general semantic system that Halliday (1974, 1977, 1981) asserts helps to fulfill the textual function of language, one of three basic functions of language (the others being the ideational and the interpersonal functions). The textual function is that by which language is formed into texts that are relevant to a particular situation. The textual function is an enabling function; it enables us to create texts as distinct from lists of unrelated sentences, and to use these texts to convey ideational and interpersonal meanings.

A Question About Given and New Information

One significant question about given and new information concerns how the segments of connected English sentences conveying each kind of information should be positioned so that the sentences can perform their communicative functions most effectively. A traditional linguistic hypothesis holds that the segment bearing given information should precede the segment conveying new information (Quirk, Greenbaum, Leech, & Svartvik, 1972; Prince, 1978; Chafe, 1979; Kuno, 1980; Bock & Irwin, 1980). Some prominent rhetoricians and composition specialists have listed a given-before-new guideline in their advice to writers (Flesch, 1946; Strunk & White, 1959). Finally, there has been some research into the styles of well-known writers of English in terms of the positioning of given and new information. This research has shown that some of these writers generally follow the given-before-new hypothesis (see Smith, 1971, for an interesting analysis of an essay by Bertrand Russell).

However, not all writers always express given before new information. Both Gray (1982) and Ruzich (1984) found several writers, including older novice writers and professionals, frequently placing new information before given information in sentences. Moreover, expressing given before new information is significantly easier in languages such as Czech or Russian, languages with relatively free word orders, than it is in English, a language with a relatively fixed word order. This fact has led some theorists to hypothesize that in English there must be considerable tension between word-order principles and the hypotheses of FSP, among which would normally be included the given-before-new hypothesis. Some theorists, in fact, have even claimed that "English differs from Czech in being so little susceptible to the requirements of FSP as to frequently disregard them altogether" (Mathesius, cited in Firbas, 1974, p. 17; on this point see also Teskey, 1976). Thus the question about the ordering of given and new information in English sentences should be addressed.

The Hypothesis that Given Information
Should Ordinarily Precede New Information

Some Tests

In some recent experiments, I tried to discover whether writers should try to express given before new information whenever possible in English texts. That is, I tried to discover whether short texts structured according to the given-before-new hypothesis actually have cognitive advantages over texts structured to contradict the given-before-new hypothesis.

Much of the other experimental evidence that sheds some light on this issue comes from tests on individual sentences or pairs of sentences (Haviland & Clark, 1974; Clark & Haviland, 1974, 1977; Clark, 1977; Glatt, 1982). But to examine this issue properly, in ways that reflect how information ordinarily becomes given, and in ways that could tell us how people normally respond to given and new information, we should examine whole texts, the means by which people most often achieve communicative ends.

Therefore, I tried to work with texts long enough and natural enough to make it at least conceivable that they could appear in the worlds of natural discourse. If it could be shown that a text in which each sentence after the first moves from given to new information has cognitive benefits over its variant, we would have strong evidence for the hypothesis that even in English, writers should ordinarily try to express given before new information. The variant text would convey essentially the same propositional information but would do so with sentences after the first that move from new to given information.

At this point, we should take note of several things. First, I have commented on "sentences after the first" since initial sentences pose their own interesting questions about given and new information. Many of these are answerable only when one knows a great deal about the extralinguistic situations of texts. Second, I decided to test for "cognitive benefits" in terms of how easily readers read the texts and retained information from them.

If the given-before-new hypothesis could be supported with evidence based on experiments using texts, we would have largely avoided some troubling characteristics of earlier work testing the hypothesis. Some evidence for the hypothesis resulted from work on isolated sentences or pairs of sentences. Often in such tests, the sentences were unnaturally simple, the sentences expressed either all given or all new information, or the sentences had to be read as fast as possible and perhaps in a way different from the way people normally read texts. These characteristics of the work on sentences, of course, make it too easy to question the validity and more especially the applicability of the resultant evidence for the given-before-new hypothesis. If we can avoid such possibilities and support the hypothesis, such support would have significant implications for composition researchers and teachers.

To the best of my knowledge, the only other tests that have sought to answer questions about given and new information using texts approaching naturalness are reported in Kieras (1978) and de Beaugrande (1979). Although these come close to meeting our needs, neither provides the specific information sought here. De Beaugrande composed passages by ordering the same set of sentences differently, thereby probably producing passages with different intersentence logical connections and overall semantic structures. Moreover, his guidelines for rearranging information are not sufficiently explicit. Kieras also composed passages by ordering the same set of sentences differently. He treated the information in a sentence as either wholly given or wholly new, and he presented sentences to subjects one at a time.

Experimental Materials

For this test I constructed several pairs of expository paragraphs. In one kind that for convenience I will call topically linked, identical or closely related information (represented through lexical repetition, pronoun substitution, or the naming of necessary, probable, or possible parts and characteristics of things) appears early in the syntactic subject position of each sentence after the first. Each of these sentences moves on to some new information. For example, consider paragraph 1 (with its expressions of given information italicized):

> Currently the Marathon is the best waxless ski for recreational cross-country skiing. *Its weight* is a mere two pounds. Yet *its width* allows the skier to break a trail through even the heaviest snow. *Its most nearly unique characteristic* is the fishscale design for its bottom. *The Marathon* is almost as effective as most waxable skis. In fact, *it* is even better than some waxable skis when the snow is very wet. *The Marathon* can be used with most conventional bindings. However, *it* works best with the Suomi double-lock. Finally, *the Marathon* is available in six different colors.

In the variant of the topically linked paragraph, the positions of given and new information are switched around; that is, the new information is now expressed in the full syntactic subject. In such a paragraph, all sentences after the first will move from new to given information. For example, consider paragraph 2, the variant of paragraph 1 (with its full syntactic subjects, in all sentences after the first, italicized to highlight the positions of new information):

Currently the best waxless ski for recreational cross-country skiing is the Marathon. *A mere two pounds* is its weight. Yet *the skier* can break a trail through even the heaviest snow with its width. *The fishscale design for its bottom* is its most nearly unique characteristic. *Most waxable skis* are only slightly more effective than the Marathon. In fact, *some waxable skis* are not as good as it when the snow is very wet. *Most conventional bindings* can be used with the Marathon. However, *the Suomi double-lock* works best with it. Finally, *six different colors* are available for the Marathon.

In another kind of paragraph, one that I for convenience will call a chaining paragraph, the information in the predicate of the first sentence is carried over to the syntactic subject of the second. There, of course, it represents given information. This pattern of linking information from the predicate of one sentence to the subject of the next continues throughout the paragraph, producing a chain of given and new information. As in a topically linked paragraph, each sentence after the first in a chaining paragraph moves from some given to some new information. In a topically linked paragraph the given information is identical or nearly identical in each sentence after the first. But in a chaining paragraph this is not the case. Each expression of given information becomes given by being carried over from the preceding sentence predicate, but each is not identical to the others. For an example of a chaining paragraph, consider paragraph 3 (with its expressions of given information italicized):

"The Odyssey" is an excellent example of an epic poem. *Epic poems* usually include a long narrative or story. *This story* is almost always marked by certain conventions. *One of these* is the epic simile. *It* is normally used to enhance the stature of a great hero. *Such a hero* personifies the ideals of particular societies. *Among these ideals,* naturally, is the trait of bravery. But *bravery* is always accompanied by courtesy. And *this courtesy* includes many particular ways of acting.

In the variant of the chaining paragraph, the positions of the expressions of given and new information are reversed. In such a paragraph, therefore, all sentences after the first move from new to given information. For example, consider paragraph 4 (with its full syntactic subjects, in all sentences after the first, italicized to highlight the positions of the new information):

An excellent example of an epic poem is "The Odyssey." *A long narrative or story* is usually included in epic poems. *Certain conventions* almost always mark this story. *The epic simile* is one of these. *The stature of a great hero* is enhanced through its use. *The ideals of particular societies* are personified in such a hero. *The trait of bravery,* naturally, is among these ideals. But *courtesy* always accompanies bravery. And *many particular ways* of acting are included in this courtesy.

Corresponding sentences in paragraphs 1 and 2 and in paragraphs 3 and 4 differ primarily in the positions of given and new information. Moreover, because, as Sachs (1967, p. 438) has found, "two sentences can have different forms but express the same meaning," I postulate that paragraphs 1 and 2, as well as paragraphs 3 and 4, have essentially the same referential meaning.

To make this claim more credible, I tried to ensure that each topically linked paragraph and its variant and each chaining paragraph and its variant used in experiments were identical or very similar to each other in numbers of words, clauses, sentences, nominalizations, and reversible and nonreversible passives, as well as in numbers of introductory conjunctions, adverbs, and prepositions. Additionally, the corresponding sentences in each pair were about equally long and contained many of the same words and full verbs.

Perhaps more important for the purposes of this study, all experimental paragraphs were checked for naturalness. Usually several of my colleagues read a paragraph in which the given information preceded the new, and several others read its variant. They examined the paragraph as often as they wished within a period of about three days, keeping in mind that they were to note in writing if any words, phrases, single sentences, or sequences of sentences struck them as being markedly awkward, or impossible in a conceivable natural situation. They were also to suggest substitutes for or alterations of the constructions that they objected to. They might have reacted differently if they had had both paragraphs in a pair to contrast. And they might have reacted differently if they had had their attention called to particular stylistic devices or linkages. But in this case, they wrote no more comments or more serious comments about awkwardness or unnaturalness for a variant of a topically linked or chaining paragraph than they did for the topically linked or chaining paragraph itself. Whenever any evaluator objected to a word, phrase, or part of a sentence in any paragraph, I changed it to what he or she suggested and then had the paragraph reevaluated. Thus, neither paragraph in an experimental pair should have had the advantage in experiments of seeming markedly more graceful or natural than its correspondent.

Therefore, contrasting these paragraphs in tests of readability and retention should be an excellent way to test the given-before-new hypothesis. Both paragraphs in an experimental pair were constructed according to explicit guidelines. The order of corresponding sentences in both paragraphs is the same. Each sentence after the first in both contains some given and some new information. Each paragraph was judged by several people to be natural. And in the tests, subjects read paragraphs without interruptions.

Experimental Procedures

I conducted five readability and three retention experiments, using large numbers of high school students as subjects. There was no necessary reason for using these particular numbers of tests, nor was there a logical connection between the nature of the readability tests and that of the retention tests. My first goal was to select tests that seemed likely to reveal how easily readers read the experimental paragraphs and retained information from them, but whenever possible I also sought tests that were easy to use with large numbers of high school students and that were frequently used in experimental work.

In the first readability test, subjects were alerted, before being allowed to read (once) a pair of paragraphs (a topically linked or chaining paragraph and its variant), that they would have to indicate which of the paragraphs was easier to read or indicate that they could detect no significant difference in readability between them. In the second test, the procedure was identical except that students read a pair of paragraphs once before learning that they should judge readability. In the third, the procedure was identical except that students were alerted to judge readability before reading the pair of paragraphs—which they could do as often as they wished for eight minutes. Whenever students had to read a pair of paragraphs, the order of presentation of the paragraphs was counterbalanced. In the fourth test, subjects read aloud one or the other of a pair of paragraphs, trying to read as accurately and rapidly as possible. Their readings were taped and scored for accuracy and speed. Finally, in the fifth readability test, subjects typed as accurately and rapidly as possible one or the other of a pair of paragraphs. Their typed pages were scored for accuracy and for the amount typed.

In the first retention test, subjects read carefully, but only once, either a topically linked paragraph, a chaining paragraph, or the variant of either of these. Then they took a recognition test on it. For this test they received a sheet showing thirty randomly ordered words or short phrases. Ten of these elements, the targets in the test, expressed new information and had appeared late in sentences in topically linked or chaining paragraphs and early in sentences in variant paragraphs. The other twenty elements were distractors. The students learned that some of the elements on the sheet had appeared in the paragraph they had read but that others had not, and they were told to try to circle the targets and avoid the distractors.

In the second retention test, subjects read one of a pair of paragraphs and then had to provide short answers to ten randomly ordered questions. The answers were numbers, words, and short phrases, each of which expressed new information, information that had appeared late in sentences in topically linked and chaining paragraphs and early in the variants of these paragraphs.

Finally, in the third retention test, subjects read one of a pair of paragraphs and immediately afterward wrote a recall protocol for it. These were later scored for accuracy and amount of information recalled.

Results

Since many of the experimental data are reported elsewhere (Vande Kopple, 1982a, 1982b, 1983), I will only summarize the results here. Paragraphs following the given-before-new hypothesis emerged as significantly more readable and memorable than their variants (some results were significant at greater than the .0001 level).

The exceptions to this generalization were few and statistically insignificant. Variants of topically linked paragraphs were typed somewhat more accurately and led to very slightly better written recall. Variants of chaining paragraphs were typed somewhat more rapidly and led to a few more correct answers on the short-answer test. Thus, although more tests on longer materials would be useful, these tests provide substantial evidence for the given-before-new hypothesis.

The Given-New Strategy of Comprehension

A promising explanation for these test results can be developed if we extend the application of Clark and Haviland's given-new strategy of comprehension from pairs of sentences to natural paragraphs (Haviland & Clark, 1974; Clark, 1977; Clark & Haviland, 1974, 1977). We must, however, note with Chafe (1976) that sometimes what Clark and Haviland call an expression of given information is more accurately an expression of contrastiveness. But in the main the details of their given-new strategy are accurately described and work well to explain the results of the tests described above.

According to Clark and Haviland, when we read a declarative sentence, we divide it into its given and new information. We view the given as a pointer to a direct antecedent in memory and search for it (see Carpenter & Just, 1977, for interesting material on discourse pointers). When we find it, we attach the new information to it. If we cannot find a direct antecedent, we can do a number of things: We can try to form an indirect antecedent by constructing an inferential bridge from something we do know; we can view all the information in the sentence as new and add a new node or nodes to memory; more rarely, we can try to restructure the information so that we do have a complete antecedent for the given information. Thus a sentence will be relatively easy to process and comprehend if its given information is easy to recognize and matches a direct antecedent in memory. Moreover, the sentence will be easy to process and comprehend if the given information occurs before the new.

When new comes before given, the reader faces some difficulty. He or she "must hold the new information in abeyance while he waits for the given information and searches for its antecedent. This increases the load on memory and makes comprehension less than optimal" (Clark & Haviland, 1977, p. 13).

At this point it is easy to see that the topically linked and the chaining paragraphs facilitate this strategy of comprehension. In such paragraphs, given information is clearly marked, is directly matched by information in storage, and is expressed in sentences before the new information. On the other hand, because the variant paragraphs have new information before given information, it is

also easy to see that they will frustrate the given-new strategy to some
extent.

Thus we have reason to believe that one of the ways our minds
move efficiently is from given to new information. There is some
evidence for this statement in some of the comments that students
wrote to explain or defend their choices in the first three readability
tests. Of course, the students had both paragraphs in an experimental pair to examine before writing comments. And because most of
them had chosen one paragraph in a pair as more readable than the
other and had to defend their choice, they were probably more
sensitive to style than people ordinarily are. At any rate, their comments are most illuminating.

Some praised topically linked paragraphs because each of their
sentences "lets you know right away what it is about," and because
each sentence "tells what you will be discussing first." One student
criticized a variant of a topically linked paragraph because it "caused
me to look back several times before I could follow it," and another
criticized such a variant because he "would start to read and then
wonder what the sentence is talking about."

Other students noted that in chaining paragraphs "one piece of
information led to another," and that "the end of a sentence leads
right into the beginning of the next." Still others criticized variants of
these paragraphs by writing that they "backtracked a lot," had "detached ideas," and "seemed broken up."

But the best evidence that subjects added new information to an
anchor of old is found in the written protocols of those who read and
recalled variant paragraphs from memory. Many of them actually
rearranged information, reading sentences moving from new to
given information but often writing sentences moving from given to
new information. They took expressions of given information expressed in the full predicates of the sentences that they had read and
moved those expressions into early subject positions in their protocols. For example, one student wrote the following, printed
exactly as received, after reading paragraph 2:

> Currently the best waxless ski for recreational cross-country skiing is
> the Marathon. It's weight is a mere 2 lbs. It can cut through the
> thickest snow. It can be used with most conventional bindings al-
> though the Suomi is best. It works better than some waxable skis on
> wet snow.

In the five clauses following the first sentence, the writer reversed the order of given and new information in every case except in the subordinate clause about the Suomi binding.

In related research, Bock & Irwin (1980) have analyzed given and new information in sentence production. On the basis of some test results, they propose that when speakers and writers express given information early in sentences, they do so not only because they are honoring an implicit contract with their addressees to do so, but also because processes operating to produce surface structures make it easier for them to do so.

Progressions of Given Information in Texts

The preceding theoretical and experimental work provides a substantial basis for recommending to writers that if syntax allows, if no desired stylistic effects are lost, and if there is no need to call special attention to new information by placing it in a marked (early) position, they should try to express given before new information in their sentences. The evidence accumulated so far indicates that doing so, even in English with its rather rigid word order, does indeed have cognitive benefits for readers. Williams is one writer on rhetoric and style who already has incorporated in a textbook advice about expressing given before new information (Williams, 1985).

If writers were to follow this advice in every sentence in their texts, they would probably produce stretches of discourse marked by one or more of the following kinds of progressions of given information that Daneš (1974) identifies (see also Dillon, 1981, pp. 106-109, for examples of these progressions in writing by master essayists).

The first kind of progression is the one governing the topically linked paragraphs described above—that is, in every sentence after the first, the same given information appears early, usually in the syntactic subject. We can represent this progression as

$$A \rightarrow B$$
$$A \rightarrow C$$
$$A \rightarrow D.$$

From some explorations in English language materials, Daneš (1974, p. 119) offers the following brief example of this kind of progression:

The Rousseauist especially feels an inner kinship with Prometheus and other Titans. He is fascinated by any form of insurgency. . . . He must show an elementary energy in his explosion against the established order and at the same time a boundless sympathy for the victims of it. . . . Further the Rousseauist is ever ready to discover beauty of soul in anyone who is under the reprobation of society.

The second progression is the one governing the construction of the chaining paragraphs. Information expressed near the end of one sentence is picked up and expressed again, now as given information, early in the next sentence. We can represent this progression as

$$A \rightarrow B$$
$$B \rightarrow C$$
$$C \rightarrow D.$$

Daneš's (1974, p. 118) example of this kind of progression from English materials is as follows:

The first of the antibiotics was discovered by Sir Alexander Flemming [*sic*] in 1928. He was busy at the time investigating a certain species of germ which is responsible for boils and other troubles.

In the third kind of progression, one sentence introduces what Daneš calls a hypertheme, and the early portions (again, usually the syntactic subjects) of subsequent sentences express subthemes that are derivable from the hypertheme. Often, once one knows the hypertheme, one can predict many of the subthemes. We can represent this progression as

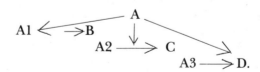

Daneš's (1974, p. 120) example of this kind of progression, with several subthemes included, is as follows:

New Jersey is flat along the coast and southern portion; the north-western region is mountainous. The coastal climate is mild, but there is considerable cold in the mountain areas during the winter months. Summers are fairly hot. The leading industrial production includes chemicals, processed food, coals, petroleum, metals and electrical equipment. The most important cities are Newark, Jersey City, Paterson, Trenton, Camden. Vacation districts include Asbury Park, Lakewood, Cape May, and others.

In this example *New Jersey* introduces the hypertheme, and subsequent sentences pick up various aspects of New Jersey to express as subthemes in their syntactic subjects.

Finally, Daneš identifies a kind of progression which combines aspects of the first and second kinds of progressions. He calls this kind the exposition of a split rheme. A representation makes this kind clear:

$$
\begin{aligned}
A &\rightarrow B (= B1 + B2) \\
B1 &\rightarrow C \\
B2 &\rightarrow D.
\end{aligned}
$$

The example of this progression given by Daneš appears below:

All substances can be divided into two classes: elementary substances and compounds. An elementary substance is a substance which consists of atoms of only one kind. . . . A compound is a substance which consists of atoms of two or more different kinds.

Of course, it is highly unlikely that one would be able or would want to adhere to one or more of these progressions without exception in constructing texts. We all face moments when we choose to write sentences expressing only the faintest trace of some given information or no given information at all.

As Daneš (1974) points out, most progressions of given information are complicated by insertions and asides. He adds that many progressions often take incomplete or modified manifestations and may demand inferences to be recognized. Moreover, there may be progressions of given information that we have not identified, complex progressions in texts with more complex sentences than those typically scrutinized thus far.

In any case, if we help students identify these progressions in natural texts and help them practice with the syntactic devices in

English that allow us to move information around in sentences (the passive construction, for example), we might be able to help them recognize a major source of text connectedness and write texts that facilitate readers' processing. My assumption is, of course, that they will try to do so unless they have a good reason to frustrate or impede readers' processing. Moreover, as researchers attend more closely to progressions of given information, they might make some interesting discoveries. They might find that certain progressions, alone or in combinations with others, correlate with particular genres, authors, purposes, or levels of writing or cognitive development.

In this connection, the work of Enkvist (1973, 1978) is interesting. He found that texts such as Boswell's *London Journal* and some works of Hemingway displayed a high proportion of the first (topically linked) kind of progression of given information. On the other hand, some work by Gibbon, Dr. Johnson, and several social scientists had a high proportion of the second (chaining) kind of progression. Enkvist (1973) writes that the first kind of progression helps to contribute to a "static" style, and that the second helps to contribute to a "dynamic" style, one common to sustained logical argument. And he wonders how long one could stick with the dynamic style without losing the connection with the starting point of a text. At this point Fries' work (1983) is also relevant. While taking care to distinguish given information from "what the sentence is about," he makes interesting headway in relating these notions to what he calls the writer's "method of development" in various kinds of texts.

Applying Knowledge about Given and New Information

Distinguishing High- and Low-Rated Texts and Revision Practices

In the light of what we now know about given and new information in sentences in texts, Goodin and Perkins (1982) are able to discuss in quite specific terms some of the ways in which a text can go wrong. In the first place, it can, at a certain point, contain little or no information that is really new. And as Witte and Faigley (1981, p. 198) discovered in analyzing some low-rated informative texts with this flaw, "Although for purposes of attaining cohesion in a text some redundancy is a virtue, the redundancy in the low-rated essays seems to be a flaw because these writers failed to supply additional information at the point where it would be expected to appear."

In the second place, Goodin and Perkins (1982) note that some texts can be deficient in given information. In sentences in such texts, there is no connection to earlier material; each sentence strikes readers as a topic sentence or an unmarked aside. To provide an example of this flaw, Goodin and Perkins offer the following short passage:

> One unique difference of the versions of *Cinderella* is the length of the story. Walt Disney's object of the story was to simplify the understanding for children. Perrault's form of Cinderella explained detailed information that was constructed in a more advanced and detailed manner. The styles of the writings contrasted greatly in this type of formality. Even though Walt Disney wrote in a brief style, the story still revealed the same plot as Perrault described in his version.

Goodin and Perkin point out that the first sentence of this passage leads readers to expect to learn what the versions are as well as which is shorter and which longer. The next two sentences identify the versions but do not provide the information about the length of each version that readers need to understand the claim about the purpose of each version. There is a deficiency in given information, most notably in the second sentence.

For work on such flaws, recently Sodowski and Witte (1983), applying some of Lautamatti's (1978) ideas, have provided more precise tools for examination and, perhaps, remediation. Sometimes they conflate the notion of given information with that of "what the sentence is about," but they make it clear that they are doing this, and generally their method is useful for those analyzing texts in terms of given and new information. They add insights into the ways in which bits of given information in successive or separated sentences can be semantically related to each other. They mention that, in some progressions of given information, the given information will be identical from one occurrence to the next. This is true of the topically linked progressions described above, for example. And they mention that writers can break such progressions with insertions of other material and then start the progressions up again.

What is perhaps most significant about their method is that they begin to specify what the semantic relationships between bits of related but not identical given information are. For example, they show that one bit of information can be considered to be given by being clearly and predictably subordinate to information expressed earlier.

Other bits of information can be considered to be given by being recoverable from earlier information through valid and predictable inferences. Witte and Sodowski admit that the category of inferences is a nebulous one, but they give several examples of pairs of sentences that we would connect by means of inferences. In one such case, we infer a connection between information about an action in one sentence and information about the agents of that action in the next sentence. The agents become given information by means of a valid inference (that actions have agents). This is true, for example, of the following two sentences (with the linked action and agents italicized):

A conscious way of escaping reality that harms no one is *reading and watching movies.*

Many people like to go to a movie to have a good cry. (Sodowski & Witte, 1983, p. 4)

When Witte and Sodowski examined some students' high- and low-rated informative texts in terms of these various progressions and relationships, they found that low-rated essays were noticeably different from the high-rated essays in several ways. First, the low-rated essays had more sentences in which there was no given information. Perhaps more important, they took longer to establish the semantic context necessary to make the high load of new information in such sentences understandable. Additionally, more sentences in the low-rated essays demanded inferences in order to be processed than did sentences in the high-rated essays. It seemed as if the writers of the low-rated essays did not care that their readers had to work hard to follow the information through their texts. Moreover, the low-rated essays had fewer bits of that kind of information that is considered given by virtue of being clearly subordinate to information expressed earlier. Finally, the low-rated essays displayed fewer chaining progressions of given information. Witte and Sodowski speculate that the chaining progression marks the mind at work, the mind moving from point to point. Such speculations would be interesting to follow up. It would be valuable to apply their method to more than just informative texts or to texts produced by writers in nonschool situations. Perhaps we would be able to be even more specific about kinds of flawed texts, reasons for them, and effects of them on readers.

Thus far, the method of Witte and Sodowski has been described in terms of how it can help us analyze texts. But they stress that most of the distinctions they make can be used in the classroom. They have students analyze other texts in terms of these progressions and relationships, then analyze their own texts in the same terms, and then work to mend such things as broken linkages and linkages requiring difficult inferences.

In a more complex study, using all the progressions and relationships described above as well as some other distinctions, Witte (1983) examined students' revisions of a particular text. The students were told to read the text carefully and then to revise it "so that it would be 'easier to read and understand' but would retain 'its character as a piece of informative discourse'" (p. 322). Witte's goal was to examine their revisions, contrast them to the original passage, and then identify the textual features students manipulated in order to make the text easier to read and to understand. He also hoped "to chart more efficiently the actual decisions writers make as they revise texts" (p. 321).

After the students had produced their revisions, Witte had them evaluated in terms of how easy to read and understand they were. Then he divided the revisions into two groups, a low-rated and a high-rated group. Finally, he analyzed these groups according to several criteria, some of which are relevant to the distinction between given and new information.

Witte found, for example, that the highly rated revisions elaborated more on fewer bits of given information and that these bits of given information were usually very closely related to the gist of the passage. Moreover, these essays had a lower percentage of chaining links between sentences. If one recalls Sodowski and Witte's work (1983), this lower percentage might seem like a deficiency. But Witte points out that the low-rated revisions tended to bury information closely related to the gist of the passage in chaining progressions; in these essays this did not lead to a smooth progression from point to point but to a blurring of focus. Witte concludes that the students who wrote poor revisions neither perceived the progressions of given information in the original text nor created a suitable set of progressions for their own revisions. And he speculates that perhaps these students revised as they did because they had never learned to read texts in their entirety, to recognize the progressions of given information and the semantic relationships between closely related but not identical bits of given information.

Again, these speculations would be worth checking. It would also be worth extending Witte's analysis to revisions of other kinds of texts besides the informative. Extending the analysis might help us discover how different kinds of writers revise different kinds of texts for several different purposes. The analysis could move us closer to an understanding of the decisions writers make as they revise features of texts.

Some Necessary Refinements in the Definition and Analysis of Given and New Information in Texts

The method illustrated thus far of defining given and new information and of applying these definitions is not entirely satisfactory. For example, the method rests on the assumption that the distinction between given and new information is binary: The method rests on a dichotomous model of information. But when one examines complex sentences in complex texts, it is easy to imagine that the model might more accurately be trichotomous or even n-chotomous. Furthermore, the definitions used here do not necessarily lead to illustrations about the ways (in English) in which given information is linguistically marked. Without additional details in this area, it is impossible to determine whether some linguistic markers call more attention to given information than others.

More important, perhaps, is that the method illustrated here allows or encourages one to view readers as complex information-processing machines, chunking through sentences, mechanically connecting various bits of information to each other. As Dillon (1981) points out, it is probably more accurate and appropriate to see readers as those who travel a path with writers and have their perspectives directed and enriched in various ways by them.

If we connect several of these points, we can suggest one of the ways in which the analysis of given and new information can be more explicitly related to the pragmatics of text production and reception.

By relating various linguistic markers of given information to finer distinctions among kinds of given information, we may be able to explore writers' apparent assumptions about their readers' stances, knowledge, beliefs, and strategies (compare Prince, 1981, p. 224), and also explore the extent to which the writers have to call readers' attention to information that is identical to, subordinate to, or available through inference from information expressed earlier. Refinements of this sort would have significant implications for the study of text production and reception.

Studies of Topic Continuity

Recently, large strides toward these refinements have been taken by Givón and several of his associates (see Givón, 1983a). Given that in their studies they use the term *topic* for the focus of their attention, I will also use that term in this section. They use the term to refer to what the rest of a clause comments on, but since they identify and analyze topics primarily in terms of given information, their work is most relevant here.

The basic questions Givón and his coworkers have tried to answer are the following: (1) How can we best measure how difficult it is for a reader to identify a sentence topic? (2) What are the linguistic markers of topics in various languages? (3) Are there correlations across languages between the difficulty of identifying topics and the various topic markers? (4) If such correlations exist, do important psychological principles underlie them? In other words, Givón tries to correlate the degree of recoverability of topics with the markedness of the linguistic topic markers. He suspects that these correlations can give us a good idea about the assumptions writers make at certain points in texts about how strongly they have to call or re-call certain bits of information to their readers' immediate attention. Because the degree of recoverability of a topic depends to a great extent on how continuous the information from one topic to the next is, Givón calls these investigations studies of topic continuity.

One of the first concerns in such a study is determining how difficult it is for readers to identify information in a topic. Givón hypothesizes that this difficulty depends primarily on four things. First, the longer that information is absent from a text, the more difficult it will be to identify. Second, if other bits of information can fulfill the same role as the information in the target topic, the target topic will be more difficult to identify. Third, the difficulty diminishes if bits of nearby information help identify the target topic. Finally, the difficulty depends on the extent to which the meaning of a passage as a whole helps identify the target topic.

To provide some objective measures of the difficulty a reader will probably have in identifying the information in a topic, Givón makes several counts in a text. First, he counts how many clauses he has to look at to the left of a topic in order to find the information that helps him identify that topic. He calls this the "lookback measure." This measure clearly shows the connection between studies of topic continuity and the idea of given information, and to a certain extent it unites points that Halliday (1977) makes about systems of information and cohesion. Second, Givón counts the number of topics near the target topic that could interfere with it semantically. Potentially interfering topics are semantically compatible with the information to which the target topic is attached. He usually checks the topics in the five clauses to the left of the target topic. Finally, Givón counts the number of clauses to the right of a topic in which the information in that topic maintains an uninterrupted presence. This he calls the persistence measure. This measure, too, is closely connected to the idea of given information. In these terms, topical information that does not look back far, that has little semantic interference from other topics, and that persists over many subsequent sentences is very continuous and is relatively easy to identify.

Givón's striking hypothesis is that across many languages there is a continuum relating the difficulty of topic identification and various linguistic topic markers. In other words, he suspects that in English and several other languages highly continuous topics are marked differently than are highly discontinuous topics. He believes that some linguistic markers signal the writer's view that readers would have little difficulty identifying topics while other markers signal the writer's view that readers would have much difficulty identifying topics. This hypothesis accords well with intuitions expressed earlier by writers such as Keenan and Schieffelin (1976) and Bolinger (1979).

A general version of Givón's continuum appears below:

Easiest topic identification (least surprising)

Zero anaphora (an anaphorical element given zero expression)

Clitic pronouns/verb agreement (uncommon in English)

Unstressed pronouns (any personal pronoun without special stress)

Stressed/independent pronouns (any personal pronoun with stress; these can be detected only when texts are read aloud)

Left dislocation (this structure has two references to the same thing within one clause; the first referent begins the clause and the second referent is generally a pronoun: *"The cheese they made there,* they sold most of *it* to the miners.")

Definite noun phrases (such as definite article plus noun phrase, demonstrative plus noun phrase)

Right dislocation (this structure has two references within one clause to the same thing; the first is usually a pronoun in the regular clause and the second is usually at the end of the clause: *"It* bothered her for weeks, *John's smile.")*

Passivization (moving what would normally be an object in a clause to subject position)

Y-movement (topicalization) (moving an NP out of its normal position in word order and placing it near the beginning of the clause: "The cheese they sold mainly to the miners.")

Cleft/focus constructions (clauses which use *it* at the beginning as a place holder, followed by a noun phrase which is modified by a relative clause: "It was John's smile that bothered Mary for weeks afterwards." Others add to these the wh-clefts.

Most difficult topic identification (most surprising) (Givón, cited by Brown, 1983)

This general continuum has been used in the study of topic continuity in various texts in several languages, including Japanese, Amharic, Ute, Biblical Hebrew, Spanish, English, Hausa, and Chamarro. Depending on the language with which they have worked, the investigators sometimes have made slight adjustments to the continuum. They add a category or two (for example, Brown, 1983, adds generics), or subdivide categories more finely than Givón did with the original (Brown, 1983, divides the definite noun phrase category into five categories). However, the striking result of the various investigations is that in general they confirm the validity of the continuum. Across languages writers and speakers seem to mark topics that are about equally difficult to identify with the same or similar linguistic devices.

Givón relates this finding to a fundamental hierarchy of orders of information, which he expresses as follows: comment (zero topic) > comment-topic > topic-comment > topic (topic repetition). This he explains with the following psychological principle: "Tend first to the most urgent task" (Givón, 1983b, p. 361). In other words, provide for your readers what they most need to know at a particular point in a text. This principle is fundamentally a pragmatic one, as it will cause the structures and meanings of texts to vary in response to writers' assumptions about particular readers and situations. It is not far removed from but yet goes beyond Dahl's (1976, p. 46) laziness principle: "Omit everything that the addressee can figure out for himself."

If we transcribe Givón's hierarchy from the *topic* and *comment* terms to those of *given* and *new,* it would appear as follows:

new information > new-given > given-new > given information.

The advantages of looking at given and new information from this perspective are significant. This perspective allows us to focus on both the writer and the reader at the same time. We can look to a text to learn what assumptions the writer probably had about the difficulty readers would have in identifying topics. This helps us view writers as being involved in judging where readers are looking, directing readers' attention, calling things to readers' minds with the appropriate force.

This perspective has other advantages. We have already seen that in general it is easier for readers to process information if given information appears before new information, but we can now add to that general backdrop. For in particular instances, expressing given before new information might not be attending to the most urgent task. Very general ease of processing for readers might not be a writer's most important consideration. If this is the case, we are now probably only approximating the complexity that we will have to achieve in psycholinguistic tests in the future.

Sometimes, when the given information is perfectly obvious to readers, it is probable that a writer can justifiably choose to omit it. Or if it is close to being obvious, he or she can justifiably choose to highlight the new information without sacrificing readers' awareness of the given by expressing new before given information. It would be interesting to see whether this was the case when the writers that Gray (1982) and Ruzich (1984) studied chose to express new before given information. Further, a writer might reintroduce a bit of given information into a text but justifiably decide that it will be so difficult for readers to identify it that he or she does not attach any new information to it.

Such decisions are probably related to those governing the establishment of boundaries of large subsections and paragraphs within a text. Givón has found, for instance, that the markers of the most discontinuous topics tend to correspond to the beginnings of paragraphs. And knowing about all such decisions must surely increase one's appreciation for the skill involved in meeting readers' minds in writing. Writers can start with the assumption that given should generally precede new information, but at particular points in texts they might well have to decide to express new before given informa tion and to choose an appropriate marker for the given.

The perspective provided by studies of topic continuity also promises to help us answer other questions related to given and new information in texts. It should help us answer Chafe's (1976) question about how long and for what reasons givenness persists in consciousness and Firbas's nearly identical question (this volume) about retrievability spans for information. This perspective also gives us a more detailed look at how some texts can go wrong. Some might seem condescending to readers (they might mark topics more overtly than those topics require), while others seem to assume too much of readers (they might not mark certain topics overtly or strongly enough, or they might omit topics that readers cannot identify).

Of course, Givón stresses that much more work is needed in this area. Studies of topic continuity have to be conducted in many more languages. We need more details about the degrees of difficulty possible for the identification of topics, about the causes of these degrees of difficulty, and about the linguistic markers that normally correlate to these degrees of difficulty. And all of this work could be complicated by the probability that not all writers possess the same ability to evaluate the difficulty of topic identification and to select appropriate linguistic topic markers. We really do not know how or when writers develop such abilities. Finally, we really do not know whether Givón's continuum holds for all kinds of texts in a particular language. Perhaps some kinds require rearrangements among the items on the continuum. Studies of topic continuity, therefore, open up many related areas that require much additional work.

Further Refinements in the Definition
and Analysis of Given and New Information

Another refinement needed in the definition and analysis of given and new information is related to the question of whether or not the distinction between given and new leads to a dichotomous, trichotomous, or n-chotomous model of information. In other words, we need to take an even closer look at given and new information than we did above. There we identified several dominant bases for speaking of given and new information: assumptions about what is in addressees' consciousnesses, shared knowledge, predictability, and recoverability (the basis for most of the discussion in this chapter). To probe these more deeply, we receive most guidance from Prince (1979, 1981), who has begun constructing a taxonomy of given and new information.

Prince works primarily with the type of givenness defined on the basis of shared knowledge or, as she prefers to call it, assumed familiarity. This she defines as follows: "The speaker assumes that the hearer assumes or can infer a particular thing/ . . . (but is not necessarily thinking about it)" (1979, p. 268). She views an understanding of this kind of givenness as a prerequisite for understanding the other kinds. By reviewing her taxonomy, which she stresses needs more investigation and refinement, we can get a good idea of the probable complexity of the various definitions of given and new information, begin to see how the kinds of givenness not defined in terms of assumed familiarity might be analyzed, and learn some interesting new ways to examine the structures and meanings of texts. In the material below, I follow Prince (1979, 1981) very closely.

Prince begins her work by defining a text as a set of instructions from a writer to readers about how to construct a particular discourse model. Underlying these instructions are assumptions on the part of the writer about what readers know and need to know in order to construct the model. The model itself includes entities (such as individuals, classes of individuals, exemplars, substances, and concepts), attributes, and linkages between entities. The entities are of special interest to her, and she investigates them by identifying and analyzing the noun phrases in a text.

Prince notes that when a writer introduces an entity into a text, the entity is new. But as such it can have one of two natures. Readers might have to extract it from the knowledge they have available for building the discourse model; they know it but are not attending to it until it is introduced. Prince calls such entities *unused*. If the sentence *Noam Chomsky went to Penn* were the first in a text, the name *Noam Chomsky*, Prince says, would be unused. She notes that a writer could assume that *Noam Chomsky* is in the model of readers engaging such a text.

On the other hand, readers, upon encountering a particular noun phrase, might have to create or imagine an entity. Prince calls such entities *brand-new*. If the sentence *A guy I work with says he knows your sister* were the first in a text, *A guy I work with*, Prince says, is brand-new and has to be created by readers. These brand-new entities can also be broken down; they can be either *unanchored* or *anchored*. They are anchored if the noun phrases representing them are linked by noun phrases to other discourse entities. Prince says that *A guy I work with* is brand-new anchored because the entity readers create for it will be linked immediately to the discourse-entity for the writer. On the other hand, Prince writes that if the sentence *I got on a bus yesterday, and the driver was drunk* was first in a text, *a bus* would be brand-new unanchored.

On the other end of the scale are what Prince calls *evoked* entities. At a particular point in a text, these are already in the discourse model that readers are building. But they can be evoked in two different ways. They can be evoked through noun phrases introduced into the text: In *A guy I work with says he knows your sister*, *he* is textually evoked. Or they can be evoked by readers on the basis of participants in and features of the extratextual situation: In *Pardon, would you have change for a quarter?* *you* is situationally evoked. Entities are situationally evoked most commonly in oral texts, but they can also be evoked in this manner in written texts that are closely connected to particular situations.

The most complex category of entities is what Prince calls *inferables*. She notes that an entity is inferable if the writer can assume that readers would be able to infer it by means of logical and plausible reasoning from entities that are already evoked or that are inferable themselves. For example, if readers read about a bus, they can plausibly infer that the bus has a driver. From among the inferables

Prince identifies a subclass, which she calls *containing inferables*. She defines these by writing that the product of the inference "is properly contained within the inferable NP itself" (1981, p. 236). Working with the sentence *Hey, one of these eggs is broken,* she writes that *one of these eggs* is a containing inferable, "as it is inferable, by a set-member inference, from *these eggs,* which is contained within the NP and which, in the usual case, is situationally evoked" (1981, p. 236).

Prince's taxonomy, then, includes the following seven descriptors: *brand-new unanchored, brand-new anchored, unused, (noncontaining) inferables, containing inferables, textually evoked,* and *situationally evoked.* The first three can be grouped together as new, the second two as inferable, and the last two as evoked. Therefore, for information defined in terms of assumed familiarity, we can make seven very fine and three more general distinctions.

Using this taxonomy, Prince (1981) has begun to explore some of the differences between kinds of texts. To do so, she examines the noun phrases in a text, and distinguishes between the noun phrases that are syntactic subjects and those that are not.

In an oral narrative, for example, she finds that almost all of the subject noun phrases are evoked, while less than one-half of the nonsubjects are. In contrast, one-sixth of the nonsubjects but none of the subjects are new. Inferable noun phrases make up one-third of the nonsubjects but only one-fifteenth of the subjects.

In a written sample (a portion of Hymes's *Foundations in Sociolinguistics: An Ethnographic Approach),* on the other hand, Prince finds a general decrease in evoked entities and an increase in inferable ones. More specifically, one-half of the subject noun phrases are evoked, but only one-eighth of the nonsubjects are. Over two-fifths of the subject noun phrases are inferable, and most are of the containing inferable type. There are no brand-new entities, and only a few unused ones in both subject and nonsubject slots. Prince generalizes that in this written text the entities are more abstract and are represented by long and complex noun phrases. Moreover, the line between what is unused and what is inferable becomes blurred. What is unused for one reader might be inferable for another. It seems that the writer of such a text must make sweeping assumptions about the knowledge readers can use to base inferences on.

As a result of exploring how noun phrases are introduced into texts, Prince offers a preliminary scale of preferences—at least in English—for the kind of entities used. The hierarchy, from top to bottom, runs as follows: the textually and situationally evoked entities, the unused, the noncontaining inferables, the containing inferables, the brand-new anchored, and finally, the brand-new unanchored. Prince's general thesis is that, in English, those producing texts will tend to use noun phrases and entities as high on this scale as possible. She suspects that when writers choose to use a noun phrase lower on this scale than what they can safely assume is available to readers, those writers will be seen as deviant in some way, as being evasive, acting childish, or creating suspense. In this area, with its focus on assumptions writers make about what their readers know and on how writers decide about what kind of information to convey, Prince's work is similar to Givón's.

And like Givón's work, Prince's opens up several significant areas for further investigation. For example, we could use her taxonomy to distinguish speech and writing from one another more precisely, to compare and contrast different kinds of texts, to examine the differences between writers of various ages and abilities, and to investigate fine differences between styles. And as Prince (1979, 1981) makes clear, thus far she has concentrated on entities; it is possible that attributes associated with entities have altogether different kinds of status as information.

ADDITIONAL AREAS FOR FUTURE RESEARCH

Thus far we have seen that investigating various aspects and uses of given and new information opens up several areas for future research. Some of these areas deserve to be described more fully, and there are others that have yet to be mentioned. One of the attractions of all these areas is that they should encourage collaborative work by investigators from several fields. For example, they should bring together workers representing functional theories of language, cognitive psychology, information processing, discourse analysis, stylistics, studies of the development of writing abilities, and studies of the differences between speech and writing. To conclude this chapter, I shall briefly describe seven areas in which future work seems promising.

In the first place, we need to learn more about the relation between kinds of given and new information and processes in the brain. At various times, researchers have claimed that the flow of information in language reveals the flow of thought (see Weil, cited in Firbas, 1974). If this is true, it would be interesting to see if there are mental correlates of such styles as those provisionally described by Enkvist (1973) as static and dynamic. If there are, it would be important to identify what causes people to depend on one or the other of such styles.

Chafe (1973, 1974, 1979) has already done interesting work relating given and new information to consciousness and to memory. But in order to relate kinds of given and new information to the production and reception of long texts (see Matsuhashi & Quinn, 1984), we shall need more work, both theoretical and empirical. Such work might also clarify how language helps us know things. We might learn more about how the various kinds of given and new information achieve their status as information and what the essence of linguistic information is.

Second, we must address such concerns within social and cultural settings. It may be that people with similar social, educational, and cultural backgrounds develop similar hierarchies of given information. They might have similar schemata. And it is possible that such hierarchies are among the more serious areas of interference for people encountering them with their own different hierarchies already in place. If such is the case, we face additional questions about how people can change such hierarchies, and about the extent to which it is practical and ethical to do so.

A third area is linked more directly to the structures of texts. The basic question here is whether we can more precisely and explicitly relate the expressions and progressions of given information in sentences in a text to the overall topic or gist of that text. Van Dijk (1977a, 1977b, 1979), Givón (1983a), and Witte (1983) have all begun fashioning answers to this question and have helped point the way to further refinements.

The fourth area is closely related. Some researchers have suggested that if we examine the semantic relations holding between consecutive expressions of given information in various kinds of texts, we should be able to distinguish general kinds of texts. Červenka (1982), for example, has begun some interesting work contrasting descriptive and narrative texts.

Fifth, as workers refine the analytical tools needed to examine the semantic relations among expressions of given information, it should become easier to discover if there are patterns of semantic relations between adjacent expressions of new information in a text. Daneš (1974) suggests that there might be. More recently, Ruzich (1984) has uncovered some evidence that such patterns exist and that advanced and basic student writers create different kinds of patterns. I have suggested (1983) that work in this particular area might lead to a more precise method of describing how various kinds of texts are generated.

Most of the current work on given and new information has centered on how elements function within the textual and ideational semantic systems of language. But it is also possible that in the interpersonal elements and metadiscourse in a text (see Vande Kopple, 1985), there are distinctions comparable to those between given and new ideational and textual elements, and that there are patterns of these elements. As Dillon (1981, p. 114) notes, such patterns may "overlay or intersect" the progressions of material functioning ideationally and textually. And such patterns might correspond to different kinds of social beings.

Finally, Kuno (1972, 1976, 1977) has begun to look at sentences and texts in terms of what he calls the writer's empathy. For example, Kuno (1972) writes that the sentence *John hit Mary* is close to a neutral or objective description of an event. The sentence *John hit his wife,* however, describes the event more from John's angle. It shows a writer empathizing with John. And the sentence *Mary's husband hit her* describes the same event from Mary's perspective. It reveals a writer empathizing with Mary. In this area much remains to be investigated. But some of what has been discovered is related to given and new information, for in developing a hierarchy of causes for kinds of empathy, Kuno (1976) hypothesizes that it is easier for writers to empathize with something or someone that they have been writing about than with something or someone that they have just introduced.

Work in all of these areas, it seems, could lead to significant discoveries about writers, information, texts, and responses to texts, in English and in other languages. And as it proceeds, such work will surely open up even more areas for research.

REFERENCES

Bock, J. K., & Irwin, D. E. (1980). Syntactic effects of information availability in sentence production. *Journal of Verbal Learning and Verbal Behavior, 19*, 467-484.

Bolinger, D. (1979). Pronouns in discourse. In T. Givón (Ed.) *Syntax and semantics: Vol. 12. Discourse and syntax* (pp. 289-309). New York: Academic Press.

Brown, C. (1983). Topic continuity in written English narrative. In T. Givón (Ed.), *Topic continuity in discourse: A quantitative cross-language study* (pp. 313-341). Amsterdam: John Benjamins.

Carpenter, P. A., & Just, M. A. (1977). Integrative processes in comprehension. In D. Laberge & S. J. Samuels (Eds.), *Basic processes in reading: Perception and comprehension* (pp. 217-241). Hillsdale, NJ: Lawrence Erlbaum.

Červenka, M. (1982). Narration and description from the standpoint of functional sentence perspective. In P. Steiner, M. Červenka, & R. Vroon (Eds.), *Linguistic and literary studies in Eastern Europe: Vol. 8. The structure of the literary process* (pp. 15-44). Amsterdam/Philadelphia: John Benjamins.

Chafe, W. L. (1973). Language and memory. *Language, 49*, 261-281.

Chafe, W. L. (1974). Language and consciousness. *Language, 50*, 111-133.

Chafe, W. L. (1976). Givenness, contrastiveness, definiteness, subjects, topics, and point of view. In C. N. Li (Ed.), *Subject and topic* (pp. 25-55). New York: Academic Press.

Chafe, W. L. (1979). The flow of thought and the flow of language. In T. Givón (Ed.), *Syntax and semantics: Vol. 12. Discourse and syntax* (pp. 159-181). New York: Academic Press.

Clark, H. H. (1977). Inferences in comprehension. In D. Laberge & S. J. Samuels (Eds.), *Basic processes in reading: Perception and comprehension* (pp. 243-263). Hillsdale, NJ: Lawrence Erlbaum.

Clark, H. H., & Haviland, S. E. (1974). Psychological processes as linguistic explanation. In D. Cohen (Ed.), *Explaining linguistic phenomena* (pp. 91-124). New York: John Wiley.

Clark, H. H., & Haviland, S. E. (1977). Comprehension and the given-new contract. In R. O. Freedle (Ed.), *Discourse processes: Advances in research and theory: Vol. 1. Discourse production and comprehension* (pp. 1-40). Norwood, NJ: Ablex.

Dahl, Ö. (1976). What is new information? In N. E. Enkvist & V. Kohonen (Eds.), *Reports on text linguistics: Approaches to word order* (pp. 37-49). Turku, Finland: Åbo Akademi.

Daneš, F. (1974). Functional sentence perspective and the organization of the text. In F. Daneš (Ed.), *Papers on functional sentence perspective* (pp. 106-128). The Hague: Mouton.

de Beaugrande, R. (1979). Psychology and composition. *College Composition and Communication, 30*, 50-57.

Dijk, T. A. van. (1977a). Text and context: Explorations in the semantics and pragmatics of discourse. London: Longmans.

Dijk, T. A. van (1977b). Sentence topic and discourse topic. *Papers in Slavic Philology, 1*, 49-61.

Dijk, T. A. van. (1979). Relevance assignment in discourse comprehension. *Discourse Processes, 2*, 113-126.

Dillon, G. L. (1981). *Constructing texts, elements of a theory of composition and style.* Bloomington: Indiana University Press.

Enkvist, N. E. (1973). 'Theme dynamics' and style: An experiment. *Studia Anglica Posnaniensia, 5,* 127-135.

Enkvist, N. E. (1978). Stylistics and text linguistics. In W. U. Dressler (Ed.), *Research in text theory: Vol. 2. Current trends in textlinguistics* (pp. 174-190). New York: Walter de Gruyter.

Firbas, J. (1974). Some aspects of the Czechoslovak approach to problems of functional sentence perspective. In F. Daneš (Ed.), *Papers on functional sentence perspective* (pp. 11-37). The Hague: Mouton.

Firbas, J. (1982). Has every sentence a theme and a rheme? In J. Anderson (Ed.), *Current issues in linguistic theory: Vol. 15. Language form and linguistic variation,* (pp. 97-115). Amsterdam: John Benjamins.

Firbas, J. (This volume). On the dynamics of communication in the light of the theory of functional sentence perspective.

Flesch, R. (1946). *How to write, speak, and think more effectively.* New York: Harper.

Fries, P. H. (1983). On the status of theme in English: Arguments from discourse. *Forum Linguisticum, 6,* 1-38.

Givón, T. (1983a). Topic continuity in discourse: An introduction. In T. Givón (Ed.), *Topic continuity in discourse: A quantitative cross-language study* (pp. 1-41). Amsterdam: John Benjamins.

Givón, T. (1983b). Topic continuity in spoken English. In T. Givón (Ed.), *Topic continuity in discourse: A quantitative cross-language study* (pp. 343-363). Amsterdam: John Benjamins.

Glatt, B. S. (1982). Defining thematic progressions and their relationship to reader comprehension. In M. Nystrand (Ed.), *What writers know: The language, process, and structure of written discourse* (pp. 87-103). New York: Academic Press.

Goodin, G., & Perkins, K. (1982). Discourse analysis and the art of coherence. *College English, 44,* 57-63.

Gray, A. K. (1982, March). *Sequencing and staging information in explanatory discourse.* Paper presented at the convention of the Conference on College Composition and Communication, San Francisco.

Halliday, M. A. K. (1967). Notes on transitivity and theme in English, part 2. *Journal of Linguistics, 3,* 199-244.

Halliday, M.A.K. (1974). The place of "functional sentence perspective" in the system of linguistic description. In F. Daneš (Ed.), *Papers on functional sentence perspective* (pp. 43-53). The Hague: Mouton.

Halliday, M. A. K. (1977). Text as semantic choice in social contexts. In T. A. van Dijk & J. S. Petöfi (Eds.), *Research in text theory: Vol. 1. Grammars and descriptions* (pp. 176-225). New York: Walter de Gruyter.

Halliday, M.A.K. (1981). Options and functions in the English clause. In M.A.K. Halliday & J. R. Martin (Eds.), *Readings in systemic linguistics* (pp. 138-145). London: Batsford Academic and Educational.

Haviland, S. E., & Clark, H. H. (1974). What's new? Acquiring new information as a process in comprehension. *Journal of Verbal Learning and Verbal Behavior, 13,* 512-521.

Keenan, E. O., & Schieffelin, B. B. (1976). Topic as a discourse notion: A study of topic in the conversations of children and adults. In C. N. Li (Ed.), *Subject and topic* (pp. 335-384). New York: Academic Press.

Kieras, D. E. (1978). Good and bad structure in simple paragraphs: Effects on apparent theme, reading time, and recall. *Journal of Verbal Learning and Verbal Behavior, 17,* 13-28.

Kirkwood, H. W. (1969). Aspects of word order and its communicative function in English and German. *Journal of Linguistics, 5,* 85-107.

Kuno, S. (1972). Functional sentence perspective: A case study from Japanese and English. *Linguistic Inquiry, 3,* 269-320.

Kuno, S. (1976). Subject, theme, and the speaker's empathy: A reexamination of relativization phenomena. In C. N. Li (Ed.), *Subject and topic* (pp. 417-444). New York: Academic Press.

Kuno, S. (1977). Generative discourse analysis in America. In W. U. Dressler (Ed.), *Research in text theory: Vol. 2. Current trends in textlinguistics* (pp. 275-294). New York: Walter de Gruyter.

Kuno, S. (1980). Functional syntax. In E. A. Moravcsik & J. R. Wirth (Eds.), *Syntax and Semantics: Vol. 13. Current approaches to syntax* (pp. 117-135). New York: Academic Press.

Lautamatti, L. (1978). Observations on the development of the topic in simplified discourse. In V. Kohonen & N. E. Enkvist (Eds.), *Textlinguistics, cognitive learning and language teaching* (pp. 71-104). Turku, Finland: University of Turku.

Lyons, J. (1981). *Language and linguistics: An introduction.* Cambridge: Cambridge University Press.

Matsuhashi, A., & Quinn, K. (1984). Cognitive questions from discourse analysis: A review and a study. *Written Communication, 1,* 307-339.

Prince, E. F. (1978). A comparison of wh-clefts and *it*-clefts in discourse. *Language, 54,* 883-906.

Prince, E. F. (1979). On the given/new distinction. In P. R. Clyne, W. F. Hanks, & C. L. Hofbauer (Eds.), *Papers from the fifteenth regional meeting, Chicago linguistic society* (pp. 267-278). Chicago: Chicago Linguistic Society.

Prince, E. F. (1981). Toward a taxonomy of given-new information. In P. Cole (Ed.), *Radical pragmatics* (pp. 223-255). New York: Academic Press.

Quirk, R., Greenbaum, S., Leech, G., & Svartvik, J. (1972). *A grammar of contemporary English.* New York: Seminar Press.

Ruzich, C. (1984, March). *Writer re-scanning: How does it affect text cohesion?* Paper presented at the convention of the Conference on College Composition and Communication, New York City.

Sachs, J. S. (1967). Recognition memory for syntactic and semantic aspects of connected discourse. *Perception and Psychophysics, 2,* 437-442.

Smith, C. S. (1971). Sentences in discourse: An analysis of a discourse by Bertrand Russell. *Journal of Linguistics, 7,* 213-235.

Sodowsky, R. E., & Witte, S. P. (1983, March). *Topical chains in the high- and low-quality informative texts of college freshman.* Paper presented at the convention of the Conference on College Composition and Communication, Detroit.

Strunk, W., & White, E. B. (1959). *The elements of style.* New York: Macmillan.

Teskey, P. D. (1976). *Theme and rheme in Spanish and English* (Occasional Papers in Linguistics and Language Learning No. 1). Coleraine, N. Ireland: Board of Studies in Linguistics, New University of Ulster.

Vande Kopple, W. J. (1982a). Functional sentence perspective, composition, and reading. *College Composition and Communication, 33,* 50-63.

Vande Kopple, W. J. (1982b). The given-new strategy of comprehension and some natural expository paragraphs. *Journal of Psycholinguistic Research, 11,* 501-520.

Vande Kopple, W. J. (1983). Something old, something new: Functional sentence perspective. *Research in the Teaching of English, 17,* 85-99.

Vande Kopple, W. J. (1985). Some exploratory discourse on metadiscourse. *College Composition and Communication, 36,* 82-93.

Weil, H. (1887). *The order of words in the ancient languages compared with that of the modern languages* (C. W. Super, Trans.). Boston: Ginn. (Original work published 1844)

Williams, J. M. (1985). *Style: Ten lessons in clarity and grace* (2nd ed.). Glenview, IL: Scott, Foresman.

Witte, S. P. (1983). Topical structure and revision: An exploratory study. *College Composition and Communication, 34,* 313-341.

Witte, S. P., & Faigley, L. (1981). Coherence, cohesion, and writing quality. *College Composition and Communication, 32,* 189-204.

4

Writing Processes and Written Products in Composition Research

STEPHEN P. WITTE
ROGER D. CHERRY

The underlying assumption of the present essay is that important insights into writing processes can be gleaned from careful analyses of written products. Because this assumption is not uncontroversial, we see the present essay as fundamentally exploratory, even speculative, in nature. At its most general level, the essay explores—by looking at relationships among framing (Bracewell, Frederiksen, & Frederiksen, 1982), planning, and translating (Flower & Hayes, 1981a)—some possible connections between writing processes and written products. At a more specific level, it explores topical focus analysis as one possible way of mapping some of the uncharted territory that lies between writing processes and written products.

The essay consists of seven major sections. The first section introduces the process/product distinction that informs much of the current research on writing in the United States and identifies some of the problems that attend the drawing of inferences about writing processes from analyses of written products. The second section reviews in a rather cursory fashion the literature on written products, and the third section outlines the current understanding of writing processes. The fourth section discusses topical focus analysis. The fifth section shows how topical focus analyses of texts might be used to make inferences about framing processes. The sixth section looks at the composing processes of two writers in light of their ability to make decisions about framing and topicalization. And the last section ties together the discussions of ideas that are the focus of the earlier sections.

THE PROCESS VERSUS PRODUCT DISTINCTION

Perhaps the most exciting development in the field of composition studies in the United States during the past two decades has been the rediscovery of process in writing. We use the term "rediscovery" because the idea of process in text construction did not originate with the modern era of writing research; constructing texts is, after all, central to Aristotle's *Rhetoric* (1954), a work that has informed rhetorical theory and practice since classical antiquity (see Corbett, 1971; Kinneavy, 1980b; Winterowd, 1968). Yet the rediscovery of process was necessary because by the last quarter of the nineteenth century, rhetorical study of writing had been reduced almost exclusively to a concern with products (see Young, 1978). Some of the historical reasons for this emphasis on product at the expense of process are identified by Parker (1967) implicitly and by Witte (1985a, 1985b) explicitly.

During the past decade, the pendulum seems to have swung the other way, at least in the United States. Together with terms designating specific processes, the term *process* itself has become something of a buzzword in both composition research and teaching. Since the seminal work of Rohman and Wleck (1964; Rohman, 1965), Emig (1969), and Graves (1975), attention to writing processes has become a major thrust in writing research. Similarly, textbook writers—following dicta such as Murray's (1984) to "teach writing as process not product"—now regularly offer extended discussions of writing processes, even though they run the risk of "dismantling" process by forcing it to conform to the linearity of the printed page (Rose, 1981), as well as the risk of denying students access to the kinds of product knowledge that can lead to the development of cognitive strategies that enable writers to construct goals for producing particular products (see Bereiter & Scardamalia, 1984; Scardamalia & Bereiter, in press). So important has the rediscovery of process become that Kuhn's (1970) concept of paradigm shifts in scientific fields is now regularly invoked (for example, Emig, 1980; Hairston, 1982; Young, 1978) to characterize the significance of the renewed interest in process in writing research and instruction.

Composition research and teaching in the United States have, to be sure, benefited enormously from the rediscovery of process in writing.

Research on writing processes has demonstrated the complexity involved in producing written text, even for skilled writers (see Flower & Hayes, 1981a, 1984; Berkenkotter, 1983). In teaching, the rediscovery of process has led to the incorporation of process as a field of study in training programs for teachers (for example, see Judy & Judy, 1979; Lindemann, 1982; Neman, 1980), to greater focus on process in writing curricula (see Witte, Meyer, & Miller, 1982), and to the use of conferencing in writing instruction (for example, Cooper, 1977; Carnicelli, 1980; Duke, 1975).

However, not all the effects of the process/product distinction have been salutary ones. One of the least fortunate effects has been the frequent dichotomizing of process and product because of difficulties encountered in drawing inferences about writing processes from written products. Much of the research on writing processes in fact assumes that processes cannot be inferred from products. This literature often takes the view recently articulated by Murray (1980, p. 3): "The process of making meaning with written language can not be understood by looking backward from a finished page. Process can not be inferred from product any more than a pig can be inferred from a sausage." Such a view, it seems to us, is tenable only if one knows nothing at all about pigs or making sausage, or writing.

Although for many reasons the process/product separation represents a useful theoretical distinction, the dichotomy is in some sense false, even if the connection between them may be a somewhat uneasy one. Odell (1983, p. 53) has addressed the problem quite succinctly:

> The distinction between written products and the writing process is not so great as we sometimes assume. By examining written products, we can identify analytic skills that writers might use both in exploring facts, ideas, and feelings and in formulating their thoughts on a given subject. Of course, there are certain kinds of information which cannot be obtained by analyzing a completed piece of writing. For one thing, we cannot learn about the sequence of activities a writer went through in the process of producing a draft. . . . [To learn about those activities], we will have to observe writers while they are engaged in the act of composing. Moreover, we cannot assume that a written product reflects all of the writer's conscious analytic activity. For example, analogies or distinctions that occurred to a writer early in the composing process may later be discarded because they seem irrelevant or invalid.

Although Odell recognizes that writing processes and written products are in some fundamental ways distinctive phenomena and although he recognizes the pitfalls associated with basing inferences about processes on products, he quite rightly also sees considerable value in not constructing rigid boundaries between writing processes and written products. For Odell (1983, p. 53) "writers' choices of language, syntax, and content have epistemological significance," a conviction that he was able to support with results reported in an earlier essay (Odell, 1977). Odell does not stand alone with this conviction. Taking a similar position, Gorrell (1983, p. 274) has recently issued a "mild warning" to writing researchers: "Many current studies of the writing process try so hard to avoid over-emphasis on the product that they neglect important and tangible processes. Observing writers in action is not the only way to find out about how writing is done. Some writing processes are understood most readily as we examine the product."

To explore some possible relationships between writing processes and products in composing and to explore the possibility of inferring process from product, we shall first have to examine general tendencies in the literature on both written products and writing processes.

WRITTEN PRODUCTS IN WRITING RESEARCH

Apart from studies that examine text features such as handwriting (McColly, 1970; Remondino, 1959) and errors (Bartholomae, 1980; Grobe, 1981; Shaughnessy, 1977; Williams, 1981), two lines of research on written products have developed, one focusing on syntactic features and one focusing on relationships across sentence boundaries. Research focusing on syntactic features has not produced results capable of providing insight into composing processes. Research on features that reach beyond sentence boundaries, on the other hand, frequently assumes that written products can and do provide insights into production processes.

Studies of syntax in written texts have appeared regularly since the 1930s (for example, see the reviews in Kerek, Daiker, & Morenberg, 1980; McCarthy, 1954; O'Hare, 1973; Witte & Davis, 1980). For the most part, these studies have sought to identify features of texts—particularly those produced by students—that are useful

either in detecting developmental differences across texts written by
writers of different ages or in making qualitative distinctions among
texts.

In the years following the publication of Hunt's (1965, 1970)
developmental research, which is based on Chomsky's (1957) theory
of transformational grammar, such studies proliferated. Hunt identified what he viewed as a gross measure of syntactic development,
mean number of words per t-unit. He defined a t-unit as an independent clause plus all of its subordinate and embedded elements.
An increase over time in mean t-unit length seemed to Hunt and
others to reflect the ability to employ various transformations that
reduce clauses to less-than-clause status and thereby allow the resulting structures to be embedded in or attached to other clauses.
Together with related indices (mean number of words per clause
and mean number of clauses per t-unit), mean t-unit length became
variously associated with "syntactic maturity," "syntactic complexity,"
and "syntactic fluency." Although such terms were never defined
very precisely (see Faigley, 1980), they were believed to represent
positive values.

On the basis of studies employing such gross indices as mean
t-unit length, Hunt and others posited a linear relationship between
age and "syntactic maturity" (or complexity or fluency), concluding
that as people grow older, the average length of their written t-units
increases.[1] Although the logical consequence of positing such a
linear relationship is "syntactic senility" (Kinneavy, 1979, p. 70),
there subsequently emerged a plethora of articles that urged ac-
celerating increases in mean t-unit length and hence written language development either through transformational sentence-
combining practice (for example, Morenberg, Daiker, & Kerek,
1978; Mellon, 1969; O'Hare, 1973)[2] or through pedagogical tech-
niques based on Christensen's (1963) "generative rhetoric of the
sentence" (for example, Faigley, 1979).

Such recent studies of syntactic features of written products,
while perhaps useful for identifying some general developmental
trends, have provided very little insight into the processes of producing written texts. Moreover, it is quite unlikely that they could, for a
number of reasons. Most important, studies of syntactic features
based on transformational grammar, like transformational grammar itself, focus on text features independently of the ideational,
interpersonal, and textual functions that Halliday (1973) associates
with language use. Chomsky's famous "Colorless green ideas sleep

furiously"—a perfectly "formed" English sentence—illustrates the limitations of syntax in accounting for the meaningfulness of a given utterance or text.

Syntactic analyses based on theories of transformational grammar by definition can, at most, focus on formal structural relationships at or below the level of the sentence or t-unit. Written texts, on the other hand, consist of sequences of semantically related sentences or t-units linked together to meet some communicative purpose. In writing, as in speaking, accessing syntactic form is generally accomplished with little or no conscious effort. Indeed, studies (for example, Flower & Hayes, 1984; Green, 1982; Kintsch & Van Dijk, 1978) of processes involved in producing connected written discourse strongly suggest that during production more of a writer's conscious attention is devoted to creating semantic relationships across the boundaries of sentences than is devoted to mapping meaning onto particular syntactic forms. Writers may, of course, choose to re-form their sentences or t-units, before or after committing them to paper (see Witte, 1985b); but when a writer does re-form a sentence or t-unit, he or she does so primarily because the sentence has been judged incongruous with the demands of context and, further, because the writer can figure out a way of altering the sentence to better answer the demands of context (see Nold, 1981). Divorced from communicative contexts, analyses of syntactic structures or features of texts can, it would appear, produce few if any useful inferences about production processes.

In contrast to those studies that have looked to sentence-level features as the basis for examining written products, a second line of inquiry has looked beyond the sentence to larger units of discourse. Echoing some of the concerns of Harris (1952/1964), this second line of research identifies an object of study that thus lies beyond the reach of grammatical analyses of sentences. According to Harris (1952/1964, p. 357), "discourse analysis" is concerned with "connected discourse" because "language does not occur in stray words or sentences, but in connected discourse." By "connected discourse," Harris means an extended communicative act that is both purposeful and cohesive. Harris's perspective on discourse anticipates, for example, Kinneavy's theory of aims and modes in extended discourse (Kinneavy, 1969, 1980b; Kinneavy, Cope, & Campbell, 1976), Halliday's theories about the ideational, textual, and interpersonal functions of language (Halliday, 1973, 1974, 1978), and van Dijk's theory of macrostructures (1977, 1980; van Dijk & Kintsch, 1983). These perspectives on discourse assume a fundamentally semiotic view of language use as consisting of interactions among the syntactic, semantic, and pragmatic dimensions.

Harris's interest in connected sequences of sentences is of a piece with the emergence during the 1960s of similar interests among researchers in both reading and writing. The underlying assumption shared by most such researchers is that the structures that characterize sequences of connected sentences represent a kind of knowledge that guides readers in comprehending text and writers in producing it, an assumption that is best articulated in the research that has focused primarily on comprehension as a meaning-constructing process (for example, Bracewell et al., 1982; Clements, 1979; Frederiksen, 1977; Grimes, 1975; Kintsch, 1974, 1977; Mandler & Johnson, 1977; Stein & Glenn, 1979; Thorndyke, 1977; van Dijk, 1977, 1980; van Dijk & Kintsch, 1983).

Among composition researchers in the United States, attention to larger units of discourse such as the paragraph has taken basically four forms. One approach looks at relationships among sentences on the basis of functional slots or semantic levels of generality (for example, Christensen, 1965; Becker, 1965; D'Angelo, 1974; Fahnestock, 1983; Grady, 1971; Karrfalt, 1968; Nold & Davis, 1980; Pitkin, 1969, 1977a, 1977b; Rodgers, 1966, 1967; Young & Becker, 1965). A second approach, which draws heavily on traditional rhetorical theory, conceptualizes discourse "modes" to explain the ideational structure of texts (for instance, D'Angelo, 1975, 1979; Kinneavy et al., 1976; Moffett, 1968). Neither the first nor the second approach has resulted in empirical studies that test the theories that underlie them. A third approach, which in recent years has been based on the work of Halliday and Hasan (1976) on cohesion, identifies words or phrases capable of carrying meaning across sentence or t-unit boundaries (for example, King & Rentel, 1981, 1982; Lybbert & Cummings, 1969; Markels, 1982; Rentel & King, 1983; Starling, 1980; Stotsky, 1983; Tierney & Mosenthal, 1983; Winterowd, 1970/1975; Witte & Faigley, 1981). A fourth approach draws, in part, on distinctions between given and new information to account for textual coherence in extended texts (for instance, Dillon, 1981; Prince, 1981; Vande Kopple, 1982a, 1982b, 1985; Williams, 1979a, 1979b; Witte, 1983a, 1983b). Both the third and fourth approaches have resulted in empirical studies that test their underlying theoretical assumptions.

Informing many of the studies that look beyond the level of the sentence in their examinations of written products is the sometimes explicit but usually implicit assumption that suprasentential structural patterns in written texts reflect thinking processes of the mind that produced the text. A few examples will illustrate. Christensen (1965) argues that sentences within paragraphs stand in relation to one another such that the sentence which introduces the principal topic exists at a higher level of generality than all of the other sentences. For Christensen, such semantic relationships in extended texts not only provide a basis for describing paragraph structure, but they also serve a generative function by guiding the writer in discovering content. The same may be said of Becker and Young's (Becker, 1965; Young & Becker, 1965) treatment of such patterns of expository paragraphs as topic/restriction/illustration and of D'Angelo's (1979) treatment of "structural paradigms." For D'Angelo, such paradigms serve both as organizational patterns for texts and as modern counterparts for the *topoi* of invention in the classical rhetorical tradition. In this, D'Angelo agrees with Winterowd's (1975, p. 225) claim that "any theory of form is, ipso facto, a theory of invention." In his theory of discourse modes, D'Angelo (1975) goes even further in asserting a connection between formal properties of extended texts and thought, arguing explicitly that patterns of arrangement in written texts manifest ways of thinking. D'Angelo's view of the relationship between thinking and discourse forms accords with Kinneavy's conceptualization of the modes of discourse (Kinneavy et al., 1976). Kinneavy argues that modes of organization—description, classification, narration, and evaluation—represent different ways of "viewing reality." It follows, therefore, that the instantiation of the modes in written texts reflects these different ways of thinking about the external world.

Also suggesting a relationship between visible features of written products and the processes of composing is Witte and Faigley's (1981) contention that cohesion analyses are useful in identifying differences in invention skills, a claim developed more fully by Welchen (1982). Similarly, King and Rentel (1981, 1982) employ cohesion analyses of children's texts as a basis for inferences about cognitive development, in particular the thinking strategies writers use during text production. In addition, Witte has posited topical structural analysis of written products as a basis for making inferences about the way revisers construct meaning for a text to be revised and about the decisions writers make as they revise a text (Witte, 1983a); he has also suggested that a text's topical structure reflects critical decisions that writers make during text production (Witte, 1983a, 1983b, 1985b).

In short, a fair amount of the research on writing that focuses on extended written texts sees formal properties, particularly semantic properties, of texts as reflections of the thinking processes that produced them. However, to see how analyses of written products can be useful in understanding composing processes, we shall have to direct our attention to the literature on writing processes.

WRITING PROCESSES IN WRITING RESEARCH

Since the publication of Janet Emig's *The Composing Processes of Twelfth Graders* (1971), researchers have become increasingly interested in writing processes and the kinds of thinking writers do as they write. The energy devoted to studying writing processes has produced important results. Indeed, several recent surveys of the literature on composing processes (de Beaugrande, 1984; Bracewell et al., 1982; Faigley, Cherry, Jolliffe, & Skinner, in press; Humes, 1983; Scardamalia & Bereiter, in press; Witte, 1985b) indicate that current knowledge of how writers write is much more sophisticated than it was even a decade ago.

Advances in knowledge of composing are reflected in challenges to linear-stage conceptions of writing. Recent theoretical and applied research (for example, de Beaugrande, 1984; Bracewell et al., 1982; Flower & Hayes, 1981a, 1984; Hayes & Flower, 1980; Nold, 1981; Perl, 1980; Sommers, 1980; Tierney & Pearson, 1983; Witte, 1985b) has shown that earlier, simplistic linear-stage models of composing (Britton, Burgess, Martin, McLeod, & Rosen, 1975; Murray, 1968, 1978; Rohman, 1965) serve better as models of the emergence of the written product than they do as models of the thinking processes that writers employ in producing written texts. Such linear-stage models represent writing as consisting of a series of discreet stages such as prewriting, writing, and rewriting. These linear-stage conceptualizations of writing seem merely to codify misunderstandings of the classical (Aristotle, trans. Roberts & Bywater, 1954) division of rhetoric into invention, arrangement, and style (see Nystrand, 1982; Sommers, 1980; Witte, 1985b). Linear-stage models see writing primarily as a problem in either arrangement (Flower & Hayes, 1981b) or style (Witte, 1985b), but seldom as a problem in invention (Young, 1978; Flower & Hayes, 1980, 1981a, 1981b, 1981c).

Although contemporary writing researchers and theorists have had some difficulty in overcoming the powerful influence of stage conceptions of writing (see Witte, 1985b), composing is now viewed primarily as a knowledge/thinking problem and a communication problem (Flower & Hayes, 1981b). Accordingly, composing processes are best seen as cognitive processes. These processes have been shown to recur in a nonlinear fashion during the act of writing (see Flower & Hayes, 1981a; Witte, 1985b). They have also been shown to interact with one another (see de Beaugrande, 1984; Flower & Hayes, 1981a; Scardamalia, 1981; Witte 1985b). Perhaps most important, composing processes have been shown to be organized hierarchically rather than linearly such that writing processes and subprocesses can be embedded within one another (see deBeaugrande, 1984; Flower & Hayes, 1981a, 1984; Hayes & Flower, 1980; Witte, 1985b).

One especially powerful recent model of composing is that developed by Flower and Hayes (1981a; Hayes & Flower, 1980) from their studies of thinking-aloud protocols (on protocols as data for research, see Ericcson & Simon, 1980, 1981, 1984; Hayes & Flower, 1983; Schweiger, 1983; Swarts, Flower, & Hayes, 1984) collected from writers in the act of writing. The Flower and Hayes cognitive process model represents writing as consisting essentially of three interacting components—the task environment, the writer's long-term memory (LTM), and the composing processes themselves. The Flower and Hayes model appears in Figure 4.1. As Figure 4.1 shows, the task environment contains two components: the rhetorical problem—which consists of the writing topic, the audience, and exigency—and the text that the writer has "produced so far." The writer's LTM consists of knowledge of topic, audience, and writing plans. As the bidirectional arrows indicate, both the task environment and the writer's LTM affect and are affected by the writing processes themselves. These writing processes are three in number: planning, translating, and reviewing. Planning includes the subprocesses of generating ideas and plans, organizing ideas and goals, and setting procedural and substantive plans. Translating involves expressing ideas and goals in verbal forms. And reviewing includes

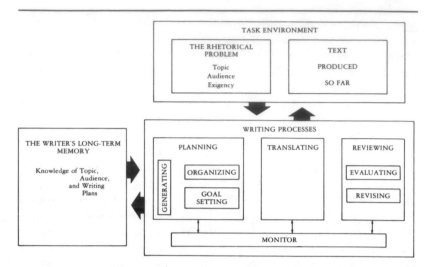

SOURCE: Linda Flower and John R. Hayes, "A Cognitive Process Theory of Writing." *College Composition and Communication*, December 1981. Copyright © 1981 by the National Council of Teachers of English. Reprinted by permission.

Figure 4.1   The Flower and Hayes Cognitive Process Model of the Writing Process

the subprocesses of evaluating and revising, which can take as their focus either plans or text. Through the use of a monitor, the writer is able to switch back and forth among the processes and to embed one process or subprocess within another such that, for example, reviewing can become a subprocess or subroutine during planning.

Clearly more robust than the linear-stage models that antedate it, the Flower and Hayes cognitive process model appears to represent the internal processes of the writer's mind working to solve communication problems, and it appears to represent the internal and external components that may affect and be affected by those processes. According to Scardamalia and Bereiter (in press), the Flower and Hayes model "appears to do what it is supposed to do, which is to serve as a frame for working out more detailed and possibly more controversial accounts of how the mind copes with writing tasks." Although Flower and Hayes's theoretical model differs in some particulars from other recent theories (for instance, de Beaugrande, 1984; Bracewell et al., 1982; Tierney & Pearson, 1983), it is not incompatible with those other theories. Most important, the Flower and Hayes model represents composing as an exceedingly complex problem-solving activity invoked in response to a rhetorical situation that demands a communicative utterance in the form of an extended written text. Accordingly, the model suggests that the way a writer represents a rhetorical problem affects both the writing processes and the written product and, further, that the text will reflect decisions writers make either planning or translating.

Three recent reviews (Faigley et al., in press; Humes, 1983; Scardamalia & Bereiter, in press) suggest that of the composing processes and subprocesses specified in the Flower and Hayes model, only three—planning, translating, and revising—have received extensive treatment in the literature. Although translating and the "text produced so far" are critical components of the Flower and Hayes model, research has generally not been much concerned either with identifying possible subprocesses of translating or with the influence of the "text produced so far" on the other processes of composing. In particular, research on writing processes has generally not relied on careful examinations of texts to help explain production processes. As Bracewell et al. (1982, p. 151) point out, "While research on the writing process has described planning and some translating processes in detail, generally, in contrast to research on comprehension, processes at all levels have not been related to the text structure and features the writer produces." A case in point is Flower and Hayes's early work on planning.

Flower and Hayes (1981b, p. 42) identify three general categories of plans: "plans for generating ideas," "plans for producing a paper," and "plans controlling the composing act." In the Flower and Hayes conceptualization of planning, the three categories of plans constantly interact during composing such that planning of one kind affects planning of the other two kinds. According to Flower and Hayes (p. 42), plans for generating ideas and for producing a paper consist of "procedural plans" and "content-specific plans," while plans for controlling composing consist only of procedural plans.

Two of the content-specific plans that Flower and Hayes identify are critical to an understanding of the relationship between composing processes and written products: "finding a focus" (p. 42), which is part of planning for generating ideas, and "forming for use," which is part of planning for producing a paper. Flower and Hayes see finding a focus as "one of the crucial acts that can bridge the gap between generating ideas and turning them into a paper" and as "a task with which many writers have trouble" (p. 45). They also note that "the plan to *find a focus* is not an operational plan," because "such a plan does not account for the thinking process a writer must go through to achieve a focus" (p. 45). Flower and Hayes see forming for use as involving plans that address two questions: *"what to use* (out of all the available ideas and language already generated) and *how to use it"* (p. 47). Flower and Hayes's discussion of such plans does not go much beyond the identification of forming for use with these two questions, perhaps because their principal interest is in planning and not in the connections between planning and translating processes and, further, because their principal interest diverts attention away from connections between these two processes and specific features of texts. Accordingly, both their cognitive process model of composing and their conceptualization of planning lack a certain specificity.

Bracewell et al.'s (1982) recent work helps add specificity to the Flower and Hayes theoretical model by hypothesizing certain relationships among planning, translating, and text. Bracewell et al. see translating as influenced by both "regulating" and "framing" processes. They illustrate these processes by referring to research on conversation. Conversation involves more than content; it also involves the "important processes" that regulate the "flow" of the conversation and create a "framework" by which the various "utterances can be interpreted and understood" (Bracewell et al., 1982, p. 148). They elaborate:

> In conversations, successful communication requires both the establishment of a common frame or structure (Frake, 1977) and the smooth regulation of the flow of turn-taking, side sequences, openings, closings, and topic shifts (Sacks, Schegloff & Jefferson, 1974). Regulating processes are characteristic of adult conversations and are learned as children acquire principles for turn-taking and producing speech that is topically and conversationally related to their own and others' speech acts.
>
> In addition to these regulative aspects, conversations typically are structured in terms of larger topically related units such as scenes, events, and entire speech activities (such as might occur in a lesson or a task-oriented dialogue). The term *frame* has been used to refer to the structure of such units that provide a context within which individual speech acts are coherent parts. To account for variability and change in contextual frames over the course of a conversation, the concept of frame had to be extended from a fixed notion to one of frame as *constructed* by participants through their interactions. (Bracewell et al., 1982, p. 148)

According to Bracewell et al. (1982), regulating and framing processes that govern the structure, content, and direction of conversations also figure importantly in the comprehension and production of written discourse:

> In comprehension of written text, it is principally the text structure that has to support the reader's comprehension, and in writing, the text structure is the principal means for expressing a conceptual structure or frame. Viewed somewhat more deeply, the reader must use the text structure to infer a writer's conceptual structure, and a writer must produce a text that is able to sustain a reader's inferences about the underlying conceptual structure. (Bracewell et al., 1982, pp. 148-149)

However important framing and regulating processes are in comprehending and producing written texts, the processes function differently during reading than they do during writing. As Bracewell et al. (1982, p. 150) explain:

> The discourse features, propositional structure, and underlying frame structures identified as important to comprehension are central to a description of discourse production. A writer must acquire a capacity (a) to generate conceptual frame structures and propositions to represent them, and (b) to select and manipulate language features using them to encode propositions and signal underlying conceptual frames. Processes of frame construction are likely to occur both in production and comprehension; the principal difference between them is the degree of constraint on frame construction. In reading, the text constrains frame construction; in writing, frame construction is constrained . . . by the writer's knowledge and the text he or she has previously written (Frederiksen & Dominic, 1981). Regulating processes in comprehension involve text-based control of comprehension; in writing they involve the writer's use of language features and text structure to control the reader's processing.

The problem of framing, and hence regulating, discourse for the writer is considerably more difficult than for the speaker. For speakers, audiences are immediate, both psychologically and physically, and capable of exerting considerable influence on the context, structure, and direction of a conversation. For writers, audiences are much more distant—in fact, almost remote. For speakers, the rhetorical problem is immediately inferrable from context. For writers, the rhetorical problem and its context are often constructed by the writer who is physically separated from an immediate communicative context. For speakers, the content of a conversation is controlled by a communicative context in which the speaker is an active participant. For writers, content is typically controlled by what the writer is able to access from long-term memory. For speakers, the stretch of discourse that must be controlled before another speaker takes a turn is relatively short in comparison to the stretches of discourse that must be controlled by writers. During production, writers, unlike speakers, have to rely solely on their own evaluations of their discourses to determine whether enough or appropriate content has been presented and whether it has been adequately framed. Speakers, on the other hand, have access to context-bound evaluation signals or cues (for instance, frowns, nods, inattentiveness) to determine whether their utterances are effective. Speakers can respond immediately to situational context; writers have to project themselves imaginatively into such a context.

These differences between speaking and writing would seem to affect production processes. In writing, planning is likely to be more extensive and more difficult because of the writer's inability to "negotiate and establish a *framework*" (Bracewell et al., 1982, p. 148) through interaction with an audience physically present during production. In writing, translating is likely to proceed more slowly, particularly if the writer must discover a framework through translating. Moreover, if in writing framing occurs simultaneously with or after translating text, the writer will likely have to retranslate (revise) portions of the "text produced so far" to adjust them to the emergent framework or be content with a text that lacks coherence (see Witte, 1985b).

As a result of their theoretical investigation of discourse comprehension processes, Bracewell et al. (1982, p. 150) conclude that "topical organization or 'staging' . . . influences the pattern of text-based inference by establishing a sequence and topical focus in presenting propositional information in text." Bracewell et al. use the terms "topical organization or 'staging'" in much the same manner as they are used by Grimes (1975) and Clements (1979) to describe, in essence, topicalization in clauses and topical relations across clauses. Based on their theoretical considerations of comprehension processes, Bracewell et al. (1982, p. 151) hypothesize that a close connection [exists] between frame construction processes in comprehension and planning the conceptual content of a paper. The sequential organization of conceptual content ought to involve generating a propositional representation and establishing a staging for these propositions. Translating processes provide the link between the conceptual frame (on the one hand), and the staging and use of language devices (on the other).

We see Bracewell et al.'s hypothesis as addressing the critical juncture between planning and translating. As such, it contributes needed specificity to the Flower and Hayes cognitive process theory of composing by showing how the major processes of planning and translating are related and in turn how those two processes relate to text. In the sections that follow, we investigate the Bracewell et al. hypothesis about the connection between framing and topicalization, first by looking at the notion of topic in written products and then by looking at how decisions about topical focus are made during composing.

TOPICAL FOCUS

The notion of topic[3] in extended discourse is not an uncommon one. For teachers of writing and for countless generations of writing students, it has informed the idea of the topic sentence. However, in such fields of study as textlinguistics, discourse analysis, reading comprehension, and stylistics, *topic* has come to be used in somewhat more specialized ways. Although there is considerable disagreement about the precise meaning of the term and about the way it ought to be applied in the study of discourse (see de Beaugrande, 1980; Chafe, 1976; Enkvist, 1974; Grimes, 1975; van Dijk, 1977, 1980), the frequency with which the term appears in the literature suggests that the concept of topic is a useful and valid one for discussing individual sentences within a discourse, semantic relationships among sentences in a discourse, and whole discourses.

For the purposes of the present essay, the concept of topic is perhaps best understood initially in terms of individual sentences or t-units, rather than as a feature of each clause as it is treated in the work of Clements (1979). The topic of a sentence or t-unit is usually, though not always (see Lautamatti, 1978; Witte, 1983a, 1983b), its grammatical subject, and it usually functions—to greater or lesser degrees (see Prince, 1981)—to express old or given information, information that is either explicit in preceding text or recoverable through inference from the preceding text or the surrounding situational context (see the discussions of given and new information in Chafe, 1974, 1976; Clark, 1977; Clark & Haviland, 1977; Daneš, 1974a; Haviland & Clark, 1974; Vande Kopple, 1982). In addition, the topic of an individual sentence may be seen as the place "where we [i.e., readers or listeners] stand as we look toward the rest of the sentence" (Dillon, 1981, p. 105). In short, a second principal function of the topic in a sentence or t-unit is to announce what the sentence or t-unit is about (see Daneš, 1974a; following Mathesius, 1929, 1964). Consider the following three example sentences, which deliver essentially the same information but seem to assume different textual and situational contexts. In contrast to the topic portion of the sentence, a comment portion typically delivers essentially new information not recoverable from the preceding textual or situational context. Each of the following sentences is well formed, but each seems to assume a somewhat different context.

(a) *Paul* struck the bell with a stick.
(b) The *bell* was struck by Paul with a stick.
(c) A *stick* was used by Paul to strike the bell.

Although sentence topics sometimes appear in places other than the head of the sentence or t-unit, each of the above three sentences fronts a different lexical item, and these lexical items tend to control the way readers approach or process the remaining portions of the sentences. The sentence topics, which are italicized, provide the perspective from which the rest of the sentence is viewed. Accordingly, most readers would probably say that (a) is "about" Paul, that (b) is "about" the bell, and that (c) is "about" the stick used to strike the bell. In addition to the relatively high frequency with which topics and grammatical subjects are identical, a second characteristic of topics is that they are typically, though not always, the first noun appearing in a sentence.

In order to understand how writers and speakers decide what to topicalize in a given sentence or t-unit, it is necessary to understand two other functions of the topics of individual sentences or t-units in

connected discourse. Consider, for example, the following sequence
of sentences:

> *Paul Mayes* visited a small border town in southwest Texas. When *he*
> arrived late in the evening, he discovered that the water can he had
> carried with him through Big Bend National Park was empty. *He*
> stopped at a mission church at the edge of town, hoping to find fresh
> water. The *church*, like the town, was dark and appeared deserted, and
> *Paul* was unable to stir anyone from sleep by knocking on any of the
> doors. As *he* scanned the front of one of the doors, he made out the
> shape of a bell. *Paul* immediately thought of arousing someone within
> by ringing it, and the *bell* was struck by Paul with a stick.

This text, written for purposes of illustration, shows that sentence or
t-unit topics provide one means of creating local coherence between
one sentence or t-unit and the next. When sentence topics do not
function in this way, they disrupt processing. Given the t-units that
precede that last one in the above text, most readers would expect as
a last sentence in this text sentence (a) above instead of (b) or (c). The
reason is found in another function of sentence topics in discourse,
namely, that they guide the reader's construction of a text's "gist" or
global meaning, which in the above text is conditioned by the "dis
course topic" (see van Dijk, 1980; Lautamatti, 1978; Witte, 1983a,
1983b). The topic of the last sentence, *bell*, does not accord well with
either the discourse topic or the "gist" or "macrostructure" (van Dijk,
1980) that the preceding sentences have led the reader to construct.
That is to say, the topic of the last t-unit in the above text is incompatible with what most readers would construe as the discourse topic
and would therefore probably not have been written as part of the
text.

The preceding discussion of topical focus identified four functions of sentence topics in extended texts. First, they announce what
an individual sentence or t unit is about. Second, they provide for
the smooth introduction of new information into a text. Third, they
help to create local coherence between individual sentences or
t-units. And fourth, they guide readers in constructing "gists" and
identifying discourse topics for the texts they read.

TOPICAL FOCUS AND TEXT

As we noted previously, Flower and Hayes (1981b) observe that one of the difficulties many writers face is "finding a focus." As the preceding discussion suggests, "focus" in Flower and Hayes's sense of the term may be related to choices writers make about "topics" at both the level of the discourse and at the level of the sentence. It seems reasonable to assume that the difficulties writers experience in "finding a focus" and alternative ways of "finding a focus" would be reflected in discernible patterns of sentence topics in texts and that these patterns would help us identify relationships between written products and writing processes.

To investigate this possibility, we decided to look for such patterns in a set of informative/descriptive texts written by writers of different ages. Our data consists of informative/descriptive texts written by students in grades 4, 8, 12, and 15.[4] All of the texts discussed below were written in response to a single explanatory writing task, one that asked students to describe to an acquaintance a place or landmark that was near their home or that they had visited while on vacation or on a day trip. The aim, mode, and (to some extent) content of the writing task were therefore constant across all grades.

Our investigation did allow us to identify four patterns of topical focus. Along with Bracewell et al. (1982), we see "staging" or topicalization as connected to framing processes during text production. We assume, therefore, that the four patterns of topical focus reveal different framing strategies that writers can use in composing descriptive/informative discourse. Because all four strategies appear at all grade levels, they cannot be construed to represent a developmental sequence. The texts below illustrate the four strategies. These texts were not chosen because they are typical; in fact, most of the 70 texts we examined evidence more than one strategy. The texts selected to illustrate the strategies were chosen because they reflect primarily a single strategy and thereby provide a clear example of it. The relationships that we see between particular framing strategies and characteristics of texts that result from them are set out in Figure 4.2.

In the following paragraphs, we discuss the hypothesized relationships between text characteristics and framing strategies. Throughout this discussion, we argue that the framing strategies result from the writers' different conceptualizations of an identical

FRAMING STRATEGIES	EFFECTS ON TEXT
Narrative Framing	Topical subject slots dominated by first-person pronoun, singular or plural. Description of place subordinated to narrative of events, experiences; e.g., "First we went into the front hallway. Then we went into the living room."
Sequence Framing	Topical subject slots dominated by second-person pronoun. "You" serves as vehicle for movement through description; e.g., "First you go into the front hallway. Then you turn left into the living room."
Locative Framing	Topical subject slots dominated by identification of location with object placed in location. "Location" serves as vehicle for movement through description; e.g., "In the front hallway is a large mirror. In the living room there is a piano."
Descriptive Framing	Focus on objects and features rather than on process or location; e.g., "A large mirror is in the front hallway. A piano is in the living room."

Figure 4.2 Textual Effects of Framing Strategies Used in Composing Descriptive/Informative Discourse

writing situation and, perhaps, different choices about specific content.

The narrative framing strategy. Many students interpreted the writing task described above as a call for a narrative describing a sequence of events surrounding a visit to the place they chose to write about. These students apparently represented the writing task to themselves in something like the following manner: "I am being asked to tell about what happened when I visited X." Such a problem representation seems to have invoked a subject matter or content that necessitated a framing strategy emphasizing the participants in a series of events at the place rather than the place itself. In texts that reflect writers' use of this strategy during planning and translating, the sentence or t-unit topic slots tend to be filled by first-person singular or plural pronouns. The following eighth-grade text suggests the writer's use of the narrative framing strategy. In this and in the other examples, we have italicized the sentence or t-unit topics.

It was three years ago when *I* went to Allegheny State Park. *We* rented a cabin and running under and around it *we* saw chipmunks. *We* were able to see a deer in the field across the road. After awhile *we* rented a double-seated bike. *We* rode all around the park until our time limit was up. That night *we* watched raccoons raid our garbage cans.

The next morning *we* ate our breakfast and then took a ride in the car. *We* were riding along when we lost our tailpipe and muffler. *We* were going to Thunder Rocks, so *we* walked the rest of the way. Then *two guys* came along and helped fix our tailpipe and muffler.

In the afternoon *we* went down to the beach and when *you* went in it was cold at first. After *you* got use to it, the water felt warm. When [*we*] got done swimming we went back to the cabin and ate our supper. When *we* got done eating we played cards or played some game.

Later that evening *we* went outside and made a bonfire and cooked hotdogs, toasted marshmallows and made some popcorn. Then *we* went to bed and my *mother and father, aunt and uncle* played cards.

The sequence framing strategy. A number of the student writers included in our sample appear to have represented the writing assignment as one that asked them to formulate a kind of "guidebook" narrative, rather than a first-person narrative. The writers using the sequence framing strategy probably conceptualized the rhetorical problem as something like the following: "Put someone within place or object X and show that person what will be seen." The framing strategy that appears to have been invoked by this conceptualization of the rhetorical problem often results in sentences that can be characterized by their focus on the second-person pronoun *you*. Accordingly, the sentence or t-unit topic slots are frequently filled by second-person pronouns, which may have been chosen because of the writer's concern for a hypothetical reader. This reader is addressed more or less directly and is led through a re-creation of the steps the writer may have followed when experiencing the object or place about which he or she is writing. The following twelfth-grade text seems to reflect the writer's reliance on the sequence framing strategy during composing, even though not all of the sentence topics are second-person pronouns.

Across from *Delaware Park* is the Buffalo Zoo. When *you* first look at it you will not be very impressed. The *main entrance* is full of people, little kids, parents, teenagers, boyfriends & girlfriends and other people. As *you* go through you pay the lady and go through the turnstile. Now *you* are in the zoo. There are a *few paths* that go off in different directions it really doesn't matter *which one* you take because they all end up in the same place. The *ground* is full of old candy wrappers and cotton candy sticks. If *you* go over to the bears you can watch them catch the food people throw at them. Although there are *signs* everywhere that say "Please don't feed the animals" people seem to think it doesn't pertain to them. After the bears *you* can go to the reptile house. *I* don't like going there because it's all dark and smells funny. There is a *monkey house, a bird house and a mammal.* There is the *Kiddie Zoo* which I like the best. *You* can go in there and pet all the animals. *They* have donkeys, monkeys, shetland ponies and goats. *I* really love the little baby goats. *You* can go in there and feed them and pet them. When *you* leave the Kiddie Zoo you are quite near the elephants. So *you* might as well pay them a visit. *They* are big and [*you*] don't go to near them because there not very friendly. Then *you* can go to the pond where all the ducks are. *They* swim around and eat all the bread you throw them. The *seals* are the best. *You* can buy fish and stand by their pool. *They* jump up and catch the fish you throw them. There are *three* and *they* have beautiful black and shiny skin. *I* could stand there for hours. The *seals* are right near the exit so *you* walk out eating cotton candy feeling a little hot, stickey but very happy that you spent your day at the Buffalo Zoo.

The locative framing strategy. The locative framing strategy assumes the construction of a somewhat different rhetorical problem than either the narrative strategy or the sequence strategy. Writers who employ this framing strategy probably constructed the rhetorical problem in something like the following way: "I need to create a view of place or object X by locating its parts in relation to one another." In texts reflecting the use of the locative framing strategy, locations are given topic status in many of the sentences or t-units. These topicalized locations serve as vehicles for movement through a description of a place or object, and they provide the place in the sentence or t-unit from which the reader acquires information about specific artifacts or features of the place or object being described. Typically, such a description starts in a particular location and then moves in an orderly fashion until all pertinent elements in the scene have been located in relation to one another. The following excerpts from a grade 15 text illustrate the writer's reliance on the locative framing strategy during text production.

The *building* itself is rather large, and rectangular. The *roof* in the center is very high, and there are huge *sliding doors* in the back. . . . *All the way down* the building, except for a small section in the front and center, is a double row of stalls, with an aisle in between. Then, in the *center* of the building, and occupying pretty much the entire site, is a big, open spaced riding ring, filled with tons of soft dirt. . . .

In the *front and center* of the building is the main office, with a rectangular lounge. The *lounge* is entirely glass on one side. . . . *Behind* this lounge, and toward the front door of the club, is the office and a tack shop located directly across. Even more amazing is that *above* the lounge and office is a very large and very inhabited apartment. . . .

To the *left* as you face the building is a fairly large paddock or riding ring and *beyond* that is a field which is even a little larger. A *driveway* encircles the entire stable, and there is an oblong circular *driveway* approaching (and leaving) the main entrance. *Beyond* all this are apartments, houses, a public school, streets, a gas station, and even a fairly large plaza. . . .

The descriptive framing strategy. The descriptive framing strategy seems to assume yet another conceptualization of the rhetorical problem. Writers who rely on this strategy apparently represented the problem as follows: "I need to create an image of object or place X by calling attention to its distinguishing characteristics." Texts that result from the writers' use of the descriptive framing strategy represent what might be thought of as "description proper." In such texts, individual sentences or t-units focus on discrete objects or attributes characteristic of the place or object being described. Accordingly, objects or attributes fill the topic slots in most sentences or t-units. The following twelfth grade text results from the writer's use of the descriptive framing strategy during the writing process.

From the moment that *you* enter it and become baked by the heat, to the time you exit, splattered by paint, you'll find the stagecraft room a rather unique place. The *walls* are graffitited with impressions and names of those who have passed through those doors in theatric triumph. Not *anywhere* is a profane word to be seen. *Flats,* the painted walls of the false rooms, rest wearily against each other in bins against the wall, wedged in with an archaic N.H.S. plaque and a cardboard fireplace. *Bent nails, crumpled papers, and piles of sawdust* complement the battered wooden table used for sawing, hammering, nailing, and taking ones frustrations out on. An oil spattered *house* on rollers is wedged into one corner, opposite of a tool cabinet once robbed from the band and never returned. Above *that,* now boarded up, is what was known as "Heaven," the A.V. room from where Cyril Bodnar's resonant voice boomed out as "God." *This,* is a complete stagecraft room. *To have eaten, slept, loved, and created* in this room, is to have had it become a memorable part of your life.

Each of the above texts is clearly different from the others. The differences among the four texts cannot be explained solely in terms of differences in content or syntactic structure. Rather, the principal distinguishing characteristic seems to be choices the various writers made during composing about what to topicalize in their discourse. Our examination of these texts suggests that analyses of discourse topics and sentence topics can lead to useful inferences about writing processes. In particular, the framing strategies we have identified suggest ways in which an analysis of topical focus can be used to gain insight into the ways writers construct writing tasks for themselves and consequently "find a focus" and "form" their texts "for use." Our assumption is that the observed differences in topical focus reflect framing strategies that are in turn a reflection of the specific writing task writers have set for themselves.

TOPICAL FOCUS AND PROCESSES

The interaction of conceptual frames based on representations of the rhetorical problem, discourse topics, and sentence topics is, we believe, more explicitly illustrated in the following excerpts from two thinking-aloud protocols, transcriptions of taped recordings of writers thinking aloud as they composed. The first protocol shows a writer experiencing difficulty framing at both the global and local levels; the second shows a writer having comparatively little trouble with these processes. The protocols suggest that these framing processes are closely related to what Flower and Hayes call "finding a focus" and "forming for use," the two kinds of content-specific plans that are most closely linked to the process of translating and consequently "the text produced so far."

The protocols were taken just after the subjects had finished reading a writing assignment. The assignment asked the writer to assume that he or she was a student representative on a Faculty Disciplinary Committee that was reviewing an appeal of a failing grade received in a zoology course. "Jack," the student bringing the appeal before the Committee, was given a failing grade because another student, "Charlie," was caught using Jack's class notes during an examination. Jack had given Charlie the notes to use for studying prior to the examination. The writer was instructed to prepare a written statement designed to persuade the other members of the committee to adopt his or her view of Jack's innocence or guilt.[5] What follows is the opening segment of the first student's protocol. The numbers within parentheses identify what we see as natural divisions between idea units.

Protocol 1

(1) O.K.—so I'm a member of the faculty committee (2) and I have to figure out what— (3) what determines (4) if he'd be innocent— (5) or if he knew— (6) I think he'd be innocent— (7) and I agree with him saying (8) that he didn't know how the notes were going to be used (9) O.K.—let's see—let's see—O.K.— (10) I'll say that Jack had no control over the notes— (11) because he was trying to help out a friend (12) and didn't realize that Charlie was going to use them to cheat with— (13) and therefore he wasn't cheating by helping somebody— (14) so—how do I explain it— (15) I guess you could say—let's see— (Transcribes note) Jack was innocent—(Transcribes note) because he had no idea how Charlie was going to use the notes (Reviews transcribed note) because he had no idea how Charlie was going to use the notes (16) so, if I was on the committee— (17) I'd—I'd try to tell them that there's no way he could be guilty— (18) uh—uh—I guess—let's see— (19) if I was a committee member— (20) I could build sort of a case saying (21) that maybe—let's see—that Charlie never explicitly— let's see— (22) that Jack tried to help him— (23) let's see—he never refused to help him— (24) but he didn't want to— (25) because he didn't want to cheat— (26) so he tried to compromise by offering Charlie his class notes to use in preparing for the test— (27) O.K.— so—he was—he was trying to help Charlie—(Transcribes note) Jack was trying to help Charlie by letting him use his notes (28)—so he could study— (29) and then Jack wouldn't have to cheat that way— (30) I think—O.K.—let's see— (31) Charlie—Oh—O.K.—Jack didn't know— (32) I don't know where I can come from— (33) I don't know what point I can get to— (34) besides that Jack didn't know what Charlie was going to do (35)—and you can't always take Jack's word— (36) so—that is why the professor examined the notes that Charlie had during the test— (37) and he discovered they belonged to Jack— (38) he can't prove that Jack also had cheat notes— (39) or cheated— (40) and he only claimed— O.K.—(Transcribes note) The professor only claimed that—claimed that Jack cheated—O.K.—(Reviews note) he

claimed that Jack cheated— (41) but he couldn't prove it—
(Transcribes note) he couldn't prove that Jack cheated—O.K.—
(Reviews note) He claimed that Jack cheated—but he couldn't prove
it— (42) I still don't know how he explained this— (43) maybe—maybe
I could go from the other end— (44) maybe he was guilty— (45) I
could try from that end maybe— (46) I could write some notes on that
(47) and see what happens—let's see— (48) there is evidence that Jack
cheated—let's see—(Transcribes note) Jack could have cheated by—
(49) well—he might have known what Charlie was going to use the
notes— (50) what—I guess he could have lent Charlie his notes to help
him by cheating— (51) that way, he wouldn't get caught— (52) but he
did— (53)—that's—that's sort of cheating—I guess— (54) I don't
know—let's see— (55) well he could have—but possibly not—let's see
(Reviews assignment) It says Jack felt that he was innocent and ap-
pealed to the Faculty Disciplinary Committee which is responsible for
making a decision in cases involving academic cheating. (56)—
O.K.—well—you still can't prove he was cheating— (57) this is hard—
(58) uh—I don't know—I don't know— (59) it's just I can't figure out
which angle to come from— (60) because there could be several
angles— (61) he could be guilty or not guilty— (62) I don't—

This first protocol shows how the writer's difficulty in framing at
the discourse level leads to difficulty in framing and translating at
the sentence level. In fact, during the portion of the protocol
presented here, the writer transcribes only what she considers to be
preliminary notes. Global framing of discourse, and hence local
framing, seem to be inhibited because of the writer's ambivalence
about the content of the text she intends to write. Although the
writer seems to make a critical content decision early during planning (that is, "I think he'd be innocent"), she has difficulty translating
that content into written text. The writer is able to generate ideas
capable of supporting her initial claim that Jack is innocent, but she
apparently does not recognize that these ideas might serve as evidence to support her claim. This failure suggests that the writer has
been unable to access a conceptual framework for argument, a
framework that she could draw on in framing discourse to meet the
demands of a novel situation.

The difficulty this writer has in framing at both the global and
sentence levels may result from an inadequate representation of the
rhetorical situation and the rhetorical problem (Flower & Hayes,
1980). In part, the difficulty the writer appears to have with framing
seems to be a product of the writer's having trouble entering imagi-

natively into the rhetorical context posited by the writing assignment. Although she notes initially that "I'm a member of the faculty
committee," the writer's imagined participation on the Committee
begins to collapse as soon as she says: "I think he'd be innocent." The
modal "would" suggests that the hypothetical nature of the writing
task is now foremost in the writer's mind. Notice that by idea unit 19
she has become so tentative that she says, "If I was a committee
member . . ." These uncertainties about role create problems for the
writer in conceptualizing the relationship between writer and audience for her intended text. More precisely, the writer is unable to cast
propositions in forms that will address the requirements of the
audience in this imaginary rhetorical situation.

The writer also seems to be uncertain about her purpose, about
the problem she needs to solve. Although the writing assignment
clearly states that she is to persuade other committee members to
adopt her position, this writer formulates her purpose as follows: "I
have to figure out what—what determines if he'd be innocent." Of
course, figuring out "what determines if he'd be innocent" is in some
way necessary for completing the writing task, but it would not be the
central aim of the text the assignment asked the writer to produce.
The writer's misrepresentation of the rhetorical problem posed by
the assignment may account for her failure to access a conceptual
framework for argument, even though she generates orally the
substance of an argument. Inadequate representation of the rhetorical situation—specifically, inadequate working definitions of role
and purpose (or aim)—eventually lead this writer into such serious
difficulties with framing and translating that she begins to abandon
the content she attempts to verbalize very early in the protocol. She
ultimately reverses her original position on Jack's innocence in the
hope that the guilty finding will be easier to frame and translate, and
she does finally produce a text that asserts Jack's guilt.

Consider now the opening section of a protocol collected from a
second writer, a writer who experiences few of the difficulties encountered by the previous writer.

Protocol 2

(1) O.K.—um—so I'm a student member of a faculty disciplinary
committee— (2) and I've got to convince a bunch of faculty members
(3) that Jack is either guilty or innocent—um— (4) he's obviously

innocent— (5) and I've got to persuade them that he is— (6) let me
see—how can I persuade them— (7) I think that the facts the zoology
professor presented amounts to little more than—circumstantial evidence— (8) and Jack was never caught cheating in the way Charlie—
(9) all Jack did was give Charlie the notes— (10) Jack couldn't control
what Charlie did with the notes— (11) that's a strong point— (12) if
Jack's guilty of anything— (13) he's guilty of giving a desparate friend
a way of—a way to pass a test—what—honestly— (14) I've lent my
notes to other students many times— (15) and—and—if they used
them during a test— (16) that's their problem— (17) they're responsible for that—not me— (18) that would be like charging a—car
dealer—with manslaughter— (19) if someone who bought a car from
him—say—ran a red light and killed a pedestrian— (20) the professor
doesn't have much of a case against—what's his name—Jack— (21) let
me see now—how should I start—(Transcribes text) Fellow Committee Members: As the student member of this Committee, I believe it
my duty to speak on behalf of Jack, not because Jack is a fellow student
but because none of the evidence presented against him warrants the
failing grade he received in zoology. Let me review that evidence with
you. (22) First, the zoology professor's evidence is altogether circumstantial in nature. (Transcribes text) The evidence presented to
this Committee by Jack's zoology professor amounts to nothing more
than circumstantial evidence. Charlie, not Jack, illegally used class
notes during the examination. (23) The notes Charlie used were class
notes that Jack made— (24) as he has stated— (25) in his letter
appealing the failing grade he received—(Transcribes text) The class
notes that Charlie used were Jack's, as Jack clearly stated in his letter
appealing the grade he received in the zoology course. (26) But—Jack
also states that he lent the notes to Charlie for no other reason
than—to help him prepare for the examination— (27) and there is no
evidence— (28) that Jack gave Charlie the notes for the purpose of
cheating on the exam—(Transcribes text) Jack's statement to this
Committee indicates that his purpose in giving Charlie the notes was
to help him prepare for the examination and not to help Charlie
cheat. Indeed, neither Charlie nor the zoology professor has
presented evidence to this Committee that would allow us to conclude
that Jack conspired with Charlie in a cheating scheme. One only thing
indicating such a conspiracy is the professor's claim, a claim unsup-
ported by the evidence before us. (29) Many students—including
me—lend their notes to other students before an examination— (30)
it's a common practice— (31) but I don't expect the person I give my
notes to— (32) to take them to the exam— (33) that's like—I can use
the analogy here—(Transcribes text) The practice of lending class
notes to fellow students is not an uncommon one by any means.
(34)—and the University has no rules—

Unlike the first writer, this second writer seems to be able to represent the rhetorical situation and the rhetorical problem adequately to herself. She appears to have a clearer conception of her role as a student member of the Disciplinary Committee. She steps quickly and easily into this role and seems to have no trouble staying in the role. In fact, she works to make the role more realistic by thinking of personal experiences that will enable her to invent arguments suitable for the role. Her sense of purpose is also very clearly formulated. The clarity with which she has represented the rhetorical situation enables her to represent to herself a rhetorical problem different from the one represented by the first writer. The first writer sees her major problem to be figuring "out what—what determines if he'd be innocent," whereas the second writer represents her major problem as having "to convince a bunch of faculty that Jack is either guilty or innocent." Because the second writer is able to represent the rhetorical situation and the rhetorical problem adequately to herself, she is able to access a conceptual framework for argument that enables her to frame her discourse for the novel task demanded by the assignment in a way that seems to make translating content ("obviously, he's innocent") almost effortless.

The importance of writers' perceptions of rhetorical situations and writing problems, both of which are aspects of what Flower and Hayes call "the task environment," cannot be overemphasized. Defining, in effect, rhetorical context, they form a critical component of the Flower and Hayes model; and as aspects of context, they are a vital part of what motivates framing. As Bracewell et al. (1982, p. 148) point out, frames "provide a context within which individual speech acts are coherent parts." This notion of context is further specified when it is seen in light of Halliday's three functions or levels of language. Halliday (1970, 1973, 1974, 1978) suggests that language operates on three different levels simultaneously, that it performs three functions at once: the ideational, the interpersonal, and the textual. The ideational component of language has to do with the content of what is expressed. The interpersonal function of language attends to forming and maintaining human relationships. The textual function involves creating texts that observe conventions necessary for achieving coherence. As an aspect of context, these language functions must be accommodated in the frames speakers and writers construct in order to contextualize discourse and discoursing. We see the ability to construct sequences of sentences that use topical focus to regulate the reader's processing of and response to the text as one dimension of framing during the planning and translating of extended text. We hypothesize that framing decisions, which must operate at the global level of whole discourse and at the local level of individual sentences or t-units, are reflected in writers' decisions about topicalization.

Global framing and local framing in terms of the ideational, interpersonal, and textual functions of language become evident in the decisions about topicalization that the second writer makes as she translates ideas into verbal form and then transcribes them into written text. These decisions can be more easily seen if part of the transcribed text is excerpted from the protocol.

> Fellow Committee Members: As the *student member* of this Committee, I believe it my duty to speak on behalf of Jack, not because Jack is a fellow student but because none of the evidence presented against him warrants the failing grade he received in zoology. *[You]* Let me review that evidence with you. The *evidence* presented to this Committee by Jack's zoology professor amounts to nothing more than circumstantial evidence. *Charlie,* not Jack, illegally used class notes during the examination. The *class notes* that Charlie used were Jack's, as Jack clearly stated in his letter appealing the grade he received in the zoology course.

Rather than reiterating the "discourse topic," the sentence topics in the opening portions of the second writer's text focus attention on particular aspects of it. The second writer, unlike the first, appears able to mobilize in the service of written language the tacit knowledge that every speaker has of the ideational, interpersonal, and textual functions of language. Accordingly, the first two sentence topics frame the discourse in terms of its situational context by referring explicitly to the writer, her role on the committee, and the audience for the text, thereby contextualizing the entire discourse in terms of the interpersonal function of language. This framing of the text in terms of the participants, in turn, frames the macroproposition—"none of the evidence presented against him [Jack] warrants the failing grade he received in zoology"—which is expressed in the predicate or comment portion of the second sentence. This macroproposition expresses what becomes the discourse topic and provides a framework for the text's ideational content. The topics chosen for the subsequent sentences allow the writer to elaborate on that discourse topic by focusing on specific pieces of evidence. The choice of sentence topics and the writer's decisions about sequencing them meet the demands of the textual function of discourse. Unlike the writer represented in the first protocol, this second writer seems to have had little difficulty in "finding a focus" or in "forming" a text "for use."

This analysis of the two thinking-aloud protocols demonstrates some important connections between framing as an aspect of planning, on the one hand, and topicalization in texts, on the other. As such, the analysis provides a kind of validation for the inferences that we made about framing strategies on the basis of textual patterns of topical focus in the informative/descriptive texts. It will be recalled that we argued that topical focus in the informative/descriptive texts gave insight into the ways the various writers conceptualized the rhetorical situation and the rhetorical problem with which they were confronted. In our analysis of the informative/descriptive texts, we suggested that decisions about topics reflect more or less directly the writer's decisions about how to accommodate dimensions of the rhetorical situation. Given our analyses of the two thinking-aloud protocols, we are now prepared to argue that the four framing strategies illustrate different ways of bringing to bear on a particular writing task the writer's tacit knowledge of language functions. Together, our analyses of the informative/descriptive texts and the two thinking-aloud protocols strongly suggest that if done cautiously and carefully, analyses of texts can lead to useful and valid inferences about writing processes.

SOME CONCLUDING REMARKS

From the outset, we conceived of this essay as fundamentally exploratory. In it we have explored the possibility of using written products as the basis for making inferences about writing processes. More specifically, we have explored the possibility of using topical focus analysis of written products to gain insight into framing strategies invoked during planning and translating.

Our analyses of both completed texts and thinking-aloud protocols lead us to view the complementary processes of framing and topicalization as exceedingly rich constructs that help to establish a connection between production processes and written products. These constructs render somewhat more specific the processes of planning and translating that are critical components of Flower and

Hayes's cognitive process model of composing. Framing discourse at both the global and the local levels occurs at the critical juncture between planning and translating. Framing decisions—which are based on tacit knowledge of the ideational, interpersonal, and textual functions of language and on the writer's representation of the rhetorical problem—in turn regulate decisions about topicalization as the writer attempts to translate ideas into language and then to transcribe them as written text. At the global level these decisions result in choices regarding the discourse topic. At the local level, these decisions result in choices regarding sentence topics. Topicalization is in effect a vehicle for translating framing decisions into text.

The framing strategies we have abstracted in our analyses of informative/descriptive texts suggest how topical focus analysis can be used to gain insight into the ways writers construct writing tasks for themselves and frame texts accordingly. Our analyses suggest that topical focus reflects text production strategies that are in turn a reflection of the specific writing task writers have set for themselves. Our analyses of these texts should not imply that the texts themselves are the processes by which they are produced. Rather, our analyses should suggest that, given knowledge of how planning and translating enter into the composing process and the kinds of influences that act upon them, it is possible to make reasonable inferences about writing processes from written products. Written products, our analyses suggest, can serve as a window on some processes of composing.

The connection between written products and writing processes posited on the basis of our analyses of the informative/descriptive texts is reinforced by the two thinking-aloud protocols. We saw in the protocols evidence of the two writers drawing on tacit knowledge of language functions in their respective representations of the rhetorical problem. Those representations were then shown to affect the writers' attempts to frame at a global level the texts they wished to produce. The second protocol shows that successful framing at the global level facilitates framing at the local or sentence level. When we examined the resultant text we saw in fact that the discourse topic and the choice of sentence topic represented an earlier conceptualization of the rhetorical problem and the kind of written response that it demanded.

Our hope is that the analyses we have presented in the present essay contribute to our understanding of how writers conceptualize a rhetorical situation—including the rhetorical problem—develop frames consistent with that conceptualization, and make framing decisions at both the level of the sentence and the level of connected discourse. We see the strength of the present essay to lie in its drawing together theory and research from a number of different disciplines and bringing it to bear on the relationship between writing processes and written products. If the essay has succeeded, it has perhaps brought us one step closer to understanding the relationship between written products and writing processes and to mapping some of the uncharted territory that lies between them.

NOTES

1. In addition to Hunt's studies cited, see also the reports of Bateman and Zidonis (1966), Huddleston (1971), Hunt (1966, 1977), Loban (1963, 1976), Marckworth and Bell (1967), O'Donnell, Griffin, and Norris (1967), and Schmeling (1969).

2. In addition to the studies already cited, a plethora of such studies have been completed. Some examples are the following: Anderson (1979), Callaghan (1977), Combs (1976, 1977), Fisher (1973), Green (1972), Klein (1977), Levine (1976), Maimon and Nodine (1978), Mulder, Braun, and Holliday (1978), Pedersen (1977), Perron (1974), Smart and Ollila (1978), Stewart (1978), Straw (1978), Sullivan (1977), and Vitale, King, Shontz, and Huntley (1971). In addition, Mellon (1979) and Stotsky (1975) offer critical reviews of the literature on sentence combining. Kinneavy (1979) and Witte (1980; Harris & Witte, 1980) have argued that whatever success sentence combining has had in improving students' written texts is attributable to teaching rhetorical principles inductively through the sentence-combining exercises, a view that finds some support in Daiker, Kerek, and Morenberg (1979), Nugent (1979), and Palacas (1970).

3. Readers interested in overviews of the literature on topics will find the following references useful: Daneš (1974b), van Dijk (1977, 1980), Vande Kopple (1982), and Witte (1983a).

4. We selected the texts used in the following analyses from a larger sample consisting of 70 descriptive/informative texts, 20 at each of grades 4, 8, and 12, and 10 at grade 15. The texts on which we base the following discussion are drawn from a subgroup formed by the 35 highest rated essays in the data set. The 70 texts were collected as part of the Buffalo Cross-Sectional Study of Writing Performance. Planned as a data base for descriptive studies of writing performance, this study was designed in early 1976 by Charles R. Cooper, Lee Odell, and Cynthia Watson, who together devised the sampling plan and the writing tasks. During the 1976-1977 school year, Cooper and Watson coordinated the gathering of the sample from school districts in New York, Michigan, and Illinois. Subsequently, Cooper and Odell supervised the primary-trait scoring of the sample.

5. This assignment is taken from Faigley et al. (in press).

REFERENCES

Anderson, P. V. (1979). Out of the classroom: Sentence combining in training programs for business, industry, and government. In D. A. Draiker, A. Kerek, & M. Morenberg (Eds.), *Sentence combining and the teaching of writing*. Akron, OH: L & S.

Aristotle. (1954). *"The Rhetoric" and "The Poetics" of Aristotle* (W. R. Roberts and I. Bywater, Trans.). New York: Modern Library.

Bartholomae, D. (1980). The study of error. *College Composition and Communication, 31,* 253-269.

Bateman, D. R., & Zidonis, F. J. (1966). *The effect of a study of transformational grammar on the writing of ninth and tenth graders* (NCTE Research Report No. 6). Urbana, IL: National Council of Teachers of English.

de Beaugrande, R. (1980). *Text, discourse, and process: Toward a multidisciplinary science of texts.* Norwood, NJ: Ablex.

de Beaugrande, R. (1984). *Text production: Toward a science of composition.* Norwood, NJ: Ablex.

Becker, A. L. (1965). A tagmemic approach to paragraph analysis. *College Composition and Communication, 16,* 237-242.

Bereiter, C., & Scardamalia, M. (1984). Learning about writing from reading. *Written Communication, 1,* 163-188.

Berkenkotter, C. (1983). Decisions and revisions: The planning strategies of a publishing writer. *College Composition and Communication, 34,* 156-169.

Bracewell, R. J., Frederiksen, C. H., & Frederiksen, J. D. (1982). Cognitive processes in composing and comprehending discourse. *Educational Psychologist, 17,* 146-164.

Britton, J., Burgess, T., Martin, N., McLeod, A., & Rosen, H. (1975). *The development of writing abilities (11-18).* London: Macmillan Education.

Callaghan, T. F. (1977). *The effects of sentence-combining exercises on the syntactic maturity, quality of writing, reading ability, and attitudes of ninth grade students.* Unpublished doctoral dissertation, State University of New York at Buffalo.

Carnicelli, T. A. (1980). The writing conference: A one-to-one conversation. In T. R. Donovan & B. W. McClelland (Eds.), *Eight approaches to teaching composition.* Urbana, IL: National Council of Teachers of English.

Chafe, W. L. (1974). Language and consciousness. *Language, 50,* 11-33.

Chafe, W. L. (1976). Givenness, contrastiveness, definiteness, subjects, and topics. In C. N. Li (Ed.), *Subject and topic.* New York: Academic Press.

Chomsky, N. (1957). *Syntactic structures.* The Hague: Mouton.

Christensen, F. (1963). A generative rhetoric of the sentence. *College Composition and Communication, 16,* 155-161.

Christensen, F. (1965). A generative rhetoric of the paragraph. *College Composition and Communication, 16,* 144-156.

Clark, H. H. (1977). Inferences in comprehension. In D. LaBerge & S. J. Samuels (Eds.), *Basic processes in reading.* Hillsdale, NJ: Lawrence Erlbaum.

Clark, H. H., & Haviland, S. E. (1977). Comprehension and the given-new contract. In R. O. Freedle (Ed.), *Discourse production and comprehension.* Norwood, NJ: Ablex.

Clements, P. (1979). The effects of staging on recall from prose. In R. O. Freedle (Ed.), *New directions in discourse processing.* Norwood, NJ: Ablex.

Combs, W. E. (1976). Further effects of sentence-combining practice on writing ability. *Research in the Teaching of English, 10,* 137-149.

Combs, W. E. (1977). Sentence-combining practice: Do gains in judgments of writing "quality" persist? *Journal of Educational Research, 70,* 318-321.

Cooper, C. R. (1977). Teaching writing by conferencing. In R. Bean, A. Berger, & A. Petrosky, (Eds.), *Survival through language: The basics and beyond.* Pittsburgh, PA: University of Pittsburgh.

Corbett, E.P.J. (1971). *Classical rhetoric for the modern student.* New York: Oxford University Press.

Daiker, D. A., Kerek, A., & Morenberg, M. (1979). Using "open" sentence-combining exercises in the college composition classroom. In D. A. Daiker, A. Kerek, & M. Morenberg (Eds.), *Sentence combining and the teaching of writing.* Akron, OH: L & S.

Daneš, F. (1974a). Functional sentence perspective and the organization of the text. In F. Daneš (Ed.), *Papers on functional sentence perspective.* The Hague: Mouton.

Daneš, F. (Ed.). (1974b). *Papers on functional sentence perspective.* The Hague: Mouton.

D'Angelo, F.J. (1974). A generative rhetoric of the essay. *College Composition and Communication, 25,* 388-396.

D'Angelo, F. J. (1975). *A conceptual theory of rhetoric.* Cambridge, MA: Winthrop.

D'Angelo, F. J. (1979). Paradigms as structural counterparts of *topoi.* In D. McQuade (Ed.), *Linguistics, stylistics, and the teaching of writing.* Akron, OH: L & S.

Dijk, T. A. van. (1977). *Text and context: Exploration in the semantics and pragmatics of discourse.* London: Longmans.

Dijk, T. A. van. (1980). *Macrostructures: An interdisciplinary study of global structures in discourse interaction and cognition.* Hillsdale, NJ: Lawrence Erlbaum.

Dijk, T. A. van, & Kintsch, W. (1983). *Strategies of discourse comprehension.* New York: Academic Press.

Dillon, G. (1981). *Constructing texts: Elements of a theory of composition and style.* Bloomington: Indiana University Press.

Duke, C. (1975). The student-centered conference and the writing process. *English Journal, 64,* 44-47.

Emig, J. (1969). *Components of the composing process among twelfth-grade writers.* Unpublished doctoral dissertation, Harvard University.

Emig, J. (1971). *The composing processes of twelfth graders* (NCTE Research Report no. 13). Urbana, IL: National Council of Teachers of English.

Emig, J. (1980). The tacit tradition: The inevitability of a multi-disciplinary approach to writing research. In A. Freedman & I. Pringle (Eds.), *Reinventing the rhetorical tradition.* Conway, AR: L & S, for the Canadian Council of Teachers of English.

Enkvist, N. E. (1974). Theme dynamics and style: An experiment. *Studia Anglia Posnaniensia, 5,* 127-135.

Ericcson, K. A., & Simon, H. A. (1980). Verbal reports as data. *Psychological Review, 87,* 215-251.

Ericcson, K. A., & Simon, H. A. (1981). Sources of evidence in cognition: An historical overview. In T. V. Merluzzi, C. R. Glass, & M. Genest (Eds.), *Cognitive assessment.* New York: Guilford.

Ericcson, K. A., & Simon, H. A. (1984). *Protocol analysis: Verbal reports as data.* Cambridge: MIT Press.

Fahnestock, J. (1983). Semantic and lexical coherence. *College Composition and Communication, 34,* 400-416.

Faigley, L. (1979). The influence of generative rhetoric on the syntactic maturity and writing effectiveness of college freshmen. *Research in the Teaching of English, 13,* 197-206.

Faigley, L. (1980). Names in search of a concept: Maturity, fluency, complexity, and growth in written syntax. *College Composition and Communication, 31,* 291-300.

Faigley, L., Cherry, R. D., Jolliffe, D. A., & Skinner, A. M. (in press). *Assessing writers' knowledge and processes of composing.* Norwood, NJ: Ablex.

Fisher, K. D. (1973). *An investigation to determine if selected exercises in sentence combining can improve reading and writing.* Unpublished doctoral dissertation, Indiana University.

Flower, L., & Hayes, J. R. (1980). The dynamics of composing: Making plans and juggling constraints. In L. Gregg & E. Steinberg (Eds.), *Cognitive processes in writing: An interdisciplinary approach.* Hillsdale, NJ: Lawrence Erlbaum.

Flower, L., & Hayes, J. R. (1981a). A cognitive process theory of writing. *College Composition and Communication, 32,* 365-387.

Flower, L., & Hayes, J. R. (1981b). Plans that guide the composing process. In C. H. Frederiksen & J. F. Dominic (Eds.), *Writing: Process, development and communication.* Hillsdale, NJ: Lawrence Erlbaum.

Flower, L., & Hayes, J. R. (1981c). The pregnant pause: An inquiry into the nature of planning. *Research in the Teaching of English, 15,* 229-244.

Flower, L., & Hayes, J. R. (1983). The cognition of discovery: Defining a rhetorical problem. *College Composition and Communication, 31,* 21-32.

Flower, L., & Hayes, J. R. (1984). Images, plans, and prose: The representation of meaning in writing. *Written Communication, 1,* 120-160.

Frake, C. O. (1977). Plying frames can be dangerous. Some reflections on methodology in cognitive anthropology. *Quarterly Newsletter of the Institute for Comparative Human Development, 1,* 1-7.

Frederiksen, C. H. (1977). Structure and process in discourse production and comprehension. In M. A. Just & P. A. Carpenter (Eds.), *Cognitive processes in comprehension.* Hillsdale, NJ: Lawrence Erlbaum.

Frederiksen, C. H., & Dominic, J. F. (1981). Introduction: Perspectives on the activity of writing. In C. H. Frederiksen & J. F. Dominic (Eds.), *Writing: Process, development, and communication.* Hillsdale, NJ: Lawrence Erlbaum.

Gorrell, R. M. (1983). How to make Mulligan stew: Process and product again. *College Composition and Communication, 34,* 272-277.

Grady, M. (1971). A conceptual rhetoric of the composition. *College Composition and Communications, 22,* 348-354.

Graves, D. (1975). An examination of the writing processes of seven-year-old children. *Research in the Teaching of English, 9,* 227-241.

Green, E. (1972). *An experimental study of sentence combining to improve written syntactic fluency in fifth grade children.* Unpublished doctoral dissertation, Northern Illinois University.

Green, G. M. (1982). Linguistics and the pragmatics of language use. *Poetics, 11,* 45-76.

Grimes, J. (1975). *The thread of discourse.* The Hague: Mouton.

Grobe, C. (1981). Syntactic maturity, mechanics, and vocabulary as predictors of quality ratings. *Research in the Teaching of English, 15,* 75-85.

Graves, D. (1973). *Children's writing: Research directions and hypotheses based upon an examination of the writing process of seven year old children.* Unpublished doctoral dissertation, State University of New York at Buffalo.

Hairston, M. (1982). The winds of change: Thomas Kuhn and revolution in the teaching of writing. *College Composition and Communication, 33,* 76-88.

Halliday, M.A.K. (1970). Language and structure and language function. In J. Lyons (Ed.), *New horizons in linguistics.* Harmondsworth, England: Penguin.

Halliday, M.A.K. (1973). *Explorations in the functions of language.* London: Edward Arnold.

Halliday, M.A.K. (1974). The place of "functional sentence perspective" in the system of linguistic description. In F. Daneš (Ed.), *Papers on functional sentence perspective.* The Hague: Mouton.

Halliday, M.A.K. (1978). *Language as social semiotic: The social interpretation of language and meaning.* Baltimore: University Park Press.

Halliday, M.A.K., & Hasan, R. (1976). *Cohesion in English.* London: Longman.

Harris, S.L., & Witte, S.P. (1980). Sentence combining in a rhetorical framework: Directions for further research. In A. Freedman & I. Pringle (Eds.), *Reinventing the rhetorical tradition.* Conway, AR: L & S, for the Canadian Council of Teachers of English.

Harris, Z. (1952/1964). Discourse analysis. In J.A. Fodor & J.J. Katz (Eds.), *The structure of language.* Englewood Cliffs, NJ: Prentice-Hall.

Haviland, S.E., & Clark, H.H. (1974). What's new? Acquiring new information as a process of comprehension. *Journal of Verbal Learning and Verbal Behavior, 13,* 512-521.

Hayes, J.R., & Flower, L. (1980). Identifying the organization of writing processes. In L. Gregg & E. Steinberg (Eds.), *Cognitive processes in writing: An interdisciplinary approach.* Hillsdale, NJ: Lawrence Erlbaum.

Hayes, J.R., & Flower, L. (1983). Uncovering cognitive processes in writing: An introduction to protocol analysis. In P. Mosenthal, L. Tamor, & S. Walmsley (Eds.), *Research in writing: Principles and methods.* New York: Longmans.

Huddleston, R.D. (1971). *The sentence in written English: A syntactic study based on an analysis of scientific texts.* Cambridge: Cambridge University Press.

Humes, A. (1983). Research on the composing process. *Review of Educational Research, 53*(2), 201-216.

Hunt, K.W. (1965). *Grammatical structures written at three grade levels* (NCTE Research Report No. 3). Urbana, IL: National Council of Teachers of English.

Hunt, K.W. (1966). Recent measures of syntactic development. *Elementary English, 43,* 732-739.

Hunt, K.W. (1970). Syntactic maturity in schoolchildren and adults. *Monographs of the Society for Research in Child Development.*

Hunt, K.W. (1977). Early blooming and late blooming syntactic structures. In C.R. Cooper & L. Odell (Eds.), *Evaluating writing: Describing, measuring, judging.* Urbana, IL: National Council of Teachers of English.

Judy, S.N., & Judy, S.J. (1979). *The English teachers' handbook: Ideas and resources for teaching English.* Cambridge, MA: Winthrop.

Karrfalt, D. (1968). The generation of paragraphs and larger units. *College Composition and Communication, 19,* 211-217.

Kerek, A., Daiker, D.A., & Morenberg, M. (1980). Sentence combining and college composition. *Perceptual and Motor Skills, 51* (Monograph Suppl. 1), 1059-1157.

King, M.L., & Rentel, V.M. (1981). *How children learn to write: A longitudinal study.* Columbus: Ohio State University, Research Foundation.

King, M.L., & Rentel, V.M. (1982). *Transition to writing.* Columbus: Ohio State University, Research Foundation.

Kinneavy, J. L. (1969). The basic aims of discourse. *College Composition and Communication, 20,* 297-304.

Kinneavy, J. L. (1979). Sentence combining in a comprehensive language framework. In D. A. Daiker, A. Kerek, & M. Morenberg (Eds.), *Sentence combining and the teaching of writing.* Akron, OH: L & S.

Kinneavy, J. L. (1980a). A pluralistic synthesis of four contemporary models for teaching composition. In A. Freedman & I. Pringle (Eds.), *Reinventing the rhetorical tradition.* Akron, OH: L. & S, for the Canadian Council of Teachers of English.

Kinneavy, J. L. (1980b). *A theory of discourse* (2nd ed.). New York: Norton.

Kinneavy, J. L., Cope, J. Q., & Campbell, J. W. (1976). *Writing: Basic modes of organization.* Dubuque, IA: Kendall/Hunt.

Kintsch, W. (1974). *The representation of meaning in memory.* Hillsdale, NJ: Lawrence Erlbaum.

Kintsch, W. (1977). *Memory and cognition.* New York: John Wiley.

Kintsch, W. & van Dijk, T. A. (1978). Towards a model of discourse comprehension and production. *Psychological Review, 85,* 363-394.

Klein, M. (1977). *Teaching sentence structure and sentence combining in middle grades.* Madison: Wisconsin State Department of Public Instruction.

Kuhn, T. S. (1970). *The structure of scientific revolutions* (2nd ed.). Chicago: University of Chicago Press.

Lautamatti, L. (1978). Observations on the development of the topic in simplified discourse. In V. Kohonen & N. E. Enkvist (Eds.), *Text linguistics, cognitive learning, and language teaching.* Turku, Finland: Åbo Akademi.

Levine, S. S. (1976). *The effect of transformational sentence-combining exercises on the reading comprehension and written composition of third-grade children.* Unpublished doctoral dissertation, Hofstra University.

Lindemann, E. (1982). *A rhetoric for writing teachers.* New York: Oxford University Press.

Loban, W. (1963). *The language of elementary school children* (NCTE Research Report No. 1). Urbana, IL: National Council of Teachers of English.

Loban, W. (1976). *Language development: Kindergarten through grade twelve* (NCTE Research Report No. 18). Urbana, IL: National Council of Teachers of English.

Lybbert, E., & Cummings, D. (1969). On repetition and coherence. *College Composition and Communication, 20,* 35-38.

Maimon, E. P., & Nodine, B. F. (1978). Measuring syntactic growth: Errors and expectations in sentence-combining practice with college freshmen. *Research in the Teaching of English, 12,* 233-244.

Mandler, J. M., & Johnson, N. S. (1977). Remembrance of things parsed: Story structure and recall. *Cognitive Psychology, 9,* 111-151.

Markworth, M. L., & Bell, L. M. (1967). Sentence-length distribution in the corpus. In H. Kucera & W. N. Francis (Eds.), *Computational analysis of present-day American English.* Providence, RI: Brown University Press.

Markels, R. (1982). *Cohesion patterns in English expository paragraphs.* Unpublished doctoral dissertation, Ohio State University.

Mathesius, V. (1929). Sur satzperspektiv in modernen Englisch. *Archiv für das Studium der neueren Sprachen und Literaturen, 155,* 202-210.

Mathesius, V. (1964). On linguistic characterology with illustrations from modern English. In J. Vachek (Ed.), *A Prague school reader in linguistics.* Bloomington: University of Indiana Press. (Original work published 1928)

McCarthy, D. (1954). Language development in children. In L. Carmichael (Ed.), *Manual of child psychology.* New York: John Wiley.

McColly, W. (1970). What does educational research say about the judging of writing ability? *Journal of Educational Research, 64,* 148-156.

Mellon, J.C. (1969). *Transformational sentence-combining: A method for enhancing the development of syntactic fluency in English composition* (NCTE Research Report No. 10). Urbana, IL: National Council of Teachers of English.

Mellon, J.C. (1979). Issues in the theory and practice of sentence combining: A twenty-year perspective. In D.A. Daiker, A. Kerek, & M. Morenberg (Eds.), *Sentence combining and the teaching of writing.* Akron, OH: L & S.

Moffett, J. (1968). *Teaching the universe of discourse.* Boston: Houghton Mifflin.

Morenberg, M., Daiker, D.A., & Kerek, A. (1978). Sentence combining at the college level: An experimental study. *Research in the Teaching of English, 12,* 245-256.

Mulder, J.E.M., Braun, C., & Holliday, W.G. (1978). The effects of sentence-combining practice on linguistic maturity level of adult students. *Adult Education, 28,* 111-120.

Murray, D.M. (1968). *A writer teaches writing: A practical method of teaching composition.* Boston: Houghton Mifflin.

Murray, D.M. (1978). Internal revision: A process of discovery. In C.R. Cooper & L. Odell (Eds.), *Research on composing: Points of departure.* Urbana, IL: National Council of Teachers of English.

Murray, D.M. (1980). Writing as process: How writing finds its own meaning. In T.R. Donovan & B.W. McClelland (Eds.), *Eight approaches to teaching composition.* Urbana, IL: National Council of Teachers of English.

Murray, D.M. (1984). Teach writing as process not product. In R.L. Graves (Ed.), *Rhetoric and composition: A sourcebook for teachers* (2nd ed.). Upper Montclair, NJ: Boynton/Cook.

Neman, B. (1980). *Teaching students to write.* Columbus, OH: Charles E. Merrill.

Nold, E.W. (1981). Revising. In C.H. Frederiksen & J.F. Dominic (Eds.), *Writing: Processes, development, and communication.* Hillsdale, NJ: Lawrence Erlbaum.

Nold, E.W., & Davis, B.E. (1980). The discourse matrix. *College Composition and Communication, 31,* 141-152.

Nugent, H.E. (1979). The role of old and new information in sentence combining. In D.A. Daiker, A. Kerek, & M. Morenberg (Eds.), *Sentence combining and the teaching of writing.* Akron, OH: L & S.

Nystrand, M. (1982). Rhetoric's "audience" and linguistics' "speech community": Implications for understanding writing, reading, and text. In M. Nystrand (Ed.), *What writers know: The language, process, and structure of written discourse.* New York: Academic Press.

Odell, L. (1977). Measuring changes in intellectual processes as one dimension of growth in writing. In C.R. Cooper & L. Odell (Eds.), *Evaluating writing: Describing, measuring, judging.* Urbana, IL: National Council of Teachers of English.

Odell, L. (1983). Written products and the writing process. In J.N. Hayes, P.A. Roth, J.R. Ramsey, & R.D. Foulke (Eds.), *The writer's mind: Writing as a mode of thinking.* Urbana, IL: National Council of Teachers of English.

O'Donnell, R.C., Griffin, W.J., & Norris, R.C. (1967). *Syntax of kindergarten and elementary school children: A transformational analysis* (NCTE Research Report). Urbana, IL: National Council of Teachers of English.

O'Hare, F. (1973). *Sentence combining: Improving student writing without formal grammar instruction* (NCTE Research Report No. 15). Urbana, IL: National Council of Teachers of English.

Palacas, A. L. (1970). Towards teaching the logic of sentence connection. In D. A. Daiker, A. Kerek, & M. Morenberg (Eds.), *Sentence combining and the teaching of writing.* Akron, OH: L & S.

Parker, W. R. (1967). Where do English departments come from? *College English, 28,* 339-351.

Pedersen, E. L. (1977). *Improving syntactic and semantic fluency in the writing of language arts students through extended practice in sentence combining.* Unpublished doctoral dissertation, University of Minnesota.

Perl, S. (1980). Understanding composing. *College Composition and Communication, 31,* 363-369.

Perron, J. D. (1974). *An exploratory approach to extending the syntactic development of fourth-grade students through the use of sentence-combining methods.* Unpublished doctoral dissertation, Indiana University.

Pitkin, W., Jr. (1969). Discourse blocs. *College Composition and Communication, 20,* 138-148.

Pitkin, W., Jr. (1977a). Hierarchies and the discourse hierarchy. *College English, 38,* 649-659.

Pitkin, W., Jr. (1977b). X/Y: Some basic strategies of discourse. *College English, 38,* 660-672.

Prince, E. F. (1981). Toward a taxonomy of given-new information. In P. Cole (Ed.), *Radical pragmatics.* New York: Academic Press.

Remondino, C. (1959). A factor analysis of the evaluation of scholastic compositions in the mother tongue. *British Journal of Educational Psychology, 29,* 242-251.

Rentel, V. M., & King, M. L. (1983). *A longitudinal study of coherence in children's written narratives.* Columbus, OH: Ohio State University, Research Foundation.

Rodgers, P., Jr. (1966). A discourse-centered rhetoric of the paragraph. *College Composition and Communication, 17,* 2-11.

Rodgers, P., Jr. (1967). The stadium of discourse. *College Composition and Communication, 18,* 178-185.

Rohman, D. G. (1965). Pre-writing: The stage of discovery in the writing process. *College Composition and Communication, 16,* 106-112.

Rohman, D. G., & Wlecke, A. O. (1964). *Pre-writing: The construction and application of models for concept formation in writing* (U.S. Office of Education Cooperative Research Project No. 2174). East Lansing: Michigan State University.

Rose, M. (1981). Sophisticated, ineffective books: The dismantling of process in composition texts. *College Composition and Communication, 32,* 65-74.

Sacks, H., Schegloff, E. A., & Jefferson, G. (1974). A simplest systematics for the organization of turn taking in conversation. *Language, 50,* 696-735.

Scardamalia, M. (1981). How children cope with the cognitive demands of writing. In C. H. Frederiksen & J. F. Dominic (Eds.), *Writing: Processes, development, and communication.* Hillsdale, NJ: Lawrence Erlbaum.

Scardamalia, M., & Bereiter, C. (in press). Written composition. In M. Wittrock (Ed.), *Handbook of research on teaching* (3rd ed.). New York: Macmillan Education.

Schmeling, H. H. (1969). *A study of the relationship between certain syntactic features and overall quality of college freshman writing.* Unpublished doctoral dissertation, George Peabody College for Teachers.

Schweiger, D. (1983). Is the stimulus verbal protocol a viable method for studying managerial problem-solving and decision-making? *Academy of Management Journal, 26,* 185-192.

Shaughnessy, M. P. (1977). *Errors and expectations: A guide for the teacher of basic writing.* New York: Oxford University Press.

Smart, W. D., & Ollila, L. D. (1978). The effect of sentence-combining practice on written compositions and reading comprehension. *Alberta Journal of Educational Research, 24,* 113-120.

Sommers, N. I. (1980). Revision strategies of student writers and experienced adult writers. *College Composition and Communication, 31,* 378-388.

Starling, B. R. J. (1980). *An analysis of cohesion in selected texts of referential discourse.* Unpublished doctoral dissertation, University of Texas at Austin.

Stein, N. L., & Glenn, C. G. (1979). An analysis of story comprehension in elementary school children. In R. O. Freedle, (Ed.), *New directions in discourse processing.* Norwood, NJ: Ablex.

Stewart, M. F. (1978). Freshman sentence combining: A Canadian project. *Research in the Teaching of English, 12,* 257-268.

Stotsky, S. L. (1975). Sentence combining as a curricular activity: Its effect on written language development and reading comprehension. *Research in the Teaching of English, 9,* 30-71.

Stotsky, S. L. (1983). Types of lexical cohesion in expository writing: Implications for developing the vocabulary of academic discourse. *College Composition and Communication, 34,* 430-446.

Straw, S. B. (1978). *The effect of sentence-combining and sentence-reduction instruction on measures of syntactic fluency, reading comprehension, and listening comprehension in fourth-grade students.* Unpublished doctoral dissertation, University of Minnesota.

Sullivan, M. A. (1977). *The effects of sentence-combining exercises on syntactic maturity, writing quality, reading ability, and attitudes of students in grade eleven.* Unpublished doctoral dissertation, State University of New York at Buffalo.

Swarts, H., Flower, L. S., & Hayes, J. R. (1984). Designing protocol studies of the writing process: An introduction. In R. Beach & L. Bridwell (Eds.), *New directions in composition research.* New York: Guilford.

Thorndyke, P. W. (1977). Cognitive structures in comprehension and memory of narrative discourse. *Cognitive Psychology, 9,* 77-110.

Tierney, R. J., & Mosenthal, J. H. (1983). Cohesion and textual coherence. *Research in the Teaching of English, 17,* 215-229.

Tierney, R. J., & Pearson, P. D. (1983). Toward a composing model of reading. *Language Arts, 60,* 568-580.

Vande Kopple, W. J. (1982a). Functional sentence perspective, composing, and reading. *College Composition and Communication, 33,* 50-63.

Vande Kopple, W. J. (1982b). The given-new strategy of comprehension and some natural expository paragraphs. *Journal of Psycholinguistic Research, 11,* 501-520.

Vande Kopple, W. J. (1985). Sentence topics, syntactic subjects, and domains in texts. *Written Communication, 2,* 339-357.

Vitale, M. R., King, F.-J., Shontz, D. W., & Huntley, G. M. (1971). Effects of sentence-combining exercises upon several restricted written composition tasks. *Journal of Educational Psychology, 62,* 521-525.

Welchen, A. (1982). Formuleervaardigheid en de cognitieve balans bij het schrijven. *Tijdscript voor Taalheheersing, 4*, 131-162.

Williams, J. M. (1979a). Defining complexity. *College English, 40*, 595-609.

Williams, J. M. (1979b). Non-linguistic linguistics and the teaching of style. In D. McQuade (Ed.), *Linguistics, stylistics, and the teaching of writing.* Akron, OH: L & S.

Williams, J. M. (1981). The phenomenology of error. *College Composition and Communication, 32*, 152-168.

Winterowd, W. R. (1968). *Rhetoric: A synthesis.* New York: Holt, Rinehart & Winston.

Winterowd, W. R. (1970/1975). The grammar of coherence. In W. R. Winterowd (Ed.), *Contemporary rhetoric: A background with readings.* New York: Harcourt Brace Jovanovich.

Witte, S. P. (1980). *Review of Sentence combining and the teaching of writing,* edited by D. A. Daiker, A. Kerek, and M. Morenberg. *College Composition and Communication, 31*, 433-437.

Witte, S. P. (1983a). Topical structure and revision: An exploratory study. *College Composition and Communication, 34*, 313-341

Witte, S. P. (1983b). Topical structure and writing quality: Some possible text-based explanations of readers' judgments of students' writing. *Visible Language, 17*, 177-205.

Witte, S. P. (1985a). *A critical review of recent representations of the University of Texas' "composition problem."* Unpublished manuscript.

Witte, S. P. (1985b). Revising, composing theory, and research design. In S. W. Freedman (Ed.), *The acquisition of written language.* Norwood, NJ: Ablex.

Witte, S. P., Daly, J. A., & Cherry, R. D. (in press). Syntactic complexity and writing quality. In D. McQuade (Ed.), *Linguistics, stylistics, and the teaching of writing* (2nd ed.). Carbondale: Southern Illinois University Press.

Witte, S. P., & Davis, A. S. (1980). The stability of t-unit length: A preliminary investigation. *Research in the Teaching of English, 14*, 5-17.

Witte, S. P., & Faigley, L. L. (1981). Coherence, cohesion, and writing quality. *College Composition and Communication, 32*, 189-204.

Witte, S. P., Meyer, P. R., with Miller, T. P. (1982). *A national survey of college and university teachers of writing* (ERIC Document 219 779). Austin, University of Texas, Writing Program Assessment Project.

Young, R. E. (1978). Paradigms and problems: Needed research in rhetorical invention. In C. R. Cooper & L. Odell (Eds.), *Research on composing: Points of departure.* Urbana, IL: National Council of Teachers of English.

Young, R. L., & Becker, A. L. (1965). Toward a modern theory of rhetoric: A tagmemic contribution. *Harvard Educational Review, 35*, 450-468.

5

News Schemata

TEUN A. van DIJK

INTRODUCTION

In this chapter I examine and further elaborate the hypothesis that news reports in the press are organized by a conventional news schema. In previous work on the structures of news, I postulated that such a schema is a typical example of textual superstructures (van Dijk, 1980a, 1983a, 1985a, b). Such schematic superstructures are the conventional global form of a discourse. The global content that may be inserted into such a form is defined in terms of semantic macrostructures, which have been introduced to explain notions such as topic, theme, or gist of a discourse. Textual schemata, or superstructures (two notions that I use interchangeably here), order and categorize the topics of a text. For instance, the category of "Introduction," the caption for this section of the chapter, may be considered as a conventional schematic category of several discourse genres, such as scholarly papers and lectures. In news reports in the press, we usually find initial schematic categories like Headline and Lead. These conventional news categories are obvious and well known, but we should also ask whether the body of the report also exhibits schematic organization. If so, we should introduce other typical news categories, as well as rules for their ordering in an overall news schema. In addition, we should show how such categories are related to the global content, the thematic macrostructure, of news discourse. And finally, we should discuss how news schemata are exhibited in the actual surface structures of news reports in the press.

I indeed believe that it is empirically and theoretically warranted to assume that news schemata exist. They can be described as abstract structural properties of discourse, as representations, and as socially shared systems of rules, norms, or strategies for the use of news.

For most citizens, news is perhaps the type of written discourse with which they are confronted most frequently, and insight into its structures is therefore an important task of discourse analysis. Yet the study of news schemata is not merely an important contribution to the analysis of mass media discourse. It is relevant also for our understanding of the organization of written discourse in general. Many discourse types, such as stories, scientific texts, or documents, exhibit conventionalized schematic patterns. These not only play a role in comprehension and memorization, but also in processes of production. Once made explicit, the rules, strategies, and categories of schematic organization of written discourse may play a role in the (normative) foundation of concrete writing programs for such discourse types.

The notion of textual schemata is not new, although as yet seldom applied to the kind of discourse we are confronted with daily: the news texts we read in our newspapers. Most earlier work on schemata in written or spoken discourse has dealt with stories. The structures of drama or novels have been analyzed, from Aristotle to the present century, from a literary point of view, but since the 1960s and 1970s several disciplines have focused on conventional narrative categories and their organization in stories (Propp, 1958; Communications, 1966). In the last decade there have been a vast number of studies, especially in cognitive psychology and Artificial Intelligence, that have examined the structural and cognitive nature of stories and investigated the comprehension of them. The notion of a schema in this research essentially goes back to Bartlett (1932), who uses it to refer to the mental organization of our accumulated experiences; that is, to the structure of our knowledge (Norman & Rumelhart, 1975; Schank & Abelson, 1977). Since this early work on memory for stories, the notion of schema has been used in many different senses, but it usually denotes some specific organization of knowledge. A rather fierce debate has arisen about whether stories have conventional, schematic categories, whether these can be described by some kind of narrative grammar, and whether such narrative schemata play a role in the production and understanding of stories (Rumelhart, 1975; van Dijk & Kintsch, 1978; Mandler, 1978; Mandler & Johnson, 1977; Black & Wilensky, 1979; see van Dijk, 1980b, for a survey, and the commentaries following Wilensky, 1983).

Although I cannot go into the details of this debate, I of course take account of the major results of past work on narrative discourse, since stories and news reports have several properties in common (Thorndyke, 1979). My analysis also draws on my own earlier studies on discourse structures (e.g., van Dijk, 1972, 1977, 1980a, 1981) and the psychology of discourse processing (van Dijk & Kintsch, 1983).

In my current research on news reports, I have paid detailed attention to the structures of domestic and international news, to the representations in the press of ethnic minorities and squatters, as well as to the processes of news production and comprehension (for details, see van Dijk, 1983b, 1984, 1985c). The data for my analysis of news schemata are partly derived from this empirical work, and involve hundreds of newspapers from about one hundred countries. Hence my conception of news schema is not limited to the newspapers of Western Europe.

There is increasing research into the nature of news in the mass media (see van Dijk, 1985c, for a survey). However, only a few studies have focused on the detailed discourse properties of news (Glasgow University Media Group, 1976, 1980, 1982; Hartley, 1982). Most work deals with news in terms of sociology, economics, or mass communication (Tuchman, 1978; Gans, 1979; Fishman, 1980). News discourse itself is seldom studied in its own right, so that no attention is paid to the detailed relationships between processes of news production, whether sociological or psychological, and the resulting structures of news reports. Similarly, comprehension or further processing by the readers has been neglected, although work in this area has received some more attention in the last few years (Findahl & Höijer, 1984, Höijer & Findahl, 1984). My analysis of news schemata should also be seen within the context of news processing by newsmakers and readers and the constraints of the production of news and its uses in social situations and institutions. The nature of news schemata can only be fully understood as a function of their role in the production and uses of news discourse in mass communication and society.

THEORETICAL FRAMEWORK

Much like syntactic structures of sentences, the superstructures of discourse are defined by formal categories and a set of formation rules. These define which superstructures of a given genre of discourse are well formed. Thus, for stories, we postulate that a canonical narrative shema should at least feature a Setting, a Complication and a Resolution, in this order (Labov & Waletzky, 1967; Labov, 1972). Similarly, argumentative discourse usually features several Premise categories and a Conclusion category; in the standard case the Conclusion follows (and follows from) the Premises. In news schemata the categories of Headline and Lead obviously precede the other categories. Canonical structures may be transformed by specific transformation rules. In literary narratives, for instance, we often find that a story begins *"in media res,"* that is, with a fragment of the Complication or the Resolution. Also, in everyday argumentation, a Conclusion may precede the Premises that are given to support the Conclusion. These categories and rules are conventional for a given culture; stories of one culture may be more difficult to understand for those in a different culture (Kintsch & Greene, 1978; Chafe, 1980).

Schematic superstructures, thus, are conventional forms that characterize a specific discourse genre. They order textual sequences of sentences, and assign specific functions to such sequences. They are not directly related to words or sentences (or their meanings), since they organize higher level units such as "episodes" (van Dijk, 1982), a notion that we define below. We therefore need a link between a textual schema and its textual manifestation in words and sentences. This link is established in two steps. First, the global schema is filled with global content, much as the syntactic structures of a sentence are interpreted as semantic structures. This global content is defined by the topics or themes of a discourse and is theoretically accounted for by semantic macrostructures. Each episode—that is, each coherent sequence of propositions—of a text is assigned an overall macroproposition, which is in turn part of a hierarchically organized macrostructure. The macroproposition may be seen as a semantic summary of the whole sequence. Macropropositions are structurally identical to ordinary propositions, only their content is more abstract or general and they are derived from the propositions expressed in the text by macrorules. These rules delete, generalize, or construct detailed, local, or microinformation at a more abstract level, with the help of shared social information or scripts (Schank & Abelson, 1977).

Since macrorules link the semantic microstructure of sentences with the overall macrostructure of sequences of sentences, they represent the second step of the link between schemata and textual surface structures. Schematic categories such as Summary, Introduction, Conclusion, or Resolution assign functions to macro-propositions that are inferred from sequences of propositions expressed in the sentences of a text or contained in the knowledge of the world that is necessary to interpret a text passage. The Complication of a story, for instance, may consist of many sentences, expressing many propositions, but it is only the whole episode that functions as a Complication, and not the individual propositions or sentences as such. To summarize: Each schema category is filled by one or more themes, and each theme is specified by an episode, which is finally expressed by a sequence of sentences (for details, see van Dijk, 1980a).

My abstract characterization of schematic superstructures is similar to the traditional approach of structural or generative grammars. I assume, however, that actual discourse production and understanding have a number of additional and specific properties. Instead of fixed categories and rules, a cognitive theory operates in terms of mental representations and flexible strategies (van Dijk & Kintsch, 1983). In a formal theory of textual schemata, the superstructure rules apply only to complete sequences of sentences. In actual production, speakers may start discourse production with a whole or partial schema at hand, the schema may control "top down" the formation of relevant themes and the production of sentences of each schema category. Similarly, when attempting to understand a text, a reader may before reading or after having interpreted only a few sentences, already guess which discourse genre is relevant. This guess amounts to the application of a strategy that provisionally actualizes the corresponding genre schema, which will then monitor further comprehension. The cultural nature of genre schemata guarantees that the relevant rules are shared by group members who know the genre, even when there are personal or situationally variable strategies for the application of the rules.

NEWS CATEGORIES

The theoretical framework outlined above also holds for news reports in the press. Newspapers are read daily by most adult members in our culture and in many other cultures. Readers recognize news reports as such, and are able to distinguish them from other discourse genres, including those in the same newspaper, such as the comics, the weather report or the advertisements. This implicit knowledge is based on repeated personal experiences, as well as on socially shared categorizations. Part of this implicit knowledge of news reports is defined in semantic terms: News reports are about past events of a public nature, and often feature well-known political or social actors. We also know that news reports in the press are specifically marked as such, for instance by lay-out, headlines, place in the newspaper, and sometimes by category labels, such as "International News" or "Domestic News" ("Home News") on top of the page. In other words, news schemata are only part of our implicit knowledge about news discourse.

Although not all discourse genres may have a fixed, known schematic organization, those genres that are frequently used in a culture tend to develop specific conventional categories. Similarly, from a production point of view, most forms of discourse that result from professional and institutional processing exhibit fixed categorical properties, which allow the routine production of such texts. This is particularly true for news production. Many production constraints, such as types of sources, the nature of input texts, professional routines and values, or deadlines call for standardized production of news reports. Journalists operate with conventional, shared categories that define a well-formed news report. I consider some of these categories as they may appear in news reports and then apply theoretical analysis in the description of a number of concrete news reports. To follow the theoretical discussion, therefore, it is advisable that the reader first read the sample news items (see Appendix) and then revert to them during the explanation of the respective news schema categories.

Summary

Many discourse genres have an initial Summary category. Conversational stories often begin with some kind of summary or announcement, such as "Did I tell you about . . ." or "Did you hear . . ." (Labov, 1972; Quasthoff, 1980). Scholarly papers in many disciplines are routinely prefaced by a summary or abstract, often printed separately and marked by different printing type (italics or small type). Summaries are the verbalization of the underlying semantic macrostructure of a text. They express the most important topics or themes of a text; that is, what the text is about. Cognitively, initial summaries have important strategic functions (van Dijk & Kintsch, 1983; Kieras, 1982). They convey to the reader what the intended semantic macrostructure of the text will be, so that the reader need not construct this macrostructure from the sentences of the text, a bottom-up process that is much more difficult. Since the themes are already known and activate relevant knowledge in the memory, the interpretation of the words and sentences, as well as their local coherence, can be established much faster.

Summaries have similar functions for news discourse. In general, news reports are headed by a Summary that states the main event or events in two steps. First, the various headlines, such as the main headline, and possible upper and lower headlines, constitute the conventional category of Headline. This category is typographically marked by large bold letter type, and when the article is printed in several columns, the main headline is often printed across the columns. The Headline is literally "on top" of the news report, and its size and position are therefore important strategic cues for perception and attention processes. By means of headlines we identify, separate, attend to, begin, and end a news report. Semantically, the headline is defined in terms of the highest levels of the thematic macrostructure of the report: The headline expresses the intended highest macroproposition, and therefore signals what is the most relevant or important information of the news report. Cognitively, therefore, it is the information in the headline that monitors the further processes of reading and comprehension (Kozminsky, 1977; Schwarz & Flammer, 1979). Of course, since understanding is subjective, a reader may well construct a personal macrostructure by assigning different relevance to one or more other topics not mentioned in the headline. If a headline does not express in part the highest macroproposition of the news report, but rather some lower level detail, we may conclude that the headline is biased. Theoretically, we should distinguish between the schema category Headline, and the actual, physical headlines used to express the information inserted into the schematic Headline category. Indeed, the abstract category Headline may be realized by several actual headlines. Finally, headlines are often also stylistically marked; as incomplete sentences, with articles and verbs or auxiliary verbs lacking.

The initial Summary also contains a Lead category. The Lead features the fuller expression of the thematic structure of the news report, and often repeats the highest level macroproposition as it is expressed in the headline(s). Leads have initial position, under the headlines, and are often also printed in larger or bolder type than the rest of the news story. In news formats where there is no special marking of the Lead (as in much of the English and American press), the Lead is expressed by the first sentence or paragraph of the news report, and it then has not only Summary function, but also Introduction function. According to the normative rules of newswriting, the Lead must express the major semantic categories of a news event: Who, What, Where, When, How, and so on (Garst & Bernstein, 1982). Obviously, this rule is not fully explicit, since Leads do not express all the information about participants, actions or events, locations, or other properties of news events. Lead information pertains only to the macropropositions of the text, and hence to main actors, main event, main location, and so on.

Often, newspaper readers only read the Summary part of the news report when they are skimming the paper. They interpret the major topics of the report, after which they may decide to continue or to stop reading the rest of the news report. Experiments have shown that readers after several days hardly recall much more than these main topics, even when they have read the whole news report (Kintsch & van Dijk, 1978; van Dijk & Kintsch, 1983; Reder & Anderson, 1980; Reder, 1982). Since the Headline and Lead play such a crucial role in interpretation and recall, they are obligatory and crucial categories of the news schema.

Main Events

After the Summary in the Headline and Lead, the body of a news report should minimally feature what we may call a Main Events category. This category organizes all information about the recent events that gave rise to a news report. The information in the Main Events category forms the basis for news values such as elite nation, elite actor, negativity, and geographical and ideological proximity (Galtung & Ruge, 1965). There are strict constraints upon what counts as Main Event(s). The events in this category must have taken place (or have been discovered) within the limits of one or two previous days. If there are several events that are each worth attention and that together form one macroevent or episode, it is in principle the last important event that constitutes the major event and is given most prominence (the recency principle). This is especially the case if the earlier event(s) were already covered by other media, so that primary attention given to them in the actual news report would be "old news," even if it is not old news for the readers.

Thus, in our case study of the reporting in the world's press of the assassination of President-elect Beshir Gemayel of Lebanon on September 14, 1982, it appeared that those newspapers, especially in Asia, that were too late to cover that important event on September 15 (because of time differences), paid more attention to the following invasion by the Israeli army of West Beirut, which occurred in the early hours of September 15, 1982 (van Dijk, 1984). The headline and lead in such a case downgraded the assassination to the major cause of the more recent event, by superheadlines such as AFTER THE ASSASSINATION OF GEMAYEL. In the Main Event category the invasion was mentioned first, and then the assassination of Gemayel. In other words, the news production constraints of deadline and periodicity lead to a recency preference in the decision about what is Main Event, and what are conditions, causes, or other previous events.

Since the events inserted into a Main Events category may be complex and may form a coherent sequence or episode of main events, the semantic content of Main Events may of course in turn be more complex and hierarchical, featuring major causes, major components, or various results. For instance, in the example just given about the assassination of Gemayel, the explosion of a bomb in his party headquarters is a major subtheme of the higher level theme of the assassination and simultaneously functions as the global information about the cause of Gemayel's death. Similarly, in many news reports about the assassination there is an important subtheme about the rumor that Gemayel had survived the explosion of the bomb. This subtheme is in turn hierarchically subordinate to the theme of his death, and at the same time an overall result of the explosion theme. There may also be several articles about the same major event. In that case, the other articles may be about some specific dimension of the main event, such as background, context, evaluation, and expectations. These dimensions will be chosen here as separate schematic categories of news reports. In other words, a news report may well feature Summary and Main Events only, and have its other standard categories treated in separate background articles. The intertextual coherence of this discourse cluster, as well as the functions of the articles in that cluster, are in that case also explained by the categories of the news schema.

Background: Context and History

Even short news reports usually give at least a minimum of background. I therefore consider Background as the next standard category of news reports. Journalists also routinely use this category when gathering, selecting, or combining source data for the final news report. Background may be supplied by news agencies, by reporters or correspondents who simply know such background from experience, by other media, or by documentation of various kinds. Specific newsmaking routines (phone calls, interviews, and so on) are followed to collect information for the Background category of the news report. The presence of background information is often considered a criterion for the quality of news, and that evaluation is evidence for the schematic appropriateness of a Background category in the news. In cognitive terms, background information is necessary for the reader to activate "situation models" from memory; that is, representations of accumulated personal experiences and knowledge about concrete situations (Johnson-Laird, 1983; van Dijk & Kintsch, 1983; van Dijk, 1985a). The major goal of news understanding is to update such models and to relate the model to other news situation models. For instance, most press reports about the assassination of Gemayel also mention the facts that Gemayel had just been elected president, that Moslem and leftist groups opposed his election, and that he had made many enemies (even among Christian factions) during the civil war. In general, then, it is the background information that makes news events intelligible and that allows us to update our cognitive models of the world.

I distinguish between present and past backgrounds. The present background of a news event will be called Context. The Context covers all the information in the news report about the actual situation in which the main news event takes place. These are in general socio-political states of affairs, or current events during which the specific event takes place. Thus, Gemayel was murdered in the context of his election as president of Lebanon. Similarly, the media report events in El Salvador against the background of the present context of the civil war in that country. One might even distinguish between a very complex, structural context (such as a civil war or a famine in a country) on the one hand, and some actual other events on the other hand (such as demonstrations taking place during the visit of the President). In practice, Context is marked by textual indications of temporal or local co-occurrence, expressed by words

such as *during, while, at the same time,* or simply *in.* Main events that
have little to do with each other, but which occur in the same context
(the same situation, country, etc.) are sometimes reported in the
same news report. For instance, in the news reports about the assassination of Gemayel, I also found sections about the 1982 Arab
summit in Fez, or about Reagan's plan for the Middle East.

There may be a separate category of Previous Events, in which we
find information about the events that have preceded the main news
event that now become relevant as possible conditions or causes of
the main event. Often such Previous Events are the Main Events
category of earlier news reports. Temporally, Previous Events are
restricted to events that precede the actual events by a few days to a
few weeks. Together with Context, such a Previous Events category
forms what may be called the Circumstances category for the main
news events.

In principle, we can distinguish Previous Events from the History
category. Temporally, History stretches back months or even years.
Unlike Previous Events, it does not deal with the immediate causes of
the main events. History is the past context that leads to the actual
situation and its events. Thus, the actual news about Central
America may feature historical sections about the involvement of the
United States in that region during the last decades. Structurally,
Main Events and Background belong together under a higher level
category, provisionally called Events.

Consequences

The relevance and the importance of events are often measured
by their consequences. The assassination of Gemayel was in itself a
very important event, but the political consequences were even more
serious: The presence or lack of an able successor decisively influenced the process of peacemaking in Lebanon and therefore in the
Middle East. Journalists therefore often include a Consequences
category in their news reports which covers information about the
actions and events that immediately follow the main news events,
and that may be seen as caused by the main events. Sometimes
Consequences may become so important that they downgrade the
actual main events within the same news story, or they receive attention in a separate article, much in the same way as Background.
Structurally, therefore, they may be located at the same level as the

Events that are formed by Main Events and Background. Schematic ordering, however, is not always parallel to semantic ordering: Background mostly features information that is relevant for the Consequences category, but hierarchically and according to its canonical ordering the Consequence category comes later in the schema.

There is one standard subcategory of Consequences, namely Verbal Reactions. This category contains information about the routinely gathered and quoted declarations of immediate participants and in particular of leading national and international politicians who have opinions or comments on the news events. This category satisfies the news value that gives special prominence to influential politicians, and in most newspapers in the world emphasizes the prime importance of political news and political figures. But it also has strategic value. It allows journalists to objectively measure the political implications and evaluations of an event without themselves having to formulate them. In other words, it is a safe way to provide Commentary, and a strategically effective way of choosing and quoting those that satisfy criteria of newsworthiness or credibility. It is well known that not only the U.S. press, but also the press in other countries, routinely quote the official reactions of the U.S. president on international events. At the national level, the press tends to favor the declarations of the government or relevant cabinet ministers. In domestic news, speakers for important institutions, such as the police or the courts, specialists such as doctors, technicians, or professors, and other elite news actors that are either involved or found knowledgeable are routinely asked their reactions and are sometimes extensively quoted. I have found for instance that the Verbal Reaction category was the most extensive in the dispatches of news agencies, and one of the most extensive and stable categories in international news reports (van Dijk, 1985a). Indeed, news discourse is primarily about discourse. Most of its sources are textual, and most of the events and actions reported are also textual: Most political events, for instance, consist of talks, meetings, laws and legislative procedures, verbal fights, and so on. Accidents, crime, assassination, hunger, catastrophes, and the economy are of course not textual. Yet their news construction in the press is often embedded in the reported talk of the news actors involved: interviews with or reactions of eyewitnesses, responsible authorities, and politicians. Main Events, Background and Consequences together constitute what may be called the complete news Episode, the core of a news story.

Comments

Finally, news stories often feature various Comments categories. Although there is a widespread journalistic ideology that facts and opinion should be separated, many news reports have implicit or explicit information that has evaluative dimensions. These may simply be speculations or expectations about what might happen next. Opinion in that case need not be personal, although it is necessarily political and ideological, because it presupposes beliefs and attitudes about rules and laws of a social, political, or cultural nature. If reporters write that after the assassination of Gemayel the future of Lebanon is bleak and peace is threatened, this Expectation presupposes a positive evaluation of the role of Gemayel as president of Lebanon. Although this evaluation may be shared by many others, including most news actors quoted, it still remains an evaluative part of the news report.

Yet these evaluations may remain implicit. The expectations may be derived only from what others say or from general knowledge about the political situation in a country. Therefore, it makes sense to introduce also an explicit Evaluation category under the Comments category. Here, the journalist explicitly formulates opinions (personal ones or those of the newspaper) about the actual news events. Thus, Expectations imply reference to future events, whereas Evaluation explicitly features evaluative expressions (*good, bad, unfortunate, controversial,* and so on) about the news events.

The Comments category is not obligatory. In this respect there may also be differences among types of newspapers, regions, cultures, and political systems. There are however more than enough examples to warrant the special introduction of a Comments category. As with the other schematic categories, this information may also be reserved for a special background or commentary article. Editorials have of course as their main function the formulation of the newspaper's expectations and evaluations of the events. Also, more personal reports from local or international correspondents about recent events may feature much more subjective information.

The News Schema Hierarchy

I have reviewed the major news schema categories, and explained their intuitive and more formal properties, both in terms of textual functions or expressions and in terms of cognitive and social news-making processes. The categories should now be placed in their hierarchical schema. In Figure 5.1, I have given an abstract example of such a news schema.

From this schematic representation we can see that the Summary and the actual news story should be kept apart at a rather high level of description: They indeed have quite different functions. Similarly, Comments should be distinguished from the actual Episode they are about. And the same holds for the lower categories mentioned above. I also have suggested that not all categories are obligatory. Minimally, we should have Summary and Main Events, although usually at least some Background information is also given, even when separate articles may be dedicated to such backgrounds. Some of the categories are recursive. That is, Episode and Events may be complex: One news article may be about several events, each with their own background and consequences.

The ordering of the categories follows by general rules and strategies of presentation. The schema in Figure 5.1 in this respect suggests a fixed order, but this is rather a structural tendency than a strict rule of order. Indeed, usually Main Events are treated first, and then Background, Consequences, and Comments. Sometimes important information from Consequences or some Context feature may be given first. Yet it is seldom the case that the news story starts with a long historical or contextual section, and only then presents the actual main events. This would be the possible structure of literary or everyday stories. News stories have a different structure: The main event is the most important information, and therefore should (1) be summarized in Headline and Lead, and (2) be presented first in the rest of the story. Context, History and Consequences may then follow in less strict order. Verbal reactions and especially Comments tend to occur toward the end of the article, even when an occasional element from them may be placed earlier. In other words, the schematic categories and their canonical ordering in the abstract superstructure of a news report are only one factor in the actual realization and expression of news discourse. Therefore, exactly how the news schema is actualized in news reports and how it is related to other textual structures, such as the

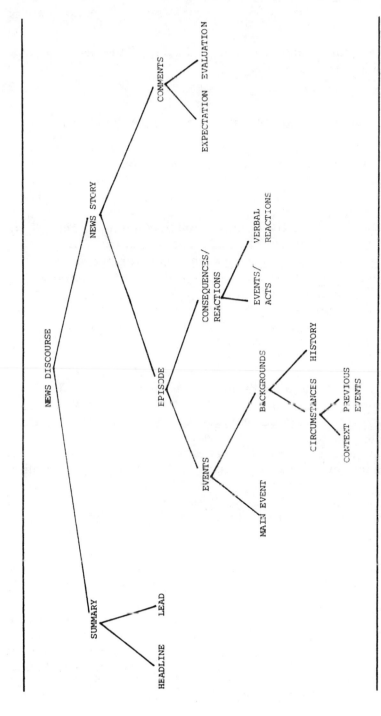

Figure 5.1 Superstructure Schema of News Discourse

overall thematic and relevance structures of the news, must be examined in more detail.

THE TEXTUAL REALIZATION OF NEWS SCHEMATA

It was suggested that news reports, unlike other story types, are not just organized to represent events in their chronological or causal order. Instead of a "natural ordering" of propositions (van Dijk, 1977; Levelt, 1982), we find what I call a relevance ordering. That is, throughout the headlines and lead and in the body of the story, we find the results of a general news production strategy that places first the information that is most important or relevant. The very separation between Summary and the actual news story is already one major factor in this relevance structure: Because the macrostructure defines the most important information, it is expressed first, as a summary, and from this summary the most important information is summarized again and placed in the headlines.

This ordering principle also characterizes the rest of the news story. Although the Main Event category tends to be actualized first, we do not get all the information from that category at once; that is, in one linearly ordered, continuous section. Rather, what we get is again the most important information of the Main Event (which often repeats the information in headlines or lead). Details of Main Event information may follow later in the article, after the realization of the higher level information from other categories. We first get some general Background information, the major Consequences (such as Verbal Reactions of the most prominent news actors), and possibly even first Comments. Then, the news article may revert to Main Events and deliver further, lower level information from that category. In other words, each category is realized in installments. Therefore, the relevance principle assigns what may be called a rather confusing zig-zag or installment structure to the news report.

The installment structure of news reports also affects the realization of their thematic structure. Each schematic category, as we have seen in Figure 5.1, dominates a hierarchical semantic structure, with macropropositions on top. This means that the thematic structure organized by the schema is also realized in installments, "top down":

The main themes are realized first (in Headlines and Lead), and then the main theme defining the Main Event, then the main theme of the Backgrounds, and so on. Usually, each textual paragraph, often consisting of one or a few long sentences, coincides with one installment of the combined thematic-schematic structures. The local coherence of news discourse may be rather fragile: Subsequent paragraphs or event sentences may not immediately cohere according to the usual coherence rules of discourse (van Dijk, 1977). We may jump from main event information to context or history, and from background to comments or consequences. Besides the natural left-right (cause-consequence) realization in the description of events, and besides the left-right and top-down realization of schematic categories, the relevance principle assigns an overall top-down organization to the text, such that in general all more important information is given first. In Figure 5.1, thus, we should read from top to bottom and from left to right, taking first the information high in the respective triangles, and then going from right to left back to the first triangle to express the next level.

This relevance ordering is the result of a general newswriting strategy. There is no fixed formal rule; variation is possible, depending on communicative context (interests, goals, personal or ideological relevance). For instance, in some examples of news stories, in particular in the popular press, we find a more narrative organization in the expression of events, a chronological ordering found in other kinds of storytelling. This creates the usual suspense about what will happen next, a narrative-rhetorical ploy to keep readers or listeners interested. Of course, stories about catastrophes, accidents, crimes, or other human interest events lend themselves better to such a narrative organization than complex reports about political situations and events. It is one of the reasons why the tabloid press prefers such news stories: They can be framed in a narrative schema.

An Example

To illustrate and further refine the theoretical framework sketched above, let us analyze a concrete example. Under the headline "U.S.-Backed Coalition Wins Grenada Election," the *International Herald Tribune* of December 5, 1984, published a brief report, taken from the Washington Post Service, about the elections in Grenada (see Example 5A). This news article also exemplifies how

Example 5A   From the *International Herald Tribune*, December 5, 1984

U.S.-Backed Coalition Wins Grenada Election

By Edward Cody
Washington Post Service

1 ST. GEORGE'S, Grenada — Herbert Blaize's New National Party was declared the winner Tuesday of parliamentary elections on this Caribbean island.

2 The party won 14 of 15 seats in the House of Representatives. The sweeping victory by the the coalition group, understood by most Grenadians to enjoy U.S. backing, represented an endorsement of the Reagan administration's invasion on Oct. 25, 1983, that crushed what remained of a Marxist-oriented revolution.

3 Mr. Blaize, 66, was sworn in Tuesday as prime minister and vowed to give the island's 90,000 inhabitants "that kind of security they have a right to expect."

4 Mr. Blaize, who concentrated his campaign on promises of stability, said at a news conference that the results represent a rejection by the Grenadian people of "postures of the extreme left or postures of the extreme right."

5 He promised to follow a moderate course designed to restore faith in government institutions after the abuses and eventual self-destruction of Prime Minister Maurice Bishop's leftist rule.

6 A revolutionary faction of Mr. Bishop's party overthrew and killed him, precipitating the U.S.-led invasion.

7 Mr. Blaize's main challenger, the Grenada United Labor Party of former prime minister Eric Gairy, won the lone remaining seat. But the victor in that district, Marcel Peters, said after conferring with Mr. Gairy that he will resign because of allegations of voting irregularities.

8 The charges were matched by Mr. Bishop's remaining followers in the Maurice Bishop Patriotic Movement, which failed to gain a seat. They have accused Mr. Blaize of receiving help from the Central Intelligence Agency, apparently referring to funds provided by two private U.S. groups with ties to Republican politics and a third linked to the AFL-CIO.

9 Mr. Blaize dismissed the charges of irregularities as carping of "disgruntled wretches" who refused to accept defeat. He noted observers from the Organization of American States and the British High Commission for the Eastern Caribbean, on hand to guarantee fair balloting, reported no serious violations of procedure.

10 [President Ronald Reagan, welcoming President Jaime Lusinchi of Venezuela on a state visit to Washington Tuesday, said that Mr. Blaize's victory "marks the first time that Marxist-Leninist government has been succeeded by a government that received its authority by a free election," United Press International reported.]

news schemata and their realization may be influenced by the political or ideological perspective of the newspaper. The U.S. invasion of Grenada and the financing by the United States of elections on that island have been widely opposed in the Carribean, South America, and Europe, and therefore constitute a controversial issue that may be covered in different ways. The different perspectives may manifest themselves in the general structure, style, semantic content (including selection and exclusion), and rhetoric as well, but I focus on the schematic structures. The analysis of the categories follows the order in which they occur in the news item. This means that, given the discontinuous (installment) nature of news categories, fragments of such categories may appear several times in our linear analysis of the news item. The reader may follow the analysis by simply taking each clause or sentence as a tentative unit of schema realization.

Summary: headline + lead. The headline summarizes the event of the victory of the NNP coalition in Grenada, an event that is also summarized, with a few more details, in the lead. One proposition that is part of the headline and that does not appear in the lead is that the NNP was backed by the United States, which, however, is a correct summary of another theme of the article. In the report that appeared in the *Guardian* of the same day we also see this emphasis on the role of the United States in these elections, this time both in the headline and in the lead (see Example 5B). That this role is relevant may also be inferred from the *Guardian*'s leader article. Now, if we take the short report in *USA Today* of December 5, this prominence of the U.S. backing is no longer present in either headline or lead paragraph. Instead, the ideologically more positive term *moderate* is chosen to qualify the NNP and its leader. In other words, what is expressed as part of the Summary depends on what is the major topic of the news article, and on what the newspaper considers relevant and important information.

Main events. After the summarizing introduction of the headline and lead, the second paragraph of the *Herald Tribune* specifies the main events: elections for what legislative body, how many seats the winning party obtained, and the U.S. backing of the elections.

Background. The same paragraph, however, also delivers first installments of various types of background information. That is,

Example 5B   From the *Guardian* [London], December 5, 1984

Reagan favourite sweeps Grenada

From Greg Chamberlain in St George's, Grenada

The US pronounced itself satisfied yesterday after Grenadian voters swept to power a rightwing coalition that Washington helped to put together on the Caribbean island.

The coalition, the New National Party (NNP), headed by Mr Herbert Blaize, who is 66 and severely crippled with arthritis, won 14 of the 15 seats in Monday's pool. One went to the conservative and populist Grenada United Labour Party of the authoritarian former prime minister, Sir Eric Gairy.

The victory was hailed by President Reagan as "an achievement of historic importance."

The left-wing Maurice Bishop Patriotic Movement (MBPM), backing the memory and programme of the prime minister murdered a week before last year's US invasion, won no seats and only 5 per cent of the vote. Only one MBPM candidate, the former army chief of staff, Mr Einstein Louison, managed to save his deposit.

Sir Eric, with 36 per cent of the vote, suffered the biggest defeat of his stormy, 35-year political career. He had not campaigned personally and the very high 85 per cent turnout swamped his disciplined supporters.

The MBPM leader, Mr Kendrick Radix, claimed that the election had been rigged by the CIA. Outside aid, especially American, for Mr Blaize's party was given openly during the campaign. A large number of MBPM supporters, however, failed to vote.

Hundreds of celebrating Grenadians poured into the steep streets of this picturesque port capital as Mr Blaize's victory became known. He flew into the island yesterday from his constituency in Grenada's sister-island of Carriacou, went to church to give thanks and was later sworn in as Prime Minister.

Mr Blaize, a lawyer and deeply religious man, is confident that he can cope with a Grenada whose youth has been subjected to heavy politicisation and has come to expect energetic government since he last ruled it as prime minister in a more genteel and economically kinder world 17 years ago.

But his conservative business supporters are unlikely to be very interested in the NNP's campaign pledge that it will seriously tackle the island's high unemployment and continue some of the popular social programmes of the revolutionary Bishop regime.

Mr Blaize, who has hinted that he will crack down on the left and continue to purge its supporters from the civil service, says he wants US troops to stay on in Grenada for at least five years because he claims the left still have weapons hidden in the island.

But the US has said it plans to pull out its 300 or so remaining troops by Easter.

Jamaica, which has 150 soldiers here, also wants to withdraw for pressing financial reasons now that the election is over. However, the new Government may appeal to them to stay on, despite growing annoyance at their presence.

Leader comment, page 12.

Example 5C   From the *Guardian*, December 5, 1984

Blaize the American way

The United States inspired and organised the invasion of Grenada a year ago.
Now it has inspired and organised the post-
invasion election. The sweeping victory for
the candidate which Mr Reagan favoured is
hardly surprising. The surprise only is that
the Reagan Administration should have felt
it necessary to commit so much money and
diplomatic attention to achieving Mr Her
bert Blaize's victory. When American troops
went in last October, it was said they
would stay for a short while only. But a
contingent has stayed until today. Though
small in number, it is relatively large for
an island as tiny as Grenada ; roughly the
equivalent of having 125,000 American
troops in Britain.

The United States forged the coalition
of three parties which Mr Blaize leads, and
subsidised his campaign. Private American
groups contributed more than $100,000 to
encourage a high turnout in the polls, a
subsidy of about three dollars for every
vote cast. Was this all necessary ? The
trauma of the murder of the former Prime
Minister, Maurice Bishop, and the virtual
suicide of the revolution which he led were
still too recent in most Grenadans' lives for
his heirs to have commanded much support. Sir Eric Gairy's dictatorial rule was
remembered too clearly. In the vacuum of
Grenadan authority which the Americans
found when they invaded, it was inevitable
that the new government which eventually
emerged would be the one which the invad-
ers favoured, especially if they were still
around at election time.

Every Grenadan knew that the only
hope for investment in their impoverished
island would be if they voted for the American candidate. The future flow of aid
money and private US capital were dependent on Mr Blaize's victory, and it has now
been duly recorded. After the upheavals of
the last decade Grenadans have voted for a
quiet political life, and the hope that as an
undisguised American protectorate they will
be luckier than the rest of the Caribbean's
small islands. But as Grenada stumbles into
the future, the crucial question is whether
the United States is indeed as dependable
as Grenadans wish it to be. Now that the
United States has won the formal seal of
approval for its invasion by being able to
say that it established democracy, will it
come forward with the cash ? Or, in the
aftermath of Mr Reagan's own election triumph, will Grenada be packed away like
last summer's opinion poll ratings ?

The social discontent and economic de-
pression which first gave rise to Maurice
Bishop's New Jewel Movement have not
gone away. They remain as palpable as the
potholes in the island's roads. For the
United States to show that it has something
to offer in the Caribbean, it will have to do
more than arm an invasion and finance an
election. It must share something of its
wealth.

Example 5D   From *USA Today*, December 5, 1984

Moderate wins Grenada parliamentary vote

Special for USA TODAY
ST. GEORGE'S, Grenada —The New National Party (NNP) of Herbert Blaize, 66, was headed for an overwhelming victory over four other parties amid a heavy voter turnout in Monday's Grenadian parliamentary elections, according to early returns.

An estimated 86 percent of the island nation's 48,000 registered voters cast ballots in Grenada's first parliamentary election in eight years. The 15-seat Parliament will replace the country's 13-month old interim governing council, which was installed after last year's U.S.-led invasion toppled a radical Marxist junta.

Early returns showed that the moderate NNP, the party favored by the Reagan administration to lead Grenada, had captured 11 seats and was leading in three other races.

Election supervisors said the NNP received about two-thirds of the vote. The Grenada United Labor Party of former Prime Minister Sir Eric Gairy, which lead by a slim margin in one district, received about 25 percent of the total vote.

the U.S. role in the elections can be interpreted as part of the Context, which makes the victory of Blaize and his coalition intelligible. Also, Previous Events or History are represented here, namely, by brief reference to the U.S. invasion and its destruction of the "Marxist revolution." That the election results "represent an endorsement of the . . . invasion" is not properly part of the Context, but should be interpreted as part of the Comment, namely, as an Evaluation of the main event. We see that a single paragraph, or even a long sentence, may combine propositions that belong to different news categories: News schemata are indeed realized in discontinuous installments. Nevertheless, the overall top-down and left-right ordering is still respected: Summary, Main Event, Context, History/Evaluation.

Main events (continued). The third paragraph continues the main event by specifying further information (age) about Blaize, as well as the usual result of elections: the winner taking office. Similarly, a first installment of Verbal Reactions is given here, in the form of a quotation by Blaize. This declaration is further summarized in the next (fourth) paragraph. The newspaper focuses on what Blaize says about security and the rejection of extreme left or extreme right postures, which is precisely what *USA Today* conceptualizes as "moderate," a notion that also occurs in the next paragraph of the *Herald Tribune* report. A relative clause appended to the head noun "Mr. Blaize" in paragraph 4 provides a contextual flashback to the election campaign, whereas the contents of the declarations of Blaize at his press conference implicitly refer to the political background (History) of these elections. Again, we witness that news categories do not always appear in neat, continuous packages. The same happens in the next (fifth) paragraph, which within a summary of

Blaize's declaration realizes both the routine plans for the future as well as a flashback to the historical background: Maurice Bishop's "self-destruction" and "leftist rule."

History. The central historical information appears in the sixth paragraph, and focuses on the assassination of Bishop and the U.S.-led invasion. Ideologically interesting is of course the fact that the verb "precipitating" indicates that the assassination itself was the cause of the U.S. invasion, instead of the U.S. fears that Grenada might move even further to the left. It seems highly unlikely that the United States would have intervened if Bishop had been assassinated by a right-wing, antirevolutionary faction. Besides the specific category of Comment/Evaluation, implicit evaluations may be expressed throughout a news discourse by the very choice of words denoting events, actions, and participants.

Main events (continued). Paragraphs 8 and 9 specify further details about the main events. The declarations and accusations of the Maurice Bishop Patriotic Movement refer to some important features of the context: the financial and other help of various U.S. organizations. Paragraph 9 may be seen as part of the Main Event— as the usual verbal results of election victories—or as part of the Verbal Reactions category. At the same time, the reaction of Blaize against the allegations of the two losing parties are in a sense lower level consequences of the act of allegation itself.

Verbal reaction. The final paragraph, marked by square brackets and coming from a different source (UPI), provides the classical international reaction category: Reagan's comments on the election. Its rhetoric is stereotypical: A Marxist-Leninist government is contrasted with the notion of free election. The brief reference to the visit of the Venezuelan president merely serves as the context for Reagan's declaration.

This brief analysis has demonstrated that most of the conventional news categories are present in the report on the elections in Grenada. Only a Consequences category seems to be absent, although we might take Blaize's election speech as such a consequence of his election. But I interpret it as an integral part of the Main Event, since according to our conventional knowledge (our script) of elections, it is customary that participants in elections give comments about the elections. Similarly, the declarations may be taken as domestic Verbal Reactions to the main event, as opposed to the international Verbal Reactions we find in the last paragraph. The analysis also shows that the canonical ordering of Summary, Main Events, Context, History, Verbal Reactions, and Comments is more or less respected, although this may happen in a discontinuous way. Third, despite the overall ordering of news schemata, Background and Comments may be mixed with Main Event information. Fourth, the Main Events category itself is realized throughout the entire article, top down, from the high level victory topic, to the specifics of who won what, who lost, and what their reactions were. Fifth, stylistic choices of words may also reveal, throughout, implicit ideological evaluations of the events. Thus the winner and his U.S. allies are associated with concepts such as "security," "moderateness," and "freedom," and the elections are characterized as "fair" because of the presence of external (objective, that is, noncommunist) observers. Of those who lost, the Bishop party is associated with Marxist-Leninism, killing, self-destruction, and so on. No negative evaluations are given of Gairy's right-wing party. On the contrary, allegations of voting irregularity are met by the single winning representative of that party by a magnanimous offer to resign if the allegations prove to be correct. In other words, the implicit Evaluation of this news report also appears in the semantic rhetoric of Contrast in the description of the major participants: The moderate is associated with positive evaluations, the right-wing extremists are not negatively characterized, and the left wing is associated with several negative concepts.

THE IDEOLOGY OF THE UNSAID

The ideological nature of discourse in general, and of news discourse in particular, is often defined by the unsaid. Information that could (or should) have been given is selectively left out. Even in a brief account of the historical and contextual background, one might have mentioned the popular support for the Movement of Maurice Bishop, and what Bishop did for the population at large, such as serious attempts to reduce unemployment. Instead, this movement is merely qualified as Marxist-Leninist, and no clear distinction is made between it and the small faction that assassinated

Bishop. Similarly, no reference is made to the devastating policies and practices of former premier Gairy. We find no mention of the worldwide condemnation of the U.S.-led invasion as an unjustified form of armed interference with the internal affairs of an autonomous state.

That such absent information is not necessarily left out because of routine constraints on news processing, such as space, deadlines, or lack of information, is shown by the different contents, style, and schematic structure of the *Guardian* report about the same event. Similar but more critical is the categorization of the winning coalition as being "Reagan favourite" in the headline. Different, however, is the political placement of the winning coalition as "right wing" in the *Guardian*, and "moderate" in *USA Today* and the *International Herald Tribune* (in an article derived from the *Washington Post*). Interesting for our schematic analysis is that the Verbal Reaction category appears first in the *Guardian*, namely, the U.S. satisfaction with the result of the election. This topicalization of the Verbal Reactions category may function as a signal of the opinion (of the *Guardian*) that not the election itself, or its winner, but the U.S. backing and the realization of U.S. goals in Grenada are the most important. This hypothesis is confirmed by the explicitly critical analysis given in the *Guardian*'s leader article on the one hand, and by the rest of the news report on the other. Indeed, former prime minister Gairy is qualified as "authoritarian." The relevance of the U.S. reaction to these elections is also signaled by the fact that Reagan's verbal reaction figures rather prominently in the third paragraph (after its first summary in the Lead).

The *Guardian* also provides more details about Main Events and especially Context. More information than in the *Herald Tribune* is given about the winning candidate and about the fact that hundreds of Grenadians celebrated in the streets. Most significant, however, is the information that Blaize's conservative business supporters are unlikely to be very interested in reducing the high unemployment rate, and that the Bishop regime had popular social programs. This information is absent in both *USA Today* and in the *Herald Tribune* (*Washington Post*) report. And finally, the unabashedly pro-U.S. policies of Blaize are specified by the information that he will "crack down on the left" and "purge" the administration of pro-Bishop people, while inviting American and Jamaican troops to stay "despite growing annoyance at their presence." In other words, the report in the *Guardian* provides much more, and for many readers more balanced, information about the political history and context of these elections. It places more emphasis on the American role in the victory of Blaize, qualifies Blaize as conservative and pro-American and not as "moderate," as the U.S. newspapers do, and also briefly mentions the positive aspects of Bishop's revolution. Apart from style and local meanings, these differences are also apparent in a different realization of the schematic structure: Significant Verbal Reactions may be put in initial lead position, and contextual and historical background may become more extensive. Also, the *Guardian* explicitly formulates a Comment/Expectation category, featuring the expectation that Blaize's business supporters are not likely to be interested in the reduction of unemployment. Indeed, neither *USA Today* nor the *Herald Tribune* pays attention to what these results will mean for the well-being of the people of Grenada, except for their participation in "historic, free elections" in a pro-U.S. and U.S.-dependent state. Details of these implications are spelled out in the *Guardian* leader. None appear in the *Herald Tribune,* whereas *USA Today* has no Context, History, Verbal Reactions, or Comments at all, except for the brief clause which says that a U.S.-led invasion toppled a "radical Marxist junta." In this respect, news reports in the widely distributed *USA Today* resemble the dominant Main Event structure of international news in the European tabloid press, which often lacks background information too, thus reducing news to headlines of (mostly spectacular) events.

CONCLUSIONS

This chapter has shown that news reports in the press may be analyzed in terms of a conventional schema, consisting of a number of hierarchically ordered categories. These superstructural categories assign functions to overall semantic macrostructures, and include a general Summary, Main Events, historical and contextual Background, Consequences, Verbal Reactions, and Comments. They are acquired, known, and used by journalists; they cognitively organize, top-down, the production of news reports; and they signal the organizational constraints on the processing of source discourses into the final news text. It seems plausible that habitual newspaper readers have implicit knowledge of such categories. Although such knowledge has been demonstrated for other discourse types, especially for stories, the experimental evidence for such knowledge of newspaper categories is still to be established. Finally, it emerges that it is a specific property of news reports that the schematic superstructure categories are not realized continuously in discrete linear units. Rather, the overall relevance structure imposes a left-right and top-down installment organization, in such a way that in each category the most important information is given first.

This analysis of the schematic structure of news reports contributes to a systematic and critical analysis of the functional organization of the topics in news discourse—for instance, by providing a discovery procedure for the categories that are present and those that are lacking in the news: In formal terms, this analysis provides an evaluation procedure for "well-formed" news reports. Obviously, this is only one aspect of a proper evaluation of the adequacy of news discourse. It does not specify what information should be given in the Main Events, Background, or Comment categories. For such an evaluation one would need to draw on political, historical, and sociocultural knowledge, as well as a critical ideological perspective. Yet, the formulation of superstructure rules does allow us to notice when specific transformations of the canonical schema occur, which then may be interpreted for special examples. Finally, I briefly suggested that specific, ideologically relevant properties of news schema organization should be linked with a thematic, stylistic, and rhetorical analysis. Although both local and global semantic content are of primary importance in a systematic and critical analysis of the news, the form of news discourse also plays an important role.

Although this analysis of news schemata is based on an extensive empirical data base, and the theoretical discussion develops earlier work on discourse schemata, it goes without saying that further work on news and news schemata is imperative. First, we need to examine many more examples from different types of newspapers and from different countries and cultures. News in the tabloid press and in the so-called quality press seems to be organized in rather different ways. We need to know which of the categories and rules are obligatory, and which are optional, and in which respect installment strategies may be different for such different types of newspapers. Second, it is possible to distinguish between different sorts of news reports. Background news articles, for instance, may not have the same schematic organization as proper news reports: They may only pay attention to Background or Context information. Third, both a theoretical and a practical problem exists in the degree of "canonicity" of news schemata. If we assume that news reports are organized by hierarchically related categories, but the actual texts only show a strategically variable, discontinuous, installment structure, the respective rules and categories are not simply a description of the manifest structural units of the news report, but rather of some abstract underlying structure. Further theoretical work is necessary to develop an appropriate framework for this kind of discontinuous schematic organization. Fourth, the relationship between schematic superstructures and other structures of news, such as the thematic macrostructure and the organization of clauses and sentences, needs further attention. For instance, we may assume, as for stories, that categories are marked in the text by specific expressions, meanings, or syntactic features. This local management of news schema categories must be examined in further detail. And finally, the cognitive and social implications of the nature and uses of news schemata require further attention: In which respects are the schemata (consciously or unconsciously) used by journalists in news production, and what exactly is the role of schematic categories when we read news reports? How are the schemata acquired, and how is their active use reproduced in routine newsmaking processes? This is to say that most empirical work on news schemata is still on the agenda.

Although this chapter is about news schemata, its results as well as its unresolved problems are also intended as a contribution to our understanding of written discourse in general. We have found evidence for the assumption that conventional, frequently used discourse types may display fixed schematic patterns, and that these may be described in terms of categories and rules, as well as by effective realization strategies. News reports in this case additionally show the particular feature of relevance-dependent installment structure. The question is whether other discourse types may also exhibit discontinuous expression of underlying schematic categories. This raises the more general issue of the role of transformations in a structural theory of discourse schemata. Finally, we have found that news schemata are subject to effective strategies and not only to rules. That is, in the actual production and understanding of news, many other levels of structure (global meanings, relevance, local meanings, and so on), as well as contextual constraints, cooperate in the resulting structure or cognitive representation of news reports. For other discourse types, too, it is important to show how different levels of analysis are cooperating in the integration of textual structures and their uses in the communicative context. The analysis of written discourse types, then, is no longer a purely structural enterprise. Rather, the dynamics of production and understanding and their textual consequences require a more flexible, strategic approach, which at the same time enables interdisciplinary integration with cognitive, communicative, and social models of discourse and discourse use.

REFERENCES

Bartlett, F. C. (1932). *Remembering*. London: Cambridge University Press.
Black, J. B., & Wilensky, R. (1979). An evaluation of story grammars. *Cognitive Science, 3*, 213-229.
Chafe, W. (Ed.). (1980). *The pear stories*. Hillsdale, NJ: Lawrence Erlbaum.
Communications 8. (1966). *L'analyse structurale du récit*. Paris: Seuil.
Dijk, T. A. van. (1972). *Some aspects of text grammars*. The Hague: Mouton.
Dijk, T. A. van. (1977). *Text and context*. London: Longman.
Dijk, T. A. van. (1980a). *Macrostructures*. Hillsdale, NJ: Lawrence Erlbaum.
Dijk, T. A. van. (Ed.). (1980b). *Story comprehension* [Special issue]. *Poetics, 8*(1-3).
Dijk, T. A. van. (1981). *Studies in the pragmatics of discourse*. Berlin/New York: Mouton.
Dijk, T. A. van. (1982). Episodes as units of discourse analysis. In D. Tannen (Ed.), *Analyzing discourse: Text and talk* (pp. 177-195). Washington, DC: Georgetown University Press.
Dijk, T. A. van. (1983a). Discourse analysis: Its development and application to the structure of news. *Journal of Communication, 33*, 20-43.
Dijk, T. A. van. (1983b). *Minderheden in de media*. Amsterdam: Socialistische Uitgeverij Amsterdam.
Dijk, T. A. van. (1984). *Structures of international news: A case study of the world's press* (Report for UNESCO). University of Amsterdam, Department of General Literary Studies, Section of Discourse Studies.
Dijk, T. A. van. (1985a). Episodic models in discourse processing. In R. Horowitz & S. J. Samuels (Eds.). *Comprehending oral and written language*. New York: Academic Press.
Dijk, T. A. van. (Ed.). (1985b). *Handbook of discourse analysis* (4 vols.). London: Academic Press.
Dijk, T. A. van (1985c). *News as discourse*. New York: Longman.
Dijk, T. A. van (1985d). Structures of news in the press. In T. A. van Dijk (Ed.), *Discourse and communication* (69-93). Berlin/New York: de Gruyter.
Dijk, T. A. van, & Kintsch, W. (1978). Cognitive psychology and discourse: Recalling and summarizing stories. In W. U. Dressler (Ed.), *Current trends in textlinguistics* (pp. 61-80). Berlin: de Gruyter.
Dijk, T. A. van, & Kintsch, W. (1983). *Strategies of discourse comprehension*. New York: Academic Press.
Findahl, O. & Höijer, B. (1984). *Begriplighetsanalys*. Stockholm: Studentlitteratur.

Fishman, M. (1980). *Manufacturing the news*. Austin: University of Texas Press.

Galtung, J., & Ruge, M. H. (1965). The structure of foreign news. *Journal of Peace Research, 2*, 64-91.

Gans, H. (1979). *Deciding what's news*. New York: Pantheon.

Garst, R. E., & Bernstein, T. M. (1982). *Headlines and deadlines* (4th ed.). New York: Columbia University Press.

Glasgow University Media Group. (1976). *Bad news*. London: Routledge & Kegan Paul.

Glasgow University Media Group. (1980). *More bad news*. London: Routledge & Kegan Paul.

Glasgow University Media Group. (1982). *Really bad news*. London: Writers & Readers.

Golding, P., & Elliott, P. (1979). *Making the news*. London: Longman.

Hartley, J. (1982). *Understanding news*. London: Methuen.

Höijer, B., & Findahl, O. (1984). *Nyheter, förståelse, och minne*. Stockholm: Studentlitteratur.

Johnson-Laird, P. N. (1983). *Mental models*. London: Cambridge.

Kieras, D. (1982). A model of reader strategy for abstracting main ideas from simple technical prose. *Text, 2*, 47-82.

Kintsch, W., & Dijk, T. A. van. (1978). Toward a model of text comprehension and production. *Psychological Review, 85*, 363-394.

Kintsch, W., & Greene, E. (1978). The role of culture specific schemata in the comprehension and recall of stories. *Discourse Processes, 1*, 1-13.

Kozminsky, E. (1977). Altering comprehension: The effect of biasing titles on text comprehension. *Memory & Cognition, 5*, 482-490.

Labov, W. (1972). The transformation of experience in narrative syntax. In W. Labov, *Language in the inner city: Studies in the Black English vernacular* (pp. 354-396). Philadelphia: University of Pennsylvania Press.

Labov, W., & Waletzky, J. (1967). Narrative analysis: Oral versions of personal experience. In J. Helm (Ed.), *Essays on the verbal and visual arts* (pp. 12-44). Seattle: University of Washington Press.

Levelt, W. J. M. (1982). Linearization in describing spatial networks. In S. Peters & E. Saarinen (Eds.), *Processes, beliefs and questions*. Dordrecht: Reidel.

Mandler, J. M. (1978). A code in the node: The use of story schema in retrieval. *Discourse Processes, 1*, 14-35.

Mandler, J. M., & Johnson, N. S. (1977). Remembrance of things parsed: Story structure and recall. *Cognitive Psychology, 9*, 11-151.

Norman, D. A., & Rumelhart, D. E. (Eds.). (1975). *Explorations in cognition*. San Francisco: Freeman.

Propp, V. (1958). *Morphology of the folktale*. Bloomington: Indiana University Press. (Original work published 1928)

Quasthoff, U. (1980). *Erzählen in Gesprächen*. Tubingen: Narr.

Reder, L. M. (1982). Elaborations: When do they help and when do they hurt? *Text, 2*, 211-224.

Reder, L. M., & Anderson, J. R. (1980). A comparison of texts and their summaries: Memorial consequences. *Journal of Verbal Learning and Verbal Behavior, 19*, 121-134.

Rumelhart, D. (1975). Notes on a schema for stories. In D. G. Bobrow & A. Collins (Eds.), *Representation and understanding* (pp. 211-236). New York: Academic Press.

Schank, R. C., & Abelson, R. P. (1977). *Scripts, plans, goals and understanding.* Hillsdale, NJ: Lawrence Erlbaum.

Schwarz, M., & Flammer, A. (1979). Erstinformationen einer Geschichte: Ihr Behalten und ihre Wirkung auf das Behalten der nachfolgenden Information. *Zeitschrift für Entwicklungspsychologie und Pädagogische Psychologie, 11,* 347-358.

Thorndyke, P. W. (1979). Knowledge acquisition from newspaper stories. *Discourse Processes, 2,* 95-112.

Tuchman, G. (1978). *Making news.* New York: Free Press.

Wilensky, R. (1983). Story grammars versus story points. *Behavioral and Brain Sciences, 6,* 579-624.

6

Overlapping Patterns of Discourse Organization and Their Implications for Clause Relational Analysis of Problem-Solution Texts

MICHAEL HOEY

THE AIM OF THIS CHAPTER

In the growing body of literature devoted to the study of written discourse (text), considerable attention has been paid in recent years to the description of a particularly common pattern of discourse organization, the problem-solution pattern, though it has not always been given this label. In Hoey (1979), I cited a number of linguists whose work had either made use of or referred to a pattern of this type: These included at that time Labov and Waletsky (1967) and Labov (1972), Longacre (1972a, 1976), Grimes (1975), van Dijk (1977), and Hutchins (1977a, 1977b). Since then, interest in the pattern has continued to increase; to refer only selectively, there have been extensive discussions by Jordan (1980, 1982, 1984), Ghadessy (1983), and myself (Hoey, 1979, 1980, 1983, 1984). These last-mentioned linguists have taken as their starting point the work of Eugene Winter, who in two unpublished works (Winter, 1969, 1976) describes the problem-solution pattern in terms of a reader's

Author's Note: This chapter has had the benefit of careful and sympathetic criticism from Sidney Greenbaum, Charles Cooper, and John Sinclair, and is much improved as a result. I am very grateful to them for their help and also to Anne Buckley for typing and proofreading each draft.

187

interaction with discourse. He elsewhere refers to the pattern as a "larger clause relation" (Winter, 1977), a view fully compatible with his reader-oriented description, because the reader looms large, as we shall see, in his definition of the clause relation.

There has been an equivalent interest in the use of the pattern in writing courses for freshmen and for other pedagogical purposes. Indeed Winter (1969, 1976) and Jordan (1984) are written with such practical purposes in mind. Young and Becker (1965), Becker (1965), and Young, Becker, and Pike (1970) introduce the pattern most directly into modern rhetoric. Use of the pattern has likewise become commonplace in teaching English to foreign learners (as in *Skills for Learning,* published by T. Nelson). Laudable though these applications to the teaching situation are, their value is on occasion vitiated by a failure to relate the pattern to the language that encodes it and by an oversimple representation of the possibilities available to writers. (A notable exception to this charge is Jordan, 1984).

In this chapter I examine the problem-solution pattern's kinship to other, less well-described, patterns and in so doing question the clarity with which the problem-solution pattern may be defined. Furthermore, I seek to show that it is necessary, if certain types of patterns are to be accounted for, to extend Winter's conception of the clause relation. The argument may suggest ways in which pedagogical applications might be modified.

A DEFINITION OF "CLAUSE RELATIONS"

The utility of the concept of the clause relation has been demonstrated in a number of places in the work of Winter:

> A clause relation is the cognitive process, and the products of that process, whereby the reader interprets the meaning of a clause, sentence, or group of sentences in the context of one or more preceding clauses, sentences, or groups of sentences in the same discourse. It is also the cognitive process, and the product of that process, whereby the choices the writer makes from grammar, lexis and intonation in the creation of a clause, sentence or group of sentences are made in the context of the other clauses, sentences, or groups of sentences in the discourse.

This definition would win no awards for elegance, but it at least incorporates a number of claims about the ways writers organize and readers process discourse. First, it makes the claim that if readers are presented with any two pieces of language in a context that suggests they belong together, they will attempt to relate them in one (or both) of two ways—by matching them or sequencing them. In other words, one's first reaction as a reader is to see what two pieces of information share and to determine whether one follows the other in time or logic. This processing strategy is independent of the language in which the information is expressed, and is not strictly a linguistic matter. But it has a direct linguistic consequence in that writers form their sentences with a view to their being so processed. The language reflects and makes more precise the interpretation that readers are expected to arrive at, and in turn the readers are attuned to the clues in the language that enable them to arrive at a precise interpretation. Consequently we can talk in terms of more precise matching or sequence relations (or rather, of more precise products of the general matching and sequence processes). Thus when we consider what two statements share, we may also decide that they match in a particular way (such as contrast, generalization-example) or are sequenced in a particular way (such as cause-consequence, condition-consequence). Writers and readers, however, are not compelled to be precise in this way. Two sentences may be presented or interpreted in such a way that only the most general relation is seen to exist between them. For the sequencing process, the most general relation is that of time sequence; for the matching process, the most general relation has no recognized name but occurs when the only feature that sentences share is a common topic.

Because clause relations are defined in terms of writer and reader, they may be seen as abstractions from the questions a writer seeks to answer, and a reader sees being answered, in a discourse.

THE NATURE OF PATTERNS

The reason for such close attention to the definition of the clause relation is that problem-solution patterns, and indeed all other patterns, are composed of clause relations. Patterns of discourse organization are made up of clause relations in combination and do not have an existence separate from them; indeed, it is possible to set up mapping conditions that allow one to show in a regular way the relationship between the pattern on the one hand and the relations that make up the pattern on the other (Hoey, 1983). In other words, the real nature of a pattern is the sense of order perceived by a reader in the way the clauses or groups of clauses in a discourse relate to each other. So to describe a pattern is to describe the relations of which it is the outcome.

A pattern of organization, such as problem-solution, does not have the status of structure. By this I mean that one cannot make predictive statements about it; written discourse patterning is not like grammatical or phonological structure or the structure of interaction, where one may say of certain combinations, "That is not English." It is more like morphology, where one may make useful generalizations and account for what has already happened, but where one's generalizations may always be undermined by a rogue example. Studies of discourse patterning do not permit the counterexample in the form of an unpredicted pattern, though the existence of a discourse with no pattern (because not related in the ways described above) would constitute a valid counterexample.[1]

THE SIGNALING OF PATTERNS

The ways in which a pattern of discourse organization may be identified have been described in some detail elsewhere (Winter, 1976, 1977; Hoey, 1979, 1983; Jordan, 1984). It is not the purpose of this chapter to contribute further to this discussion. Nevertheless a brief summary of several of the ways in which an analyst may identify a pattern may be useful at this point.

The fundamental assumption underlying all clause-relational analysis is that the sentences of a discourse have together a meaning that is more than the product of the meanings of the individual sentences taken separately. The methods we use to identify relations, or the patterns they combine to create, all center on spelling out the meaning readers find as a result of the relative placement of the sentences.

A number of methods have been suggested for identifying patterns. Crucial to the analysis of narrative by Labov and Waletsky (1967) is the identification of evaluative items, while for Longacre (1976) a variety of features, including changes of orientation, tense, and sentence length, mark the peak in a narrative pattern. For Grimes (1975, p. 238), one may begin with identification of role relations that may be observed to combine into predicates until one has "the cascading effect of layer upon layer of propositions with rhetorical predicates, whose arguments themselves are propositions of considerable complexity."

Perhaps the most basic way of identifying a pattern is to project the discourse into a question-and-answer dialogue. To show the method at its most basic, consider the following made-up example (the only virtue of which is its skeletal nature):

(1) (1) Charles was a language teacher. (2) His students came to him unable to write coherently. (3) He taught them discourse analysis. (4) Now they all write novels.

We can project this into a dialogue as follows:

(2) D(iscourse:) Charles was a language teacher.
     Q(uestion): What problem arose for him?
     D: His students came to him unable to write coherently.
     Q: What did he do about it?
     D: He taught them discourse analysis.
     Q: What was the result?
     D: Now they all write novels.

The object of such a projection into dialogue is that the questions should spell out the relationship between the sentences; the dialogue should make sense and there should be no change in the meaning of the discourse (other than that occasioned by the inevitable change in emphasis). In this case, the questions may point to a problem-solution pattern, with sentence 1 being the Situation, sentence 2 the Problem, sentence 3 the Response, and sentence 4 the positive Result. The questions are inserted retrospectively; it is not, for example, being claimed that a reader would necessarily anticipate a problem for Charles on encountering the first sentence. Rather, it is being claimed that a reader would recognize the second sentence as being connected to the first in a way reflected by the question that can be inserted between them. Clearly a number of possible questions may be asked between the pairs of sentences. Some of these represent alternative formulations of the same request for information. Thus *What was his way of dealing with this problem?* is an alternative formulation of *What did he do about it?* Others focus on different aspects of the organization. So, for example, *What did he teach in the circumstances?* (in the place of *What did he do about it?*) focuses on the general-particular relationship between the first and third sentence, where the latter spells out what being a language teacher may involve, rather than on the problem-response relationship between the second and third sentence picked up by other formulations. All the interpretations co-occur, the investigator being required to recover all the possible requests in order to make a complete analysis. Complete analyses, however, are rarely achieved and not always necessary. In this chapter certain aspects of the analyses are highlighted at the expense of others.

Winter (1977) notes that there is a special vocabulary for such questions. In those given above, we have *problem, arose, do about, result, way, dealing with,* and *circumstances.* These may be said to "signal" the relations or the patterns built out of the relations, by providing us with labels for the meanings of the relations. Such signals, however, do not have to be part of questions to do this. They are quite normally found in the body of the discourse. For example:

(3) (1) Charles was a language teacher. (2) His students came to him unable to write their names. (3) His *way* of *dealing with* this *problem* was to teach them discourse analysis, with the *result* that they now all write novels.

Whenever they occur, they may be regarded as signals by the writer of the relations or patterns to be found in the discourse.

In addition to these signals, there are also signals of evaluation. Negative evaluations may be used regularly to signal problems and, as we shall see, components of other patterns as well. Had sentence 2 in example 1 read, *Unfortunately the students came to him knowing no English, unfortunately* would have been sufficient for the reader to identify the problem-solution pattern of the discourse; an undesirable situation is one requiring improvement—a Problem requiring a Response.

Problem-Solution Patterns

We may represent the simplest types of problem-solution pattern diagrammatically as shown in Figure 6.1. Working our way down the diagram, we need to note that Situation is optional, that Aspect of Situation Requiring a Response is a longer but more accurate label for Problem, that Response is a neutral label for what is often referred to as Solution, and that the three branches represent alternative possibilities. Each of the vertical stages represents a question that is being answered, for example, "What is the Situation?"; "What is the Problem within this Situation?"; "What can be done about it?"; "How successful might this be?"; and/or "What will the result be?" If Evaluation follows directly upon Response, the question "What grounds have you for that evaluation?" is also answered. They also can be related to the clause relations of which the pattern is made up. So, for example, the relation between Problem and Response is also one of cause-consequence and that between Response and Result is also one of instrument-achievement. Because of the regularity of this relationship, it is possible, under specified conditions (Hoey, 1983, pp. 56-59), to use signals of these clause relations as signals of problem-solution patterns.

The outline of the problem-solution pattern given in Figure 6.1 is a rather primitive one, in that it is not sufficiently generalizable. Let us consider a possible alternative version of our story about the language teacher:

(4)   (1) Charles was a language teacher. (2) His students came to him unable to write their names. (3) He taught them discourse analysis. (4) This had little effect.

The same questions have been answered as before, but the presence of negative Evaluation in sentence 4 renders the discourse apparently incomplete, because it tells us of an unresolved problem. It is therefore necessary to incorporate into our description the notion of multilayering (Hoey, 1983). Multilayering occurs whenever a negative Evaluation appears after a Response; it represents the recycling of the problem-solution pattern, where a negative Evaluation sets up an expectation of a further Response, which itself has to be positively evaluated before the discourse will be deemed complete. This can be represented diagrammatically as shown in Figure 6.2. An example follows:

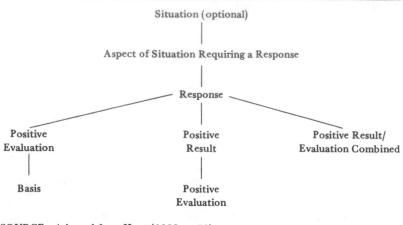

SOURCE: Adapted from Hoey (1982, p. 51).

Figure 6.1

(5) *No smell garlic*

> (1) A Tokyo rice grower, Toshia Nakagawa, reckons he has won the battle to produce a type of garlic which retains its seasoning qualities without the smell. (2) In the past, chemists have succeeded in removing the smell to reduce antagonism between lovers and non-lovers of the root: critics however have argued that the processing destroys the flavour. (3) Nakagawa started his experiments in 1958, planting heads which appeared to have less smell than others and using different types of fertilisers. (4) Now he claims the breakthrough has been made—the final tests with his new product were with a herd of cows fed with the garlic whose milk showed no odour at all (*New Scientist,* May 4, 1978, p. 295).

The pattern we find in this discourse may be represented in nonlinear fashion as follows:

Problem-Response-Negative Evaluation-Response-
Positive Evaluation

This and subsequent formulas reflect not the sequence but the pattern of relations within a discourse. Thus positive Evaluation, placed at the end of the pattern, appears not only at the end but at the beginning of the sequence. (A comparison may be drawn with

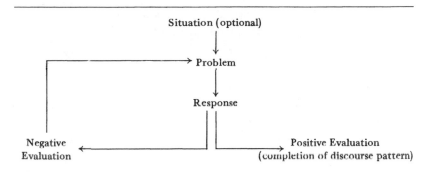

SOURCE: Adapted from Hoey (1983, p. 83).

Figure 6.2

syntax, where SVO in English may be realized by VSVO or OSV and may have optional adverbials.) Some of the elements in patterns of organization appear in various sequences, and one element may be embedded within another. Sentence 1, which traditional school rhetorics would refer to as a topic sentence, encapsulates the pattern. There is a positive Evaluation *(won)* of a Response *(battle to)* to what can only be tentatively characterized as Problem, the purpose clause being compatible with Problem but insufficient evidence for positing it. Sentence 2, however, confirms the tentative characterization; (to reduce) *antagonism* is an aspect of Situation requiring a Response—a Problem. A Response is given in the same sentence *removing the smell* (which ties in with the previous sentence's *without the smell*), and is positively evaluated *(succeeded)*. The second half of this sentence, however, offers a parallel negative Evaluation, which signals a Problem for chemists. This therefore gives rise to an expectation of a new Response. Sentence 3 meets this expectation, without any implication of success or otherwise: it answers the question "What did Nakagawa do about it?" The first half of sentence 4 provides a positive Evaluation *(breakthrough)* of this Response followed in the second half by a basis for the Evaluation.

The reader may have noticed one important way in which the analysis just given is inadequate. It fails to specify whose Problem, whose Response, and whose Evaluation. To do so is not to move from discourse features to the real world, as we require no knowledge external to the discourse to be able to make such specifications. Example 6 was represented as organized thus:

Problem-Response-Negative Evaluation-Response-Positive Evaluation
but is in fact better represented as follows:

Problem for *lovers and non-lovers of the root* [i.e. garlic]
|
Response by *chemists* to the Problem for *lovers and non-lovers of garlic.*
|
Positive Evaluation by the writer [assumed] of the Response by *chemists* to
| the Problem for *lovers and non-lovers of garlic*

Negative Evaluation by *critics* of the Response by *chemists* to the Problem
| for *lovers and non-lovers of garlic* (= Problem for chemists)

Response by *Nakagawa* to the Problem for *lovers and non-lovers of garlic*
|
Positive Evaluation by *Nakagawa* of the Response by *Nakagawa* to the
| Problem for *lovers and non-lovers of garlic*

Italics indicate explicit specification in the discourse. It will be
noticed that the positive Evaluation that is felt to complete the
discourse emanates from the same source as the Response. In other
words, while as readers we find the discourse complete, as scientists
we would be wise to reserve judgment on the completeness of the
research it reports. The absence of the writer's own Evaluation of
Nakagawa's Response leaves the reader in doubt as to the reliability
of his claims.

Cumbersome though the pattern is when presented in this fashion, it is an improvement over the simpler unattributed pattern,
which must now be regarded as shorthand. The fuller form can be
presented more elegantly and abstractly, so that it covers all cases, as
follows:

Problem for x
|
Response by y to Problem for x
|
Evaluation by z of Response by y to Problem for x

where x = or ≠ y

and z = or ≠ x or y

and any or all of x, y, and z may be the writer.

Question-Answer Patterns

Once we represent the problem-solution pattern in such a way, it
becomes apparent that it shares many features with another, hardly

studied, pattern, which we may call the question-answer pattern. I
know of no full study of this pattern (though it will be readily
recognized by any reader), but a brief account can be found in
Collier-Wright (1984). The main elements of the pattern are a Question, an Answer, and an Evaluation of the Answer, if from another
source. The similarities of this pattern to the problem-solution pattern will become apparent after we have considered an example:

(6) (1) What then are we to strive for, in accordance with the results of this
compressed analysis in the light of Christianity?

(2) Not the arrogant domination of a religion claiming an exclusive
mission and despising freedom. (3) This danger, although unintended, arises as a result of the dogmatic repression of the problem of
religion by Karl Barth and "dialectical theology". (4) We do not want a
narrow-minded, conceited, exclusive particularism which condemns
the other religions in toto, a proselytism which carries on unfair
competition and takes too restricted a view not only of the religions
but also of the Gospel.

(5) We do not want the syncretist mingling of all religions, however
much they contradict one another, harmonizing and reducing and
thus suppressing the truth.

(6) This danger, again unintended, arises from the liberal solution of
the problem of religion, advocated by Toynbee and a number of
experts in comparative religion. (7) This is a crippling, dissolvent,
agnostic-relativistic indifferentism, approving and confirming the
other religions indiscriminately, which at first seems to be liberating
and creative of happiness, but finally becomes painfully monotonous,
since it has abandoned all firm standards and norms.

(8) What we must strive for is an independent, unselfish Christian
ministry to human beings in the religions. (9) We must do this in a
spirit of open-mindedness which is more than patronizing accom-
modation; which does not lead us to deny our own faith, but also does
not impose any particular response; which turns criticism from outside into self-criticism and at the same time accepts everything positive; which destroys nothing of value in the religions, but also does
not incorporate uncritically anything worthless. (10) Christianity
therefore should perform its service among the world religions in a
dialectical unity of recognition and rejection, as critical catalyst and
crystallization point of their religious, moral, meditative, ascetic,
aesthetic values. (from Hans Kung, 1974, *On Being a Christian*,
E. Quinn, trans., pp. 111-112)[2]

This passage has an organization that may be represented as follows:

Question-Answer-Negative Evaluation-Answer-Negative Evaluation-
Answer-Positive Evaluation

where Question may be defined as aspect of situation requiring a verbal response and Answer as provision of a verbal response.

The first sentence provides the Question, marked by the combination of interrogative and the conjunct *then* (which seems often to accompany the Question of a Question-Answer pattern); the conjunct *then* is cohesive, marking a link with the previous context. Sentences 2-4 supply an Answer *(domination of a religion)* and a negative Evaluation of the Answer *(arrogant* and *not).*[3] The next paragraph follows a similar pattern. Again, an Answer is considered *(mingling of all religions)* and rejected *(not)*; the answer is further negatively evaluated by characterization as *crippling* and *monotonous.* In the final paragraph, a third Answer is given *(ministry to human beings in the religions).* This is not rejected; the pseudocleft of sentence 8 shows it to be the author's Answer, which he, slightly surprisingly, evaluates positively as *unselfish,* surprisingly because in this pattern the norm is for one's own answer to be left unevaluated.

Despite the positive Evaluation with which it concludes, the example just given is reasonably typical of the way the pattern appears, except that because it is short, the Answer and negative Evaluation have been combined on every occasion. While this is not uncommon—and has its parallel in the combination of Response and Evaluation that one often finds in short problem-solution discourses—it would be wrong to suggest that it is always, or normally, the case. In the following short extract, from a passage of many pages in length organized as a question-answer pattern, it will be seen that the Question, Answer, and negative Evaluation are all kept distinct:

> (7) (1) What, then, is the advantage which we may hope to derive from a study of the political writers of the past? (2) A view prevalent in earlier ages would have provided a simple answer to this question. (3) A work of politics, it would have been said, is the handbook of an art, the art of governing. (4) Just as a man of superior knowledge or skill in the art of carpentry may compile a work in which his knowledge is made available to those who aspire to be good carpenters, so a man of

superior wisdom in the art of politics may set down his knowledge in a book for the instruction of those whose business is to found, govern, or preserve states. (5) If this is what political theory is there is no difficulty in determining what advantage may be expected from the study of great political works. (6) They will be consulted for purposes of instruction by those who have to govern states.

(7) Some of the greatest political writers have believed themselves to be offering such a system of practical instruction, and many students of their works in the past have undoubtedly sought, and may have found in their pages that practical guidance which they have professed to offer. (8) But this is certainly not the advantage which a modern reader can be promised from a study of their works. (9) This entire conception of politics as an art and of the political philosopher as the teacher of it rests upon assumptions which it is impossible to accept. (10) If it were correct, the writers of political theory would need to be themselves past masters in the art of governing, and statesmen would need to apprentice themselves to them in order to learn their job. (11) But we find that this is not so. (12) Few political philosophers have themselves exhibited any mastery of the art of governing, and few successful statesmen have owed their success to the study of political writings. [expansion of this point omitted]

(13) If political theory is not a body of science for the instruction of statesmen what is it? (14) There is a doctrine, the "dialectical materialism" of Karl Marx, which gives a fundamentally different account of its nature. (15) According to this doctrine, political theory is not prior, but posterior, to political fact. [expansion of this point omitted]

(16) The Marxist theory thus completely reverses the relation of priority between political theory and political fact which was implied in the theory which I began by mentioning; and it is clear that a very different estimate of the value of studying political theory will follow, according as we adopt one or the other of these two conflicting views of its nature. (18) According to the former of them, it will be almost the most important study which a man can undertake, and an indispensable qualification for all who claim a share in the direction of public affairs. (18) According to the latter, since theory can in no case determine how a man will act, the study of it has no importance, and only an academic interest.

(19) I will not conceal my own opinion that, while the former doctrine errs by rating the value of this study too high, the latter errs by rating it too low (Reprinted by permission of Houghton Mifflin Company from Michael F. Foster, *Masters of Political Thought* [Vol. 1], pp. 14-17).[4]

This has the following pattern:

Question-Answer-Negative Evaluation-Answer-Negative Evaluation

Sentence I provides the Question, sentences 3-7 offer an Answer and sentences 8-12 provide a negative Evaluation of this Answer and a Basis for the Evaluation. Sentence 13 reiterates the Question and sentences 14-18 provide an alternative Answer, which sentence 19 negatively evaluates. What follows in the work from which the passage is taken is a detailed Basis for this Evaluation and the author's own Answer to his Question, which he does not evaluate.

A full account of the evidence for this analysis would largely duplicate our account of passage 6; however, it is worth noting that sentence 2 serves a function identical to signaling sentences in problem-solution patterns, characterizing what goes before as *question* and what follows as *answer*. This demonstrates that we are involved with a phenomenon similar to the problem-solution pattern.

The similarities between the two patterns go some way beyond this. I am sure no one would have made the mistake of thinking passage 7 either self-contained or finished, even if I had not described the way the passage continues. Just as we found that a problem-solution pattern was incomplete if a Response received a negative Evaluation, so we find a question-answer pattern is likewise incomplete if an Answer is negatively evaluated. This means that we can set up a diagram for the question-answer pattern comparable to that we set up for the problem-solution pattern (see Figure 6.3).

The similarities between the two pattern types continue if Answers and Evaluations are attributed. Thus, for passage 6, we can present the analysis as follows:

Question for us all (assumed)

Answer by *Barth and "dialectical theology"* to the Question for us all

Negative Evaluation by *Hans Kung* (name on title page) of the Answer by *Barth and "dialectical theology"* to the Question for us all

Answer by *Toynbee and a number of experts in comparative religion* to the Question for us all

Negative Evaluation by *Hans Kung* of the Answer by *Toynbee etc.* to the Question for us all

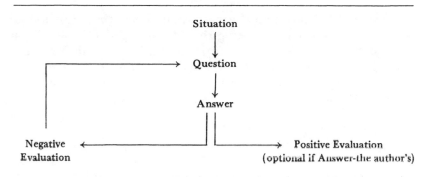

Figure 6.3

Answer by *Hans Kung* to the Question for us all

Positive Evaluation by *Hans Kung* of the Answer by *Hans Kung* to the Question for us all

For passage 7 we have the following:

Queston for us all (assumed)

Answer by people *in earlier ages* to the Question for us all

Negative Evaluation by Michael B. Foster (name on title page) to the Answer by people *in earlier ages* to the Question for us all

Answer by *Karl Marx* to the Question for us all

Negative Evaluation by Michael B. Foster *(my own opinion)* of the Answer by *Karl Marx* to the Question for us all

If we present these possibilities more abstractly, as we did the problem-solution patterns, we are again struck by the similarity of the pattern types:

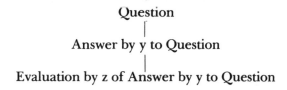

where y = or ≠ z and
y and/or z may be the author

We would need to add for this pattern, however, that Evaluation is optional in the event of y being the author and that Evaluation is obligatorily positive if y = z, y is the author and if Answer is presented without signs of hypotheticality. This last observation draws attention to another set of patterns with which question-answer shares features—the hypothetical-real patterns.

Hypothetical-Real Patterns

The hypothetical-real patterns have been altogether more fully described than the question-answer pattern, but in theses rather than readily accessible essays. Winter (1974) devotes considerable attention to hypothetical-real, regarding it as one of the two fundamental relations of discourse, the other being the situation-evaluation relation. Williames (1984) builds upon Winter's description, sticking closely to his categories most of the time, but arguing for its treatment as a pattern like the problem-solution pattern rather than as a relation such as cause-consequence or contrast. He provides detailed criteria for its identification.

The simplest form of the pattern is as follows:

John says x. This is incorrect. In fact, y.

where the first sentence represents the Hypothetical, the second the Denial of the Hypothetical, and the third the Correction. It is common for either the Denial or the Correction to be followed by a Basis, though not usually both. Sometimes the Correction is left unstated because the Basis for the Denial makes it self-evident; sometimes the Denial is omitted, its place being taken by a conjunct such as *on the contrary.*

Consider the following example of a passage with a hypothetical-real pattern:

(8)   From the Chairman
                            Stone-Platt Industries

(1) Sir, There has been a great deal of Press coverage of the Stone-Platt receivership, culminating in your leading article of March 22. (2) I welcome this opportunity to correct some important statements, which I believe to be misleading, to communicate the Board's view

more positively than has hitherto been possible, and to raise a number of broader issues which affect industry today.

(3) As regards your Leader, paragraph four is incorrect in stating that "the financial position deteriorated towards the end of last year" and that closure of the division would have involved "write-offs and redundancy costs which would have sunk the whole company." (4) In fact, the management had been successful in the last 18 months in reducing the UK manufacturing capacity of the Platt Saco Lowell division by two-thirds (closing plants at Oldham and Bolton) and had sound reasons to believe that the remaining plant at Accrington would be viable. (5) As a result of our actions, the fixed costs of the Lancashire operation had been reduced from around £20m to £7m a year and this would have come through in later profit reports (reprinted with permission of *Financial Times*, March 23, 1982).

The second paragraph of this extract from a long letter is a simple instance of the pattern and is organized in a way that may be represented:

Hypothetical-Denial-Correction

where Hypothetical may be defined as a claim by other than the author.

Sentence 3 simultaneously provides the Hypothetical and evaluates it as *incorrect*—in other words, denies it. That a Hypothetical will appear has already been signaled in sentences 1 and 2, with the reference in the first to *your leading article* and in the second to *some important statements*. The latter evidence also negatively evaluates these *statements,* in advance of giving them, as misleading and signals that they will be corrected ("opportunity to *correct*"). Sentences 4 and 5 provide the expected Correction, the onset being marked by the use of *in fact.*

It need not be the case that the Denial precedes the Hypothetical. It is nearly as common for the Hypothetical statement to come first and then to be denied; an instance is given further below. In a small number of cases, the Hypothetical may be affirmed rather than denied.

What is of interest here is not to describe the pattern type, which as noted has already been well described, but to note its relationship to the other two patterns. To begin with its relationship to the question-answer pattern, we find that if we place the two patterns together, we have:

Question   -   Answer   -   Negative Evaluation   -   Answer
                 Hypothetical   -   Denial   -   Correction

This suggests that only the vagaries of labeling prevent the hypothetical-real pattern from appearing as a question-answer pattern without the Question.

The parallels with the question-answer pattern and also with the problem-solution pattern become more striking if we represent the pattern of example 8 in such a way as to reflect the attribution of the parts of the pattern; but to do so we have to relabel the Hypothetical element as Claim:

Claim by *your leading article*

Negative Evaluation by *the chairman, Stone-Platt Industries* of claim by *your leading article*

Correction by *the chairman of Stone-Platt Industries* of claim by *your leading article*

Represented more abstractly, the pattern looks as follows:

Claim by y

Evaluation by z of Claim by y

Correction by z of Claim by y

where $y \neq z$,

and z will always be the author.

Correction is optional if Evaluation is followed by a Basis and will not occur if Evaluation is positive.

A Cline of Patterns

It will be noticed that there are greater restrictions on the identity of y and z for the hypothetical-real pattern and that these restrictions rule out the possibility of multilayering. Nevertheless the similarities between the three patterns we have considered are striking. The fact that problem-solution and question-answer resemble each other in their abstract representation might lead to the supposition that the hypothetical-real pattern is merely related to problem-solution through the mediation of question-answer. Consider, however, the following letter:

(9) (1) Sir, Mr. L. Hunt refers to the Chancellor's inability to find a practical method of indexing gains from 1965 and suggests as a simple compromise that investors could elect to pay at a reduced rate of 15 percent on the sale of holdings acquired before March 9, 1982, but without indexation for future gains.

(2) This is ingenious but fails, in my view, to give sufficient incentive to investors to pay immediately tax which they might otherwise never pay because of exemptions, death etc. (3) The only practical way both to remedy the injustice, at least in part, and to fortify the revenue, is to limit the compromise to the 1982-83 tax year. (4) The incentive would be sharpened to the Chancellor's immediate advantage and the tax system would not suffer permanent distortion.

D.A.H. Baer

This is a clear example of a Hypothetical-Real pattern. The first sentence is the Hypothetical, marked by the assignment to Mr. Hunt of the views expressed. Sentence 2 provides an Evaluation of the view, which begins positively (*ingenious*) but ends on a negative note (*"fails* to give *sufficient* incentive"). The transition from Hypothetical to Real, made up of Denial and Correction in this case, is signaled by *in my view.* Sentences 3 and 4 provide the Correction.

So far, so good. The letter conforms in every respect to what we expect of a discourse organized in terms of a hypothetical-real pattern. But it is also a clear example of a Problem-solution Pattern. Sentence 1 provides a Problem (for the Chancellor), signaled by *inability* (compare *unable* in example 1) and a suggested Response (by Mr. Hunt). Sentence 2 negatively evaluates that Response, thereby reinstating the Problem. Sentence 3 provides an alternative Response (by Mr. Baer), signaled by *way* and *remedy the injustice,* and evaluates it positively as *practical;* the positive Evaluation is continued in sentence 4.

Thus the same discourse has two closely parallel but apparently separate patterns of organization:

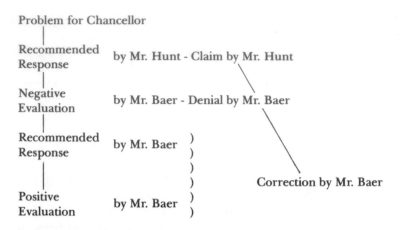

This should give us pause for thought. It suggests that the boundaries between patterns are much less distinct than has previously been suggested. We appear to have a cline as follows:

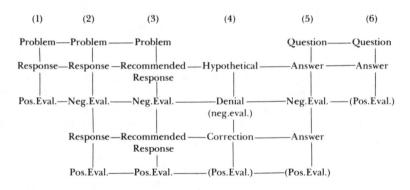

Each of these patterns may be seen as distinct from its neighbor-but-one but it may not be possible in practice to distinguish immediate neighbors in the cline.[5] This suggests that caution is necessary in positing distinct patterns. Further research into the relationships holding between patterns is certainly required; to begin with, the diagram just given is too linear in that it obscures the features we have already noted that problem-solution and question-answer patterns share (such as multilayering) with each other but not with hypothetical-real patterns.

The Interactive Nature of
the Question-Answer Pattern

All that has been said so far may modify our notion of a pattern but it leaves the concept of a clause relation unaltered. We have not yet exhausted the list of the Question-Answer pattern's friends and relatives, however, and there is one relative that poses a real problem for clause relational analysis. Up to now I have left unanalyzed the relationship between Question and Answer; it has been treated as if it were exactly parallel with that between Problem and Response, but it is not. As already noted, a cause-consequence relation always underpins Problem-Response. No such relation underpins Question and Answer; indeed no clause relation of either the Matching or Sequence kind appears to explain the relationship. Perhaps the closest analogy is Winter's (1974, 1979) replacement by addition, where one or more clauses are repeated in toto with additional information:

(10) She took just two years to reduce me to a state of nervous break-
     down, and *she did this* [repeating in toto the first half of the sentence]
     by a combination of just those characteristics which prejudice allots
     to women at work: emotionalism, capriciousness, selfishness and
     pettiness (*Guardian* [letters], May 26, 1967, p. 26, quoted in Winter,
     1979, p. 105).

One could argue that a similar process of addition was taking place in the case of Question-Answer, but such an argument would be little more than an attempt to rescue the claim that "if writers or speakers fail to relate one or more of their sentences to any of the other sentences in their discourse then they are not producing coherent discourses but fragments of a discourse" (Hoey, 1983, p. 180), where the context shows that *relate* refers to clause relations.

Though the relationship between Question and Answer may not appear easy to handle in clause relational terms, it has a very obvious parallel with the structure of interaction. Consider Table 6.1, which displays an excerpt from analyzed data in Sinclair and Coulthard (1975). Applying the categories we have been using for the question-answer pattern so far, we can arrive at the following:

Situation (sentence 1)

Question for class (sentence 2)

TABLE 6.1

Initiation				Response		Follow-up
Elicit	(1)	And now I've got this thing.	starter	(3) Iron.	reply	
	(2)	What metal is— what material is this?	elicitation			
Repeat	(4)	What is it? NV	loop bid	(6) Steel.	reply	(7) No.
	(5)	Yes.	nomination			
Elicit	(8)	It's not steel it's—	elicitation	(9) Metal. (10) Iron.	reply	(11) It is metal.
Elicit	(12)	Another name for it.	elicitation	(13) Tin. (14) Iron.	reply reply	(15) Tin yes. (16) It's metal and it's tin.

Answer by pupil A (sentence 3)

Question reiterated for class (sentence 4)
(= Implied Negative Evaluation of Answer by pupil)

Answer by pupil B (sentence 6)

Negative Evaluation by teacher of Answer by pupil (sentences 7, 8)

Answers by pupils C and D (sentences 9, 10)

Positive Evaluation by teacher of pupil C's Answer
(and therefore Implied Negative Evaluation of pupil D's Answer)

Queston reiterated for class (sentence 12)

Positive Evaluation of pupil E's Answer (sentences 15,16)

The nomination of sentence 5 does not have any parallel in the written discourses we have considered. Also, it is likely that the intonation given sentence 11 will have indicated incompleteness. In the absence of such information, however, we can still note that the pattern closely matches that of the question-answer patterns considered earlier. More to the point, it also closely matches the original analysis of the exchange by Sinclair and Coulthard:

		Move	Act
Question	——————————	Initiation	: elicit
|		|	
Answer	——————————	Response	: reply

Negative ——————————— Follow-Up	: evaluation
Evaluation	Initiation	: elicit
(Answer ———————————— Response	: reply)
(|	|	)
(Answer ———————————— Response	: reply)
Positive ——————————————— Follow-Up	: evaluation
Evaluation		

So close is the parallel between these two analyses that one might venture to suggest that the Sinclair/Coulthard analysis could benefit from the distinction between positive and negative Evaluation that we have been using. This would enable them to argue that a Follow-Up was simultaneously the Initiation of a following exchange in a manner compatible with the double function Coulthard and Brazil (1978) allow for a Response that also initiates. But whether such a suggestion was considered acceptable or not, the symmetry that already exists between the analyses is enough to demand explanation. For the Sinclair and Coulthard analysis is in terms of speech acts and describes a structure with predictive power, while the clause-relational analysis is in terms of semantic relationships and describes patterns of organization with no claims to predictive power of the same kind, though of course knowledge of basic discourse patterns does enable a reader to make predictions.

A clue to the explanation may be obtained if we consider the following passage, from a novel:

(11) (1) "What's a Sacrament?" Margaret wanted to know.

(2) "It's a little bit hard to explain," said Mummie.

(3) "It's something you can see that means something you can't see."

(4) Ronnie and Margaret looked puzzled. (5) "Something you can see that means something you can't see?" repeated Margaret. (6) "I don't understand that at all."

(7) "Well, it's like this," said Mummie. (8) "Every Sacrament has two parts—the part you can see, and the part you can't. (9) When Baby John was baptized to-day, all you saw was the water. (10) What is water used for?"

(11) "To wash with," said Margaret promptly.

(12) "Well, Baptism means 'washing'. (13) You could see the water, but you couldn't see the heavenly washing of Baby's soul. (14) And you couldn't see the Holy Spirit either, when He came to Baby John to help him to be good. (15) That's what I meant by the part you could see and the part you couldn't. (16) Every Sacrament is like that. (17) It is the way God works. (18) He takes a common ordinary thing like water, and He uses it for something else."

(19) "I see," said Margaret thoughtfully (from *Ronnie and the Sacraments*, A.C. Osborn Hann, 1954, London: S.P.C.K.).

At first sight, it would appear that we could analyze the dialogue in this passage either in terms of a question-answer pattern such as this:

Question for *Mummie* by *Margaret* (S.1)

Answer by *Mummie* of Question for *Mummie* (S.3)

Negative Evaluation of *Mummie*'s Answer by *Margaret* (and *Ronnie*) (S.4-6)

Answer by *Mummie* of Question for *Mummie*.

Positive Evaluation by *Margaret* of *Mummie*'s Answer.

or in terms of a (modified) exchange structure. But in fact the conversation is not a real exchange between two participants; it is the representation within a monologue of a fictional exchange. (See Caldas, in press, for a full working out of this distinction.)

This has important implications for the study of both written and spoken discourse. It means that the concept of clause relations must be extended if it is to account for a reader's interpretation of written dialogue. The definition of clause relations given earlier laid emphasis on the reader's interpretation of any sentence(s) in the context of preceding sentences in the discourse. It seems beyond dispute that an interpretation of written dialogue must involve some recognition of the speech acts being simulated, though not necessarily in as precise a manner as that suggested by Leech and Short (1981, p. 292), and it seems reasonable to accept that such recognition is made in light of the sentences that immediately precede the sentence in question. It follows that the recognition of speech act relations must be seen as a subcategory of clause relations. If we choose to reject this, we must unpick all the knitting. For the written dialogue has been shown to be very similar to both the hypothetical-real and the question-answer patterns, and both of these have been shown to overlap with the problem-solution pattern, which is the most quoted example of organization in terms of clause relations. The choice is then between abandonment of clause relations as a means of describing discourse organization and extension of the concept to cover speech acts perceived. The latter course allows us not only to cover the cases discussed but also to incorporate within a single framework work on discourse organization, such as that of Coulthard and Montgomery (1981) and Tadros (1985), that makes use of the notion of the speech act. It is crucial, however, to note at this juncture the difference between *perception* of related speech acts and the *performance* of a speech act. The latter would only come within the province of clause relations insofar as it was performed *in relation to* previous acts.

All this means that we must in turn reinterpret the findings of Sinclair and Coulthard (1975). We must assume that a listener eavesdropping on an exchange interprets it in the same way that a reader would on encountering a report of such an exchange. In other words, we must distinguish the observer's interpretation of the exchange in terms of clause relations from the participants' involvement in the creation of an exchange in terms of speech acts, even though the terms used to describe both may be the same. We can go further still and suggest that speakers simultaneously interpret what has just been said to them in the context of their own previous statements. In other words, for speakers to contribute appropriately to the structure being mutually built, they must first have processed what has been said by both participants in a manner similar to that they would use in processing written discourse.

CONCLUSION

What began as an apparently straightforward examination of related patterns of organization in written discourse has ended in muddy waters. I have suggested that such patterns are not as distinct as they seem. I am not, of course, denying their existence; indeed my argument has rested upon the assumption of their existence. Rather, I am reinforcing my claim that they are nonstructural and interactive in nature. They are nonstructural because the categories cannot be defined in mutually exclusive ways and because combinations described do not allow predictive statements. They are interactive because they require for their description reference not only to the reader but to the speech acts performed in spoken discourse as well.

Still less am I denying the existence or utility of clause relations; what I am doing is suggesting that what is covered by the term may be broader and more diffuse than was previously assumed. Instead of there being two ways of relating sentences—Matching and Sequencing—there may be three, the third of which might provisionally be labeled Act-evaluating. This would allow all discourses, both spoken and written, to be described in terms of clause relations, but at the expense perhaps of some useful generalizations concerning their signaling. Future research might usefully consider how the proposed third type of relation interconnects with Matching and Sequencing relations on the one hand and with speech act performance on the other. This will certainly shed light on the question of the relationship between the structure of spoken interaction and the organization of written discourse, though it will with almost equal certainty challenge some of our assumptions about both.

NOTES

1. For instance, Hoey (1985) considers the statute as an instance of an unpatterned discourse (at least in the sense in which we are using the term).

2. I have suppressed Hans Kung's shifts in typeface in the course of this example; the passage is mainly in italics with occasional shifts into roman type.

3. Rejection may be seen as the most pointed of Evaluations.

4. The question-answer pattern typically organizes quite long stretches of discourse, which is why an incomplete example is offered here. It appears to occur more commonly in religious and philosophical writing than elsewhere.

5. In case this seems a surprising claim to make about the relationship between 1 and 2 and 6, it should be remembered that an Evaluation may be both positive and negative, in which the positive almost invariably comes first. In such a circumstance, it could be argued that there is a complete pattern 1 embedded within pattern 2, or a complete pattern 6 within 5.

REFERENCES

Becker, A. L. (1965). A tagmemic approach to paragraph analysis. *College Composition and Communication, 16,* 237-242.

Beekman, J. (1970). Propositions and their relations within a discourse. *Notes on Translation, 37,* 6-23.

Caldas, C. (n.d.) *Interaction in narrative discourse: A study of conversation in the novel.* Doctoral thesis in preparation.

Collier-Wright, C. (1984). *Sermons: A study of the structure and style of four Anglican sermons with special reference to the Book of Common Prayer and the authorized version of the Bible.* Master's dissertation, University of Birmingham.

Coulthard, M., & Brazil, D. (1978). *Exchange structure.* Birmingham: University of Birmingham, English Language Research.

Coulthard, M., & Montgomery, M. (1981). The structure of monologue. In M. Coulthard & M. Montgomery (Eds.), *Studies in discourse analysis.* London: Routledge & Kegan Paul.

Dijk, T. van (1977), *Text and context: Explorations in the semantics and pragmatics of discourse.* London: Longman.

Ghadessy, M. (1983). Information structure in letters to the editor. *International Review of Applied Linguistics in Language Teaching, 21* (1), 46-56.

Graustein, G., & Thiele, W. (1981). Principles of text analysis. *Linguistiche Arbeitsberichte, 31,* 3-29.

Grimes, J. E. (1975). *The thread of discourse.* The Hague: Mouton.

Hoey, M. (1979). *Signalling in discourse* (Discourse Analysis Monographs No. 6). Birmingham: University of Birmingham, English Language Research.

Hoey, M. (1980). Viewing discourse as dialogue as an aid to English language teaching. *Aspects* (Journal of the Panhellenic Union of State Teachers of English), *5,* (2), 21-24.

Hoey, M. (1983). *On the surface of discourse.* London: George Allen & Unwin.

Hoey, M. (1984). The place of clause-relational analysis in linguistic description: The analysis of two pieces of unspoken data as evidence for doubting the value of the familiar terminological distinction between *text* and *discourse. English Language Research Journal.*

Hoey, M. (1985). The lawyer as linguist and the statute as discourse. *The Eleventh LACUS Forum 1984.*

Hoey, M., & Winter, E. (in press). Clause relations and the writing process. In B. Couture (Ed.), *Fundamental approaches to writing research.* London: Frances Pinter, and Norwood, NJ: Ablex.

Hutchins, W. J. (1977a). On the problem of "aboutness" in document analysis. *Journal of Informatics, 1,* (1), 17-35.

Hutchins, W. J. (1977b). On the structure of scientific texts. *UEA Papers in Linguistics, 5,* 18-39.

Jordan, M. P. (1980). Short texts to explain problem-solution structures and vice versa. *Instructional Science, 9,* 221-252.

Jordan, M. P. (1982). Structure, meaning and information signals of some very short texts: An introductory analysis of everyday English prose. *The Eighth LACUS Forum 1981,* 410-417.

Jordan, M. P. (1984). *Rhetoric of everyday English prose.* London: George Allen & Unwin.

Labov, W. (1972). The transformation of experience in narrative syntax. In W. Labov, *Language in the inner city: Studies in the Black English vernacular* (pp. 354-396). Philadelphia: University of Pennsylvania Press.

Labov, W., & Waletsky, J. (1967). Narrative analysis: Oral versions of personal experience. In J. Helm (Ed.), *Essays on the verbal and visual arts* (pp. 12-44). Seattle: University of Washington Press.

Leech, G., & Short, M. (1981). *Style in fiction.* London: Longman.

Longacre, R. E. (1972a). Narrative versus other discourse genres. In D. G. Hays & D. M. Lance (Eds.), *From soundstream to discourse* (pp. 167-186). Reprinted in R. M. Brend (Ed.), *Advances in tagmemics,* (pp. 357-376). Amsterdam: North-Holland.

Longacre, R. E. (1972b). *Hierarchy and universality of discourse constituents in New Guinea languages.* Washington, DC: Georgetown University Press.

Longacre, R. E. (1976). *An anatomy of speech notions.* Lisse: Peter de Ridder.

Sinclair, John M., & Coulthard, R. M. (1975). *Towards an analysis of discourse: The English used by teachers and pupils.* London: Oxford University Press.

Tadros, A. (1985). *Prediction in text* (Discourse Analysis Monographs No. 10). Birmingham: University of Birmingham, English Language Research.

Williames, J. (1984). *An enquiry into the interactive nature of written discourse: The example of the newspaper argument letter.* Unpublished master's thesis, University of Birmingham.

Winter, E. O. (1969). *Grammatical question technique as a way of teaching science students to write progress reports: The use of the short text in teaching.* Mimeo, University of Trondheim.

Winter, E. O. (1971). *Connection in science material: A proposition about the semantics of clause relations* (C.I.L.T. Papers and Reports No. 7). London: Centre for Information on Language Teaching and Research for British Association for Applied Linguistics.

Winter, E. O. (1974). *Replacement as a function of repetition: A study of some of its principal features in the clause relations of contemporary English.* Unpublished doctoral thesis, University of London.

Winter, E. O. (1976). *Fundamentals of information structure: A pilot manual for further development according to student need.* Mimeo, Hatfield Polytechnic.

Winter, E. O. (1977). A clause relational approach to English texts: A study of some predictive lexical items in written discourse. *Instructional Science, 6*(1), 1-92.

Winter, E. O. (1979). Replacement as a fundamental function of the sentence in context. *Forum Linguisticum, 4*(2), 95-133.

Young, R. E., & Becker, A. L. (1965). Toward a modern theory of rhetoric: A tagmemic contribution. *Harvard Educational Review, 35,* 450-468.

Young, R. E., Becker, A. L., & Pike, K. L. (1970). *Rhetoric: Discovery and change.* New York: Harcourt Brace Jovanovich.

7

The Discourse Status of Commentary

CHAIM RABIN

The writing of commentaries on texts of various kinds is a time-hallowed literary activity, practiced in all or most of the cultures in which writing has played a social role. The close connection of the commentary to the commentatum is in many cases made visible by writing the commentaries on the margin or below the text, or even between the lines.

That a commentary is in a way a text in itself is suggested by the fact that there are commentaries on commentaries ("supercommentaries"), as well as by the less frequent appearance of commentaries as texts or books. However, when the sections of text commented upon appear in the supercommentary they are marked off by some conventional sign, just as when short comments appear within the commentatum text they are marked off by signs.[1] The most extreme form of such a commentary is the dictionary, which might be defined as a list of words and phrases, each of which is commented upon, whether in the same language or in another language; the comments varying from bare (more or less) synonymous words or phrases to grammatical, stylistic, or historical statements.[2] As in these cases the commentatum is most probably not produced for its own sake but for the purpose of commenting upon it. This offers us a chance to analyze the relation of the two sets of elements: The purpose of the dictionary is to answer the question "What is the meaning (translation, history, etymology) of the word x?" and the headword is a conventional abbreviation of the implied question as "x," which is thus an ellipsis resolved by our knowledge of the world.

The identification of question and answer as part of the same discourse and connected by cohesion and coherence is too well known a part of discourse analysis to require elaboration. But we must note that in the dictionary the question has not been put by the actual user of the dictionary before the latter was written; the list of headwords is produced by the author according to principles he has adopted, such as a limitation on the number of words and omission of less common words, slang expressions, provincialisms, or simply words the author disapproved of. Moreover, many dictionary writers give only meanings they consider as belonging to "correct language" or to a certain sociolect, thereby rejecting the use of certain meanings as well as of certain words. We call such statements or nonstatements "normative,"[3] but the very fact that the user has to open at the headword in order to know the author's normative opinions would probably be interpreted by the author as an implied question "Is word or meaning x allowed?" Whereas the usual answer provided in the dictionary is an explanation for information, the normative answer is designed to influence, to deal with something not contained in the word itself but in the social context in which the act of commenting takes place. The author of another normative dictionary may claim the same word to be correct or elegant, while someone who would in an explicative dictionary give a different meaning would have to prove its truth.

Explanation of the meaning of words or phrases is not restricted to alphabetic dictionaries. In the Middle Ages, the words of the Hebrew Bible were sometimes written in a column in the order in which they appear in the text, and in a parallel column the same words, in the grammatical form in which they were in the text, were translated into the language of some Jewish community. Word explanations abound in commentaries on the Bible or other ancient texts. Their place may be taken by translations, although these are often annotated where the meaning given may be queried by some readers.

On the other hand, word explanation is only one facet of running commentaries on texts. Other explanations may still be within the bounds of language, such as comments on the structure of a sentence, on stylistic matters, or on the rhetoric of the text. Word explanations in a running commentary easily become discussions of the nature, purpose, or origin of the object or social or religious concept to which the word refers, or the reasons for its mention in the context, or its role in the thought of the author of the text. But commentaries often deal with matters well beyond explanation of text segments, though ostensibly the discussion is attached to a segment of the text. They deal with the situation in which a passage was written, the ideology of the author as shown in the passage, and so on. Another type of commentary, frequent in commentaries on religious texts, draws from the text spiritual and moral conclusions. As is well known, such moral discourse can also be attached to passages in the text which are merely narrative, and even to works which may not have been connected originally with religious exposition.

This brings us to the question of the relation between the text and the comment. To a great extent the problem is not perceived in a dictionary, or even in word explanations in a running commentary, because to the nonlinguist the meaning of a word is a fact; or, in other words, the semantic relation between the headword and the word or words that translate or explain its meaning is either true or untrue, and the commentator is one who "knows" the meanings of words in the language in which the text is written, just as the recipient of the commentary knows the meanings of the words employed in the comment, which are words in his or her own language. A certain sophistication is necessary to realize that in an ancient text the meaning of a word may not be fully known in our time, or even if known it may not have a one-to-one correspondence with the meaning of any word in the language in which the comment is made. Thus the commentator is in need of skills quite different from those that enable us to understand words and sentences in our own language (and this also applies to different periods of the same language). Therefore, whether a word explanation is "simple" (one word explaining another) or "complicated," the contribution of the commentator lies in applying his or her own "universe of discourse" to the text, or, to put it into a more straightforward (though not always more suitable) manner, in bringing his or her knowledge and training into play.

This is also true for comments on subject matter and on religious implications, except that here it is not only knowledge and skill that shape the comment, but also the opinions of the commentator, his or her beliefs on physical and social matters, and, to a certain extent, the commentator's feelings and preconceived attitudes toward the events and characters depicted in the text. It is clear that in these fields the explanations of different commentators, or even of the same commentator at different times, may diverge a great deal more than in word explanation, and the sophistication of the recipient of the commentary would need to be considerably greater. Often the level of reception is determined by the authority of the commentator or by adherence to a method of commentation, such as the mystical or the critical. In such cases there is often not only a dialogue between the commentator and the text, but also an accompanying dialogue between the commentator and his or her faithful public, who value their commentators in proportion to their success in getting from the text more and more information of the kind that specific readership expects.

The dialogue between the commentator and his or her text—or perhaps more truly between the text and the commentator—is paralleled by the phenomenon of "comments" in everyday speech, also called reactions or observations, which has been investigated by Roland Posner.[4] In conversation, a statement or an opinion is often met by the interlocutor(s) with short remarks that, in Posner's formulation, "reveal how the listener processes the newly-absorbed information, and how he relates it to his knowledge and his attitudes." In his book, Posner shows in detail how the comments open up implications of the sentences pronounced by the speaker and lay bare presuppositions shared or not shared by the speaker and his or her listeners.

In analyzing commentaries, we are often brought face to face with the attitude of the commentator to the text or its author and transmitters. This varies from a veneration that leads the commentator to seek significance and wisdom in the smallest items of the text, to a distrust that causes reduced respect for the form in which the text lies before the commentator. This distrust may be distrust of the author, who is believed to lie or to be prejudiced, and thus the commentary has to search for the truth behind the wording of the text. It may also be distrust of the tradition of the text, assuming it to be full of scribal errors or manipulations of "editors," a situation that forces the commentator to carry out extensive emendation before the text becomes commentable. In both these cases, the views of the commentator about the purpose and background of the text becomes predominant, though these views may be based upon other works of the same author, which the commentator (or modern scientific editor) considers in relevant passages to have suffered less from textual corruption.

The status of venerated texts, mainly "holy books," also brings about the phenomenon of inverted commentary, in which a statement is made and then proved by quoting a verse, or an actual event is stated to be the fulfillment of a verse. This implies that the verse, if properly understood, predicts the event or justifies the statement, both of which are linked to the verse by means of an implied commentary on the verse.[5]

An essential feature of commentary is that in many cases more than one explanation is possible. In contrast to a translation, which has to render everything in the source, whether it has a clear meaning allowing of only one rendering (taking into account stylistic varia tion) or can be understood in several different ways, a commentary normally passes over text sections of clear meaning and concentrates upon those whose meaning is not clear or can be understood in different ways. Different meanings, in this connection, may be imputed at the level of word meaning, of word reference (for instance, with regard to proper names), of cohesion and other features of the micro level, or they may be imputed at the macro level of explaining the place a detail holds in the text as a whole. In literary texts, poetry, and religious writings there are layers of meaning, which may result in different explanations being offered. Finally, a written text may be punctuated in different ways, especially in early texts that originally had no punctuation signs; and in the earlier stages of Semitic languages in which vowels are not indicated, the same text may be interpreted with different vocalization. Though languages have ways of indicating which elements in a sentence are stressed, stress may be shown only by intonation, which is unmarked in the written text.[6]

In what follows, illustrations of the various aspects of commentary are quoted from the work on the Hebrew Bible of a "canonized" commentator, Rashi (abbreviation of Rabbi Shelomoh Yitzchaqi, Troyes, Eastern France, ca. 1040-1105). He is considered a straightforward commentator, who gives the simple, realistic meaning (*pěshat*) of the text.[7] Let us first consider some explanations of words.

Genesis 48:8 9: "And Israel beheld Joseph's sons, and said, Who are these? And Joseph said unto his father, They are my sons, whom God hath given me *in this*." The Hebrew word translated "in this" (*ba-zeh*) means in several passages "here." Rashi comments: "He showed him the betrothal document and the marriage document," Joseph thereby proving that they were conceived in a legally valid marriage (and also probably implying that their mother had accepted the Jewish faith). Rashi's interpretation assigns a reference to the demonstrative pronoun, and understands the preposition *b-* in its alternative meaning "with," "by means of."

Genesis 42:22: "And Reuben answered them saying, Spake I not unto you, saying, Do not sin against the child [i.e., Joseph], and ye would not hear? Therefore *also* his blood is required." Rashi quotes a midrashic maxim, "the particle *gam* ("also") implies additional items," and explains: "His [Joseph's] blood and also the blood of the old man [our father] is to be avenged." Here again an ostensibly superfluous particle is given a reference.

Genesis 13:6: "And the land was not able to bear them, that they might dwell together." Rashi: "It was unable to supply pasturage to their flocks. And this is an elliptic phrase, and requires adding the word *pasturage* (which is masculine gender, as opposed to *land*, which is feminine), and for that reason *was not able* takes the masculine form of the verb." According to Rashi, ellipsis is also implied in Genesis 45:3: "And his brothers could not answer him, for they were troubled by him." *By him* is a common preposition literally meaning "from his face." Rashi's explanation "by shame" (Hebrew *mippeney ha-bushah*) supplies a reference for the pronoun, perhaps under the influence of the phrase *bosheth panim*, literally, "shame of the face."

Exegetical utilization of a common alternative construction, by which a noun and its apposition can have a preposition either once, with the headword, or twice, provides a commentary to Genesis 32:7, 12 (in A.V. 6, 11): "We came to thy brother to Esau. . . . Deliver me, I pray thee, from the hand of my brother, from the hand of Esau"; Rashi explains in both cases that Esau does not behave like a brother, but like "the wicked Esau," thus separating the phrase into two concepts.

Genesis 27:19: Jacob replies to his father's question "Who art thou, my son?" with a sentence which would normally be understood as "I am Esau, thy firstborn." Rashi, however, interprets it: "I, Esau is thy firstborn," and thus avoids imputing a lie to Jacob. In verse 24 Isaac asks: "Art thou my son Esau?" (where *thou* is emphasized by adding *this*), and Jacob answers "I," which Rashi explains: "He did not say, I am Esau, but only "I am." Thus, according to Rashi's image of Jacob's character, he did not utter a lie, though his behavior was likely to deceive his father. Here the commentary is based on the structure of the Hebrew nominal clause, in which the concept "is" is expressed by zero, so that the Hebrew sequence $I + Esau + thy$ *firstborn*, can be analyzed as "I am Esau, thy firstborn" or as "It's me. Esau is thy firstborn." and I can be taken as an elliptic form either of "I (am Esau)" or of "It's me (Jacob, and not Esau)."

Exodus 3:14: In reply to Moses' question "What is his name? What shall I say unto them?" God says, "I am that I am." This much-discussed reply is explained by Rashi: "I am with them in this trouble just as I will be with them in the oppression by other nations."[8] Rashi explains God's reply as referring to the connection between God and the people of Israel, the two actants mentioned in the passage immediately before the reply. The verb *hayah* can function as either an intransitive "exist" or the copula "be." Rashi's comment assumes that it is here the copula with omission of the implied predicative "with them" (i.e., "with the people") which can be reconstructed from the context. Note that the Biblical Hebrew "imperfect"[9] refers both to the present and the future, so that the translation given is within the range of meaning of the form: "I am . . . I will be." The words "in the oppression of other nations" (literally, "the rest of the kingdoms") are inserted from the "knowledge of the world" of the medieval theory of Jewish history. The words "just as" are not explicit in Rashi's text, which has the word *asher* as in the Biblical text, and the rendering given here is in a way a commentary upon Rashi, but is justified by the appearance of *asher* by itself in the meanings of its compound conjunctions, in this case *ka'asher* "like when, as." Possibly Rashi actually intended the use of *asher* as relative particle (also called in Hebrew grammars "relative pronoun"), as it is understood in the A.V. rendering "I am that I am," thus: "I am with them in this trouble the same one as will be with them when other nations will oppress them."

Assumptions about implication also account for the following two examples. Genesis 7:2: "[And the Lord said unto Noah . . .] Of every clean beast thou shalt take to thee seven and seven." Rashi: "Clean. That which will in future be clean for the Israelites; he thus teaches us to know that Noah studied the Torah." Both in the Noah story and in Deuteronomy 14:11, 20, the word *tahor*, here translated "clean," is used of animals and birds that Jews are allowed to eat. The knowledge of the world of Rashi and of his midrashic source implies that the permitted and forbidden animals are specified in the Pentateuch but were not known in the time of Noah. Noah must therefore have gotten the specifications from studying the Torah, which according to midrashic lore was created before the creation of the world and formed the object of studying in the "houses of learning" of the various generations of the ancestors of the people of Israel. In spite of this study, it is assumed that the Torah laws were not incumbent upon the generations before the revelation on Mt. Sinai, although another view claims that nevertheless Abraham, Isaac, and Jacob kept all those laws. The Genesis text thus raises a question in the mind of the reader, which Rashi has attempted to answer.

Genesis 45:27: "And they told him all the words of Joseph, which he had said unto them, and when he saw the ⁽agaloth which Joseph had sent to carry him, the spirit of Jacob, their father, revived. And Israel said, It is enough! Joseph, my son, is still alive." Rashi: "All the words of Joseph. He gave them a hint, showing with what he (Joseph or Jacob) had been occupied when he (Joseph) had left him, namely the chapter concerning the heifer (⁽eglah) whose neck is broken; that is what is meant by 'he saw the ⁽agaloth which Joseph had sent him', and the text does not say 'which Pharoah had sent him.'" The ⁽agaloth in this text are clearly not heifers but wagons, which Pharaoh had ordered Joseph to take from Egypt to transport the women and children as well as their aged father (verse 19). Rashi makes no remark on this same word in v. 19, and clearly is fully aware that these were wagons. According to Rashi and his midrashic sources the similiarity of the words for "wagon" (⁽agalah) and "heifer" (⁽eglah) aroused in Jacob's mind (and in Joseph's) the association with the fact that when Jacob sent Joseph on his fateful errand to his brothers, Jacob or Joseph had been studying the passage in Deuteronomy 21 that states that if a corpse has been found between two cities then the men of the nearer town break the neck of a heifer as witness that they are innocent of the murder committed within their territory. Because the place they had reached in their study that day was known only to Jacob and Joseph, this allusion was enough for Jacob to be convinced that it was Joseph who sent for him to come, and hence Jacob's spirit revived. The implied question is, Why was it just the wagons that convinced Jacob that Joseph was alive, when so many other things were sent?

Exodus 3:15: "Thus shalt thou say unto the children of Israel: The Lord, the God of your fathers . . . hath sent me unto you; this is my name for ever." Rashi: "This is my name forever. 'Forever' is written without w (le⁽olam is spelled $l⁽lm$, not the usual $l⁽wlm$), so as to say ha⁽limehu 'conceal it', namely, that the name should not be pronounced as it is spelled." The English rendering *the Lord* represents the tetragrammaton, the name of God that must never be pronounced, except by the High Priest on the Day of Atonement at a central ceremony.[10] The problems that faced the commentator were, first, that the real name of the Deity (the vowels of the tetra-grammaton) would hardly have been revealed to the entire commu-nity, since it was meant to be a secret; second, that it makes no sense in the context of Jewish religion to say that god will forever bear the same name. The word *ʿolam*, "eternity," is in the Pentateuch always spelled *ʿwlm*, with the *w* indicating a back-vowel, *o* or *u*. The combina-tion *le-ʿolam*, "forever," is spelled in the Pentateuch nine times without the *w* and only twice with the *w*; there is therefore nothing unusual in its spelling in our verse. Still, it offers the commentator a solution for both of the problems; namely, to see in it a form of the verb *ʿlm*, "to be hidden" (which in all probability is not etymologically related to *ʿolam*), and thus to make *lʿlm* state that the pronunciation of the tetragrammaton is hidden, and must be neither performed nor communicated.[11]

It is, of course, no new discovery that commentaries attempt to solve the difficulties found in texts. What we hope to have shown here is that those difficulties are not physical facts of the text, but result from disturbances in the communicative contact between the text and the reader. The reader approaches the text with certain "expectations"[12] based on social and communicative norms as to the form of a written text and its ways of transmitting a message. These expectations differ between cultures and change with times, and are probably also dependent on social class and level of education.[13] If the expectations of the listener or reader are not met, he does not understand the text; he may understand the words, but not the message. In conversation, the problem is solved by comments—remarks or questions—which cause the speaker to repeat his state-ment, or parts of it, in different formulations or with additions, to clarify what was said before. If the speaker is successful, this will be because he or she has grasped the differences between the listener's presuppositions and his or her own, and has realized which words in the statement are likely to be taken in meanings different from those that were intended.

In the case of a text, especially a text of some antiquity, the place of the speaker is taken by the commentator. This is a person who shares the expectations and presuppositions of his own society and period, and at the same time has the skill of applying them to another way of expression through long experience with texts of that culture or period or by trained intuition. He knows where to ask questions, but also gives the clarifications that ideally the author might have given if he or she had lived in the readers' ambience. In this way, we may claim, the commentary becomes continuous with the text, in the same manner as an answer is continuous with the question that occasioned it, and the speaker's clarification is continuous (in the sense of being one text) with both the listener's remark or query and with the speaker's own original statement. There is cohesion, anaphora to elements of the source text; as well as coherence, the same text elements appearing in both; and often the language of the commentary repeats grammatical elements that are alien to the language of the commentator's period (e.g., *asher* in Rashi on Exodus 3:14).

In the light of what has been said here about the changes in expectations in different generations and different climates, it is only natural that each period and each branch of Jewry has produced different commentaries on the Bible. These differ not only in the answers they provide, but also in the questions they ask; details of the text that passed without notice in an earlier commentary were discussed in later ones, and vice versa. From the commentaries we can learn a great deal as to how each period and school understood the structure of the Biblical Hebrew language: Rashi's Biblical grammar has been reconstructed from his commentaries, and the commentators of the Arabic-speaking countries, especially of medieval Spain, systematized their approach in extensive grammar books, just as a great deal of what now appears in scientific grammars of Biblical Hebrew has its origin in the work of modern critical commentators. By noticing the selection of problems with which a commentator deals, and the ways he or she deals with them, we can learn about the commentator's own world; and if he or she writes this commentary in Hebrew, we can learn about the state of the development of that language in the commentator's own time and country. Rashi, again, has been the subject of a series of volumes by the late Yitzchak Avinery, who discovered in the prose of Rashi's commentaries on the Bible and the Talmud some features that are still, or again, found in contemporary spoken Hebrew in Israel.

No doubt also in commentary literatures in other languages and cultures new insights might be gained by research on the relation between commentaries and their texts. The suggestions put forward in this chapter are only a small sample of what could be discovered by further research in this field.

NOTES

1. For example, the "gloss-wedge" which in the second millennium B.C. Akkadian cuneiform tablets marked off vernacular explanations of Akkadian words.

2. This excludes from our discussion encyclopedias or lists of technical terms with definitions, as these do not explain the words, but the subject matter.

3. The word "normative" is used here in its prescriptive sense of "language improvement," "normative grammar," and not in the descriptive sense of "social norm."

4. See *Theorie des Kommentierens: Eine Grundlagenstudie zur Semantik und Pragmatik.* (2nd ed.) Wiesbaden: Athenaion, 1980.

5. For example, the New Testament in Matthew 1:23 (where the Hebrew word *ʿalmah* is understood as "virgin," and not, as in the Jewish interpretation of Isaiah 7:14, as "young woman") and in Matthew 3:3, "A voice of one that crieth in the wilderness, Prepare ye the way of the Lord," as against the accents in the Hebrew Bible, "A voice crieth, In the wilderness prepare ye the way of the Lord" (compare the parallelism, "Make straight in the desert a high way for our God").

6. Posner gives 18 possible interpretations of the written sentence "Beate slaps Kurt's face," with different intonations and/or implications.

7. For the convenience of readers unfamiliar with Jewish Bible commentaries, I have chosen my examples from those selected by Chaim Pearl (*Rashi,* New York: Norton, 1970), but in my own translation, except where noted.

8. Pearl's translation (1970, p. 89; see note 7).

9. This is a term borrowed from Slavonic linguistics to characterize the Hebrew prefix tense (often called "future") as durative aspect.

10. The letters of the tetragrammaton—Y, H, W, H—are mostly pronounced as *adonay,* "my Lord," a name also written frequently with its own consonants, and the source of the Greek *ho kyrios,* English *the Lord.* This way of reading the tetragrammaton is indicated in Hebrew Bibles by providing it with the vowel signs *e, o, a,* which resulted in non-Jewish circles in erroneous readings such as *Jehovah.*

11. In his explanation, Rashi employs the imperative with the pronominal suffix of the verb in its causative form, a realization that does not fit *lʿm.* It is not clear what verbal or nominal form the spelling represents in Rashi's theory.

12. This is meant here in the technical meaning of the term *Erwartung* in German studies on pragmatics and on conversation analysis.

13. This has been the rationale of the *Good News Bible* ("God's Message to Modern Man") and similar projects in other Western languages.

8

Cognitive Models
and Discourse Analysis

CARL H. FREDERIKSEN

The goal of cognitive studies of written discourse is to describe how meaning and language structures are constructed by a writer and interpreted by a reader. Such a description includes a specification of the meaning and language structures, called "representations," that writers and readers construct and the rules upon which these representations are based. To achieve such a description, cognitive psychologists and researchers in the field of artificial intelligence have constructed models of cognitive representation of language and meaning. These models are used to describe cognitive processes in text comprehension and production. In experimental research on comprehension and production, the models also are used as tools for analyzing texts read or produced by subjects in the research. These methods of discourse analysis are motivated by an interest in uncovering procedures writers or readers use in discourse communication, and the cognitive representations they construct. This chapter describes cognitive models of discourse representations and illustrates how they are being applied in current research on student comprehension and writing.

In an effort to understand the process of generating, expressing, and communicating meaning, cognitive scientists have concentrated until very recently on text comprehension. Before the early 1970s, when cognitive studies of discourse comprehension became a prin-

Author's Note: The research reported in this chapter was supported by the Natural Science and Engineering Council of Canada. Many of the ideas presented in the essay were influenced by discussions with students and colleagues. These contributions are gratefully acknowledged.

cipal focus in cognitive psychology, the prevailing psycholinguistic model of discourse comprehension was an interpretive one in which text comprehension was viewed principally as a process of extracting meanings from sentences. In the early 1970s, following ideas originally presented by Bartlett (1932), an alternative constructive model was proposed in which meaning was viewed as constructed by a reader by means of contextual inferences (Bransford & Franks, 1971; Frederiksen, 1975). From experimental work designed to demonstrate the constructive nature of text comprehension emerged the notion of semantic memory representations that are related to but independent of language codes (Frederiksen, 1975; Kintsch, 1974). Thus, a major distinction was made between semantic (i.e., propositional) structures in memory and linguistic structures, and evidence accumulated supporting the importance of propositional representations in comprehension. Furthermore, semantic or propositional models and methods of propositional analysis provided tools for studying the inferences subjects make in comprehending texts (Frederiksen, 1977, 1981, 1984; Tierney & Mosenthal, 1982).

To account for the presence of large numbers of inferred propositions in subjects' text recalls, these inferences were linked, first, to text propositions (the so-called "text base"; Kintsch, 1974; Kintsch & van Dijk, 1978) and text properties ascribed to the text base such as order and topical organization (Kintsch, 1974; Meyer, 1975). The inferences were also linked to preexisting knowledge structures, called "schemata" (Rumelhart, 1980), "frames" (Minsky, 1975), or "scripts" (Schank & Abelson, 1977), that the reader brings to the comprehension task. In both of these approaches, "text-based" and "knowledge-based" theories, the assumption was that discourse comprehension involves high level conceptual structures called "macrostructures" as well as propositions that represent the literal meaning of sentences. The two theories differ in their view of how the reader constructs a macrostructure from a propositional text base.

In the text-based approach, comprehension is regarded as a process of applying inferential operations, "macrorules," or strategies that enable a reader to reduce, summarize, or elaborate a text's propositional content and thereby create a discourse macrostructure (van Dijk & Kintsch, 1984). Tasks that are usually cited as providing examples of text-based processes are creating summaries, titling essays, and writing a précis. In text-based theories, comprehension is particularly sensitive to the internal coherence and topical organization of texts. This approach has difficulty accounting for inferences that depart from the text, involving selective processing, prior knowledge, and the like.

Knowledge-based models avoid this problem by treating comprehension as a process of fitting text information into preexisting semantic structures in memory (frames, schemata). Experimental demonstrations have shown that comprehension can depend on having preexisting knowledge available in memory or on expectations related to prior knowledge of a text's content or typical structure (e.g., Anderson & Ortony, 1975; Mandler & Johnson, 1977; Stein & Glenn, 1979). However, schema theories have difficulty accounting for how one understands texts that convey new information or that have an atypical or complex form. The major problem for theories of text comprehension emphasized in constructive theories (Spiro, 1980) is not addressed, that is, how one used text as a source of new learning and knowledge.

A number of investigators recently have been studying procedures and rules that enable a reader to build cognitive representations for texts that convey new information. Collins, Brown, and Larkin (1980) studied readers' problem solving as they tried to interpret a particularly difficult ambiguous text; from this they argued that the structure-generating inferences they observed in their subjects are a general feature of comprehension. Trabasso and his colleagues (Trabasso & Sperry, 1985; van den Broek & Trabasso, 1985) have been examining inferences subjects make concerning causal relationships among events in story narratives. Bruce (1980, 1983; Bruce & Newman, 1978) has been studying readers' inferences concerning characters' plans that motivate characters' actions in stories, arguing that many stories require such inferences to be understood. In my work, I have been studying the comprehension of expository and fictional texts that convey different kinds of semantic information: narrative event structures, plans, problems, conversational structures, descriptions, procedures, and explanations. In all of this work, I study particular types of semantic representations that consist of "atomic" units of a given kind (such as events in narratives) and semantic relations that link these units together to form node-link networks called "frames." Readers are assumed to possess rules for forming such structures that they apply in making inferences during comprehension. This "rule-based" approach makes the definition of models of semantic structure and discourse analysis procedures based on them more rigorous.

MULTILEVEL MODELS OF
COGNITIVE REPRESENTATION OF DISCOURSE

There is now general agreement among cognitive researchers, supported by experimental evidence, that there are multiple levels and types of representations underlying discourse (Figure 8.1). All major theories distinguish between *conceptual* or *semantic* structures that represent the structures of meaning and knowledge expressed in texts and understood by readers or listeners, and the *textual* language structures used to encode and communicate meanings. Conceptual structures are not specific to language, but are assumed to provide the means by which knowledge acquired from both linguistic and nonlinguistic sources is represented in memory. Textual structures are assumed to reflect an individual's knowledge of language structure and to provide resources for encoding and transmitting knowledge (Frederiksen, Frederiksen, & Bracewell, 1985).

Theories also distinguish between levels within textual and conceptual representations. Texts are assumed to be structured at two levels: at the clausal/sentence level and at the level of sequences of clauses that are related by means of text-level linguistic devices such as cohesion (e.g., anaphoric expressions, conjunctions, and ellipsis; Halliday & Hasan, 1976), topicalization (patterning in topic-comment structures; Clements, 1976; Grimes, 1975), thematic units (e.g, fields of discourse), and coherence relations (Charolles, 1983; Hobbs, 1979). The latter two aspects of textual structure pertain as well to semantic representations. Conceptual/semantic representations are assumed to be at two levels as well: a propositional level representing fine-grained semantic structures (propositions) that are encoded within and between clauses (Frederiksen, 1975; van Dijk & Kintsch, 1984), and high-level semantic representations, referred to as "frames" or "schemata," that represent particular kinds of semantic-network structures that may be represented declaratively as propositions (Minsky, 1975).

Figure 8.1 depicts these levels of semantic and textual representations as they are assumed to be interrelated. These interrelations among types and levels (indicated by arrows in the figure) may be viewed in two ways: in terms of cognitive operations involved in the text production process, and formally in terms of functions mapping between representations. Mapping functions are procedures that are assumed to operate in discourse processing. Viewed in terms of mapping functions, frames are functions of propositions (i.e., there is a many-to-one mapping from sets of propositions to the frame structures they represent); and propositions are functions of clauses (i.e., there is a many-to-one mapping from sets of clauses to the propositions they encode). Other functional relations between representations are assumed to be indirect—that is, they are mediated by other representations—with one exception. As indicated in Figure 8.1, we have been exploring the hypothesis that text-level linguistic structures are used by writers to signal high-level conceptual frame structures to a reader (Frederiksen et al., 1985). As a mapping function this would imply that text structure is a function of frame structure as well as a function of clause structure.

Beyond this general schematization, theories of representation proposed within this framework need to be examined in terms of the details of their definitions and the functions linking them to one another. Only then can the discourse analysis systems based on them be understood and evaluated. This chapter will focus on semantic representations, since research linking semantic to clausal and text-level linguistic structures is less well developed. In particular, I will consider propositional and frame-level representations, and methods of semantic discourse analysis based on them (i.e., propositional analysis and frame analysis). While the emphasis in this chapter is on models of semantic representation and the discourse analysis systems based on them, these models are motivated by an interest in applying them in research on text comprehension and production. Some of these applications are described in the last section.

GENERAL CHARACTERISTICS OF SEMANTIC MODELS

Virtually all models of semantic representation proposed by cognitive psychologists employ the notation of semantic networks. Semantic networks were first introduced into psychology as models of semantic memory structure (Quillian, 1968) where they replaced earlier associative memory models. Semantic networks were used later in models for the representation of semantic knowledge underlying language and discourse comprehension (Anderson & Bower, 1973; Frederiksen, 1975; Rumelhart & Norman, 1975; Schank,

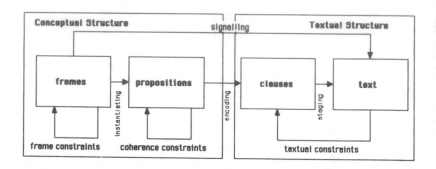

Figure 8.1   Multilevel Representations of Cognitive Structures for Text

1972). Propositional (i.e., predicate-argument) forms of representation have also been used in models of meaning in memory underlying language (Kintsch, 1974), and their equivalence to semantic network structures has been recognized. It also has been established that other proposed representations in cognitive theories may be expressed as special cases of semantic network structures (Palmer, 1978). Semantic networks, therefore, are powerful data structure representations—mathematical formalisms—that can be used to express theories of representation of semantic memory structures. However, a semantic network is not in itself a theory of representation.

To see how theories of semantic representation are specified using semantic networks, we first need to review some general properties of semantic networks as data structures. First, a semantic network is defined as a data structure composed of two kinds of entities: nodes and relational links that connect pairs of nodes. The nodes in the network are identified by labels specifying their semantic content (usually concept identifiers or pointers to items in a lexicon), and relations are labeled by relation names indicating the type of link they establish between nodes. Semantic networks also allow embedding of one network in another by permitting a node to contain a pointer to another semantic network. Network structures of various kinds are composed of specific patterns of node-link structures.

To define a particular representational model as a semantic network requires: (a) defining all relations in the network (this usually involves restrictions on the types of nodes that can be linked), (b)

specifying the entities (concepts, for example) assigned to nodes in the network, and (c) specifying rules (procedures) by which all structures in the network can be defined. The first two requirements define the content of entities represented in the network, and the last defines the form of structures that can be represented. An examination of existing theories of representation in psychology indicates that theories of representation often have been defined inadequately. Lack of an adequately precise definition of a representation is particularly serious if a discourse analysis system is to be based on it. By specifying definitions of relations, a structured lexicon, and rules for forming structures, particular types of semantic networks can be defined and tested as models of cognitive representation. Any proposal concerning models of cognitive representation can be evaluated by examination in terms of the above requirements.

Current theories of semantic representation have proposed representational models at the propositional level (Frederiksen, 1975; Kintsch, 1974) and at higher levels of semantic representation called "frames" or "schemata" (Minsky, 1975). Models of propositional structure specify "fine-grained" semantic relations that are closely linked to semantic structures encoded in sentences and that are fundamental to representing states, events and other basic semantic structures expressed in language. Particular models may adopt a propositional notation consisting of a predicate and a sequence of labeled argument slots, or a semantic network notation. Since the two representations are equivalent, the term "propositional" has come to refer to this particular level of semantic representation and not to the particular choices of formalism. Researchers employ the predicate-argument notation because it facilitates representing structures at various levels, and embedding propositions within slots.

Beyond defining propositional representations as one type of semantic network structure in memory, there have been efforts to define other semantic representations, characterized as frames or schemata. Minsky (1975) and others (e.g., Bobrow & Norman, 1975; Rumelhart, 1980) have discussed general properties of frame structures relevant to how they can be matched to input information. In frame theory, the notion was introduced that nodes in a semantic network can contain variables. Although these may have certain standard "default" values, input information (e.g., from a text) can be used to replace these standard values with new ones. Frame theories of text comprehension presuppose preexisting semantic frame structures in a reader's or listener's memory that have these properties. These structures are then matched to texts by processes of assigning symbolic values to variables in the structure. As theories of representation, frame theories do not specify rules for defining particular types of semantic network structures. Rather, they depend on the specification of particular instances of frame structures. Once a frame structure has been specified, it becomes a model for comprehension that is tested by seeing if it predicts aspects of subjects' comprehension (e.g., inferred propositions in recall).

Thus, frame theory may be viewed as a general framework for proposing and elaborating theories of semantic representation, serving as a formalism for describing cognitive representations. This framework calls attention to certain properties relevant to procedures that act on frames to enable their use in understanding texts. Since semantic networks are extremely powerful and therefore generally applicable formalisms, they do not in and of themselves constitute a theory of representation. The specification of a representational model would therefore have to involve specification of rules for forming particular structures defined as a type of semantic network. Such a model would be a rule-based model. In additional to the work to be described in this chapter, there has been work attempting to specify rules for forming particular types of frame structures. Examples of frame types that have been described are plans (Bruce, 1980), procedures (Dixon, 1982; Graesser, Hoffman, & Clark, 1980), episodes (Schank & Abelson, 1977), event chains (Trabasso & Nichols, 1978), and story schemata (Rumelhart, 1975).

In the models of propositional and frame representation I will describe, rules for forming structures are defined by means of a formalism developed in computer science for defining the syntax of programming languages (Wirth, 1976). In this formalism, known as a "BNF grammar," rules for forming structures are specified as production rules that specify how a particular symbol is composed of other symbols. Production rules may be recursive in the sense that a particular structure may "call" itself; in other words, contain a structure of the same kind embedded within it. A BNF grammar is appealing because of its simplicity and power and is formally equivalent to a procedure for parsing or producing structures (a recursive transition network) and to a context free (type 2) grammar (Winograd, 1983). In the models to be described all relational primitives are explicitly defined as well, as are aspects of concepts relevant to their incorporation into the semantic network. Representations are described at two levels: propositional structure and frame-level structure.

COGNITIVE DISCOURSE ANALYSIS

In cognitive psychology, semantic models were developed as theories of the cognitive representation of texts by readers or writers and not primarily as methods for the analysis of texts. The validity of these models is tested in experimental studies of discourse comprehension and production. If a model leads to predictions concerning discourse behavior that are confirmed, then those aspects of the model that led to the predictions are empirically supported. However, models of semantic representation are also the basis for discourse analysis procedures that are used in analyzing texts in experimental research. These analyses provide an important link in testing cognitive models of text representation. Because cognitive models are used as a basis for analyzing discourse, their ability to represent texts is an important though often ignored consideration in the methodology of cognitive studies of discourse. This section examines this problem in terms of measurement theory (Palmer, 1978), viewing discourse analysis as establishing a functional mapping from a text to a semantic model of the text. Viewed in these terms, a discourse analysis procedure is evaluated in terms of the quality of the mapping from text to model.

Figure 8.2 depicts the role of discourse analysis in the experimental study of text comprehension and writing. The top half of the figure represents the discourse communication process that is the object of investigation. In discourse communication, a writer constructs a cognitive representation of meaning and produces a text that expresses this meaning. A reader constructs a cognitive representation on the basis of this text (and other relevant sources of knowledge such as context or prior knowledge). The bottom half of the figure illustrates the use of semantic models as tools for studying the cognitive meaning structures of readers and writers, and as tools for analyzing texts. As cognitive structures cannot be observed directly, they must be inferred from some application of a semantic model to the analysis of text: either that presented to a reader or that produced by a reader or writer. For example, a reader's cognitive representation of text may be inferred by analyzing his or her recall of the text against a semantic analysis of the text; or a writer's discourse production may be analyzed in terms of models of semantic representation in order to study individual differences and effects of experimental (e.g., instructional) variables on the semantic structures produced. Thus discourse analysis is a *methodology* used to investigate cognitive theories of representation and processing of text. The models employed, however, are not tested directly but rather by means of experiments that investigate their adequacy as models of cognitive representation. In carrying out such experimental tests, a subject's knowledge structure is inferred from models of text structure.

A discourse analysis procedure may be viewed as a function mapping from an object in the world—a text—to one or more representing models. To be satisfactory as a methodology, a discourse analysis procedure must meet the following three criteria. First, the model on which it is based must be well defined. Second, the representation of a text produced by the discourse analysis must preserve relations that hold among elements of the text by linking them appropriately. Third, the functions specifying how semantic structures can be represented in text must be clearly specified. For example, if the representation is intended to define propositions, possible propositional structures must be specified by means of rules, relations among text segments that reflect propositional structure must be preserved (e.g., case relations, embedding), and language structures used to encode a particular propositional structure must be identified. Such a system of representation would satisfy the formal requirements of a measurement system (Palmer, 1978). We may refer to any such well-defined system of representation as a discourse analysis system. In the discussion of models of semantic representation which follows, attention is given both to the models themselves and to the discourse analysis procedures based on them.

Propositional Analysis

A number of reasons can be given for postulating a propositional level of semantic representation (van Dijk & Kintsch, 1984). First, there is a need for basic declarative structures representing semantic relationships and units that are expressed and manipulated in language. Such structures ought to reflect all semantic distinctions

Represented States

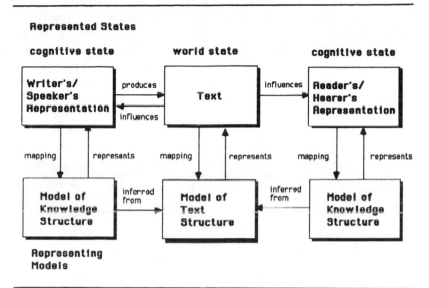

Figure 8.2   Models of Cognitive Representation in Research on Discourse Processing

marked in any language and be independent of the syntax of particular languages. Second, to account for such cognitive abilities as hypothetical and deductive reasoning based on evaluating the truth value of propositions, it is necessary to posit some semantic units having truth values associated with them. Third, expression and manipulation of language in written and oral discourse production, as well as characteristics of units of memory for semantic meaning structures, strongly suggest the need for chunks of semantic information that are independently manipulable structures. These psychological considerations suggest that there is a propositional level of semantic representation in the processing of text that has these properties.

The syntax (BNF grammar) defining the propositional representation used in our research on text comprehension and production is given in Appendix A. This grammar consists of 88 production rules that are organized hierarchically and that define the internal structure of propositions of various kinds. Thus Production Rule P1 states that a proposition consists of an identifying label (an identifying number in our system), a content, a truth value, and, optionally, tense, aspect, and modality information. (In the extended BNF notation of Wirth [1976], the curly brackets { } enclose symbols that may occur zero or arbitrarily many times; the angular brackets < > contain names for structures which, if they are not identifiers, are themselves defined by production rules, and : := indicates that a symbol is replaced with the structure to the right.) Thus every proposition has associated with it one or more truth values (given by P6), and truth values may be modified by means of one or more modals (given by P4 and P5: qualification, necessity (root), ability (can), and conditionality). The content of a proposition is specified by Production Rule P3 (the vertical bar denotes selection of one of the symbols). Thus a proposition may represent a state, an event, an algebraic relation (representing relative attributes, time, location, and so on), a dependency relation (representing relations such as causality, conditionality, and logical if, that make one proposition depend on another), identity, and propositional relations (relations specifying properties of entire propositions).

Each of these structures is specified by its own production rules. For example, stative structures are specified by P7 to consist of an object (a type of concept) and a state argument that indicates the kind of stative information specified for the object. These are given by P19 as category, part, theme, attribute, locative, temporal, duration, and number relations. The structure of events is given by production rules P38-P55: Events consist of an act (a type of concept), a case frame (given by P40 and P50) that depends on whether the act is processive (describes a process) or resultive (describes a causal system having a result), and relational arguments describing (i.e., identifying) properties of the act (these "adverbial" relations are identical to those applicable to objects, as given in P19-P31). The structure of algebraic relations is given by Production Rules P56-P64: Algebraic relations link variables (which may be represented by propositions or concepts, namely, P64) by relations of equivalence, order, and so on applied to different types of properties (such as attributes, locations, and times). Algebraic relations represent semantic structures underlying comparative structures in language. The internal structure of dependency relations is given by P65-P70: A dependency relation may be binary (linking two propositions: P65 and P66), or it may be conjoint (linking two or more propositions: P65 and P68). Binary dependency relations are given by P67: causality, conditionality, logical if, and logical if and only if; conjoint dependency relations are given by P69: and, exclusive or, and alternating or (and/or). Other types of content structures of propositions are identity relations (P71-P72) that specify the identity of concepts or propositions, and propositional relations (P73) that enable identifying relations to attach properties to propositions. The latter are important to the analysis of abstract language in which words refer to propositions rather than types of concepts (i.e., objects, acts attributes, locations, times, durations, degrees, or numbers; see P74).

Relational primitives in the propositional representation occur as upper case labels in these production rules. Every semantic relation in the model is defined explicitly by identifying the semantic relationship indicated by the label and any restrictions on its arguments (nodes in semantic network notation). For example, a CAT (category) specifies that a class of objects (or actions) is a subset of another category of objects (or actions). Definitions such as these have been developed for every relation in the representation (Frederiksen, 1975). These definitions of relations involve the classification of concepts into the categories given in Production rules P74-P82; these rules make explicit the characteristics of the lexicon that are required by the model.Thus, the propositional representation is explicitly defined according to the criteria indicated in the previous section.

To illustrate the propositional representation and its use in propositional analysis, the propositional representation of the following portion of a text used in one of our experiments on comprehension is given in Appendix B:

The Discovery of Penicillin

(1) Alexander Fleming was at work in his laboratory at Saint Mary's Hospital in London, England. (2) It was a warm day (3) and the windows were open. (4) A dish of disease germs, needed for an experiment, had been left uncovered. (5) It looked like cloudy soup. (6) As Fleming walked by (7) he glanced at the dish. (8) Something caught his eye. (9) He looked again. (10) There was a patch of blue-green Penicillium mold growing on the dish. (11) But—instead of cloudy soup, thick with germs, there was a clear circle all around the mold. (12) All of the germs near the mold were dead!

(13) Fleming knew that this was something important. (14) He scraped off the bit of mold (15) and put it in a dish of its own with some food. (16) The mold plant spread (17) and the blue-green patch grew larger. (18) When it was big enough, (19) Fleming set to work to find out why the mold had killed the germs. (20) After many weeks of difficult experiments, he finally managed to squeeze from the mold a few

drops of brownish fluid. (21) This remarkable fluid was the germ-killer. (22) Fleming named it penicillin.

(23) Penicillin turned out to be a far greater germ-killer than anything ever known before. (24) But it took so long to make even a drop of it! (25) Even though it was surely a valuable drug, (26) Fleming decided that making penicillin was not practical. (27) He went on with his other work.

This text will be used as well to illustrate frame analysis. Examples of stative propositions (see Appendix B) are propositions 1.2, 1.3, 2.0, and 3.0 (i.e., any propositions with an object as predicate followed by one or more identifying relations). Examples of events are: 1.0, 1.1, 4.0, 6.0, and 7.0 (i.e., propositions with an act as predicate followed by a list of case arguments, a % sign [separating case from identifying arguments] and possibly a list of identifying relation arguments). Examples of algebraic relations are 7.1 (representing equivalence in time) and 12.2 (representing proximity of location). Propositions 11.2 and 19.2 are examples of causal (dependency) relations, and proposition 13.1 is an example of an identity. Finally, an example of a propositional relation is proposition 20.0, in which identifying relations specify properties of "experiments," a word referring not to a simple concept, but to an entire event. Tense and aspect relations may be found in many propositions (e.g., propositions 4.0, 9.0, and 10.0). Truth value is marked only if it is not positive. Embedding of one proposition in an argument slot of another occurs frequently in the example (e.g., 13.0, 15.0, 17.0-17.2).

Developing a methodology of propositional analysis on the basis of such a model of propositional representation encounters two main difficulties. First, any realistic propositional representation is necessarily quite complex, including many primitive relations and production rules. A major hurdle is the need to learn the syntax as well as the definitions of semantic relations specified in the representation. However, because the syntax of propositions is explicit, it is possible to develop interactive computer programs to assist propositional analysis by presenting the analyst with menus of choices at different levels in the analysis (as determined by the syntax). Such a program recently has been designed (Groen, Frederiksen, & Dillinger, 1984) and is being implemented using a powerful new programming language for the analysis of texts (Plante, 1985). The second difficulty involves the mapping from text segments (clauses) to propositions. Propositional analysis is model driven; the analyst "semantically parses" a text segment by looking for different types of semantic information specified by the propositional grammar. Decisions start at the top of the BNF syntax: "What type of proposition?" and work down through decisions at increasingly detailed levels of analysis: "What type of case frame?" "What case relations are marked?" For each new component of propositional structure, the analyst must know how that particular type of semantic information can be marked in the language of the text. The variety and irregularity of such marking in English is impressive, and this marking is different for each new language analyzed. At present, we rely on native speakers' intuitions about marking of semantic information, but as we accumulate records of analyzed texts, we hope to catalogue varieties of language devices that are used to mark specific types of semantic information. Such a catalogue also can eventually form the basis for automatic procedures for propositional analysis by computer.

In summary, this propositional analysis procedure has the following characteristics. First, it is based on a well-defined representation. Second, the analysis of propositional structures of text segments is at present based on judgments by native speakers of semantic marking in their language. These judgments can be assisted by providing lists of options for marking particular semantic information. Third, the representation preserves semantic relationships, including chunking of information into independent semantic units, embedding, and case relations, that are reflected in the text. Such relationships can be tested by transforming the text to remove a particular relation and then analyzing the transformed text to verify that the relation disappears from the analysis. As the possibilities for marking propositional relations in text are catalogued, they can be incorporated into interactive computer programs for assisting in or automatically analyzing texts.

Frame Analysis

It has become increasingly clear that propositional representation is essential to account for discourse processing in text comprehension and production, and in discourse analysis, because it facilitates the analysis of higher-level types of semantic structures, namely, frames. Propositions do this by providing a declarative semantic base from which frame-level semantic representations may be derived.

Otherwise, inferential processes (and frame level discourse analysis) would have to link frame representations directly to clausal structures used to express propositions. This would require building many of the characteristics of propositions into frame representations to account for the fine-grained semantic structure of language. This advantage of basing frame analysis on a propositional base structure in discourse processing and discourse analysis was illustrated previously in Figure 8.1. In artificial intelligence, models having several levels of representation are referred to as "hybrid models" (Vilain, 1985).

In view of these arguments, the problem for frame analysis (and frame construction in text comprehension) is this: given a propositional base structure, to identify particular frame-level structures that are represented declaratively by the propositions in the base structure. Frame analysis, like propositional analysis, is based on models of particular types of frame-level semantic networks that specify structures that are represented declaratively as propositions. Frame analysis, therefore, is a mapping from a propositional text base to particular frame structures specified by a frame grammar. For example, one type of frame for which we have developed a frame grammar is the procedural frame. Procedural frames involve entities (nodes) called procedures (actions that can be executed to attain goals). These are linked together by relations such as part-whole, conditionality, and temporal order. Structures that may be composed of such node-link relations are specified by production rules in a "procedural frame grammar." To understand a procedural text, a reader is viewed as using these rules to produce a procedural frame based on a set of propositions; in other words, practicing a kind of semantic parsing.

In frame analysis, the analyst proceeds similarly from a propositional base to a frame structure of a given type. The type of frame structure is defined by a grammar and a specification of types of entities (e.g., procedures) that can occupy nodes in the network. Relations in frame structures are generally subsets of those defined in the propositional representation. In my research, I have been focusing on developing grammars for several types of frame structures that appear to be fundamental to fictional and informative text genres, including children's fiction, folktales, science, technical, and literary texts. These frame structures include the following: narrative frames (representing temporal and spatial structures for sets of definite events); procedural frames (representing the structure of procedures); state descriptive frames (representing descriptions of various types of states of the world, including attribute structures, classifications, part structures, taxonomies, locative structures, numerical structures, and similarity relations); process descriptive frames (representing descriptions of processes in the world including causally and conditionally organized systems); problem frames (representing the structure of problems and procedures for their solution); and conversational frames (representing social interaction structures composed of related turns and conversational acts as they occur in conversational discourse). We have been testing these models as representations in text comprehension and production, and are interested as well in multiple-frame texts and frame interaction in texts and text processing. In what follows, I will illustrate these models and their application to frame analysis with reference to two frame types—narrative and problem frames—describing their frame grammars and illustrating the structures resulting from frame analyses using the text given in the previous section.

Narrative frames represent the organization of sets of events in time and space. Narrative frame structures are relevant to the comprehension and production of most fictional texts and informative texts that relate sequences of events. The nodes in narrative frames consist of definite events or definite events containing other event structures embedded within them. Relations in narrative frames are all defined in the propositional syntax and include the following: order, equivalence and difference in time, dependency relations of causality and conditionality, and relations of relative location.

The syntax of narrative frames is summarized in Figure 8.3. Here syntax graphs are used to summarize a large number of production rules (see Wirth, 1976). Structures in the grammar are labeled in boldface type, and the graph below a label indicates how it is formed out of component structures. Figure 8.3 represents in graph form the topmost part of the narrative frame grammar. The first graph (Figure 8.3) labeled "narrative frame" indicates that a narrative frame is composed of an event structure and (optionally) one or more scene structures. Event structures represent temporal relations among events, and scene structures represent spatial/locative relations. Event structures (see the event structure graph in Figure 8.3) are composed of event chains (temporally ordered event sequences), elapsed time chains (events linked by difference in time relations), and coordinate event chains (events occurring at the same time or during the same time interval). As indicated in the event chain graph, event chains are composed of event nodes linked into chains by time order relations (or linked by time order and dependency relations). Because the grammar can generate many event chains that may have nodes in common, event chains may be interlinked according to branching, converging, and other complex patterns. This is also true for coordinate event chains and elapsed time chains (see the syntax graphs so labeled in Figure 8.3). As may be seen in the event node graph, event nodes consist of events and (optionally) one or more narrative frames embedded in, for instance, a theme or goal slot. This recursive possibility allows for different levels of narrative structure, as when characters' speeches form a first-level structure, and the content of their speech relates a second level of narrative. Thus event structures specify a temporal organization of events relative to one another at different levels such that individual events can be located temporally within the structure.

Scene structures consist of sets of location nodes linked by locative relations indicating proximity, equivalence, or adjacency in location (where a location node consists of an event linked to a location). Thus, like sets on a stage, scenes correspond to contiguous locations at which sets of events take place. The scenes themselves may be related spatially to one another by, for instance, containment, part, and category relations (e.g., a scene may be located within a scene). Scene structures specify a structure of space according to a kind of map in which sets of events occur at different locations on the map.

The narrative frame for "The Discovery of Penicillin" is diagrammed in Figure 8.4. Each event is listed together with its propositions, any event relations, and temporal and locative information. Events ordered in time are connected by directional arrows, events equivalent in time by bidirectional arrows. Sets of time-ordered events are referred to as episodes, and sets of events equivalent in time are referred to as coordinate event sets (CESs). Episodes connected by relations of difference in time (DIFF:TEM) are referred to as episode sequences. In the example, all events (except embedded events) occur at the same location so there is a single scene for this portion of the text.

As a discourse analysis system, narrative frame analysis is based on a well-defined representation (defined by the narrative frame grammar) and the mapping from propositional base structure to narrative frame preserves events and their temporal and spatial relations. Transformations of these properties of the text result in

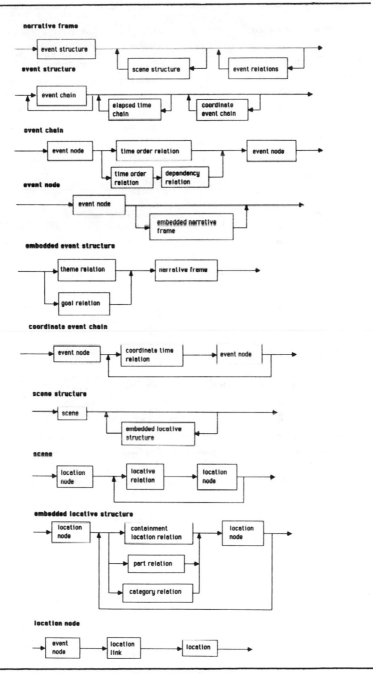

Figure 8.3 Narrative Frame Syntax Graph (Top Levels)

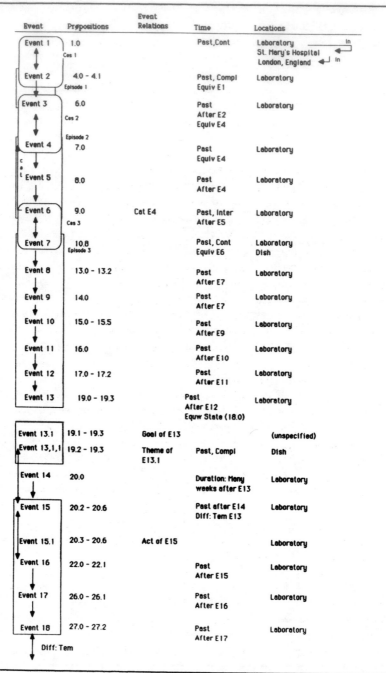

Figure 8.4   Narrative Frame for "The Discovery of Penicillin"

appropriate changes in the narrative frame. Mapping rules for narrative frame analysis were developed by listing discourse structures and conventions used to mark all relations appearing in the grammar. For example, temporal order is given by order of mention with respect to main clause representing last mentioned definite event; "and" (if prior mentioned event is completed or instantaneous); and explicit encoding (e.g., "then," "before," "after"). Equivalence in time is marked by a subordinate clause; "and" if the previously mentioned event is continuous, events with continuous aspect or modality shift; and explicit encoding (e.g., "while"). Difference in time may be marked by shift in time; explicit encoding (e.g., "later"); or an event whose duration implies a shift in time. Event relations are usually given by lexical relations or anaphoric expressions. Embedded events are marked as filling case functions such as theme or goal that are defined in the propositional representation. Marking of location of events is given explicitly, or by locating participants in an event. The analysis proceeds from a list of such markings and the assumption that by default the location of the next event is the same as the previous one unless a change is signaled. Such a list of discourse rules for marking frame relations forms the basis for mapping from propositions to narrative frame structure. These rules may be tested in text comprehension and production experiments, and are likely to be important to a theory of frame signaling processes in discourse production.

Frame analysis proceeds in a similar fashion for other types of frame structures. The analyst, using marking conventions and the propositional representation of a text, identifies elements (nodes and relations) specified by a particular frame grammar, and builds a frame representation as nodes and relations are identified. To illustrate a more complex type of frame structure, a problem frame analysis will be described for the sample text. Note that this text, like many, may be analyzed in terms of multiple frame structures. The text reflects a narrative frame, several state descriptions, and a series of problems and attempts at their solution. The problem frame reflects this last principle of structure.

Figure 8.5 presents the top-level syntax graphs for the problem frame. This frame structure includes as elements other types of frame structure generated by their own frame grammars: procedural frames and state and event description frames. BNF grammars for these frame types have been developed but will not be presented here. As may be seen from the topmost syntax graph (labeled "problem frame"), a problem frame has four components, the first of which is obligatory: (a) a goal or goal hierarchy (consisting of linked subgoals), (b) one or more problem state descriptions, (c) a set of goal-directed procedures (a procedure or procedural frame linked to a goal or subgoal), and (d) a set of problem solving events linked to goal, problem description, and procedure nodes in the network. This syntax reflects experience obtained studying a wide variety of problem texts (from stories to problem descriptions in science) and was influenced by Bruce's (1980) work on interacting plans and by models of problem solving (Newell & Simon, 1972). Consequently, the problem frame grammar is applicable to the analysis of think-aloud protocols in studies of problem solving, as well as to varieties of texts representing problems and their solutions.

The central structure in a problem frame is a goal hierarchy consisting of intersecting goal chains that form branching subgoal structures. Relations linking goal nodes in the network are conditional and temporal order relations. Linked to goal nodes are goal descriptions that represent descriptions of goal states or processes (i.e., states of the world to be attained). Also linked to goal nodes by conditional relations are problem description nodes. These are linked to descriptions of states or processes in the world upon which goals are conditioned. A goal, therefore, represents a state or process to be achieved when a problem state is encountered. Finally, also linked to goal nodes are goal-directed procedures that may consist of a single procedure or a procedural frame (i.e., a procedural hierarchy as outlined above). When the procedures are executed, the particular goal linked to them is attained. One additional aspect of the problem frame is the event component (problem-solving events) that enables the linking of events of various types to problem states, goals, and procedures. These represent various events by which one or more actors can attempt to achieve the goals represented in the problem frame. These categories of events are as follows: interpreting a problem description, adopting a goal, planning a procedure, enacting a procedure, events resolving a procedure (succeeding in achieving its goal), events blocking a procedure (preventing attainment of its goal), and responses to procedures (events that neither resolve nor block the attainment of its goal). This powerful grammar is capable of representing complex plot structure in stories in which characters adopt goals, plan and attempt to accomplish them, and

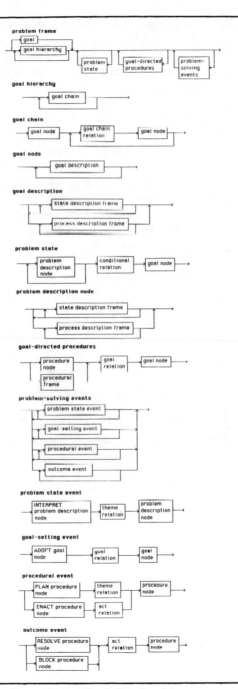

Figure 8.5   Problem Frame Syntax Graph (Top Levels)

block other characters' plans through their actions (Bruce & Newman, 1978).

The problem frame for "The Discovery of Penicillin" is summarized in outline form in Figure 8.6. In the text, two goals are identified: goal 1 (finding why the mold killed the germs, proposition 19.0) and goal 2 (finding a way to make penicillin, proposition 26.0). Goal 1 is marked by embedding in a goal case slot in proposition 19.0. The description of the goal state for goal 1 is represented in propositions 19.2-19.3. The event of proposition 19.0 marks adoption of the goal. The problem description is represented by 10.0-12.3 (descriptive frame propositions), and proposition 13.0 marks that the problem state was interpreted. Propositions 16.0-22.1 represent procedures (i.e., a procedural frame) for accomplishing goal 1. Each procedure is linked to other procedures by relations of temporal order (AFTER), conditionality (COND ON), and part-whole (HAS PART). The procedural frame grammar defines hierarchical structures consisting of patterns of procedures linked by these relations. Each of these procedures has events associated with it that enact or resolve the procedure.

Goal 2 (proposition 26.0) is not explicitly marked and therefore is inferred. It is linked to goal 1 by a conditional relation (it is conditional on goal 1) and temporal order. The description of goal 2 is represented in proposition 26.1 (indicating it was not adopted). The problem state is described in propositions 23.0-26.1, and only a single procedure is identified (proposition 27.2) which is blocked (26.0-26.1) and followed by a response (27.0-27.2).

Problem frame analysis is considerably more complex than narrative frame analysis. This complexity is attributable in part to the complexity of the problem frame syntax, and in part to the fact that texts often fail to make all aspects of the frame explicit. The problem frame does preserve aspects of the problem structure of these texts that transformations of the texts reveal. For example, a writer can modify, elaborate, or rephrase aspects of the problem structure, and the narrative frame will reflect these modifications appropriately. The mapping from a text and its propositional base involves both explicitly marked problem frame relations and inferences. Currently we keep the two distinct by marking all inferred problem frame elements (e.g., with a [in Figure 8.6). As problem frame analysis is used as a tool in research on comprehension and produc-

```
GOAL 1 "FIND CAUSE OF MOLD KILLING GERMS

        DESCRIPTION: 19 2-19 3 "CAUSE OF MOLD KILLING GERMS

            EVENT-ADOPT: 19 0

        PROBLEM: 19.1 "FIND OUT WHY

                    DESCRIPTION: 10 0-10 3
                    DESCRIPTION: 11 0-11 4
                    DESCRIPTION: 12 0-12 3

                        EVENT-INTERPRET: 13 0

        PROCEDURE: 14 0-14 1 (P1) "SCRAPE OFF MOLD

                    EVENT-ENACT: 14 0

        PROCEDURE: 15 0-15 5 (P2) "PUT WITH FOOD

                        AFTER P1
                        COND ON P1

                    EVENT-ENACT: 15 0

        [PROCEDURE (P3) "GROW MOLD

                        HAS PART P1
                        HAS PART P2

                        OUTCOME-RESOLVE: 16 0-16 1 "SPREAD
                        OUTCOME-RESOLVE: 17 0-17 3 "GROW LARGER

        PROCEDURE: 19 0 (P4) "SET TO WORK

                    AFTER P3

                    EVENT-ENACT: 19 0

        PROCEDURE: 20 0 (P5) "EXPERIMENT

                    AFTER P4

                    EVENT-ENACT: 20 0

        PROCEDURE: 20 3-20 6 (P6) "SQUEEZE DROPS

                    AFTER P5

                    EVENT-ENACT: 20 3

        PROCEDURE: 22 0-22 1 (P7) "NAME FLUID

                    AFTER P6

                    EVENT-ENACT: 22 0

        [PROCEDURE: EXTRACT GERM KILLER

                        AFTER P3
                        COND ON P3
                        PART OF P5
                        HAS PART P6

                        OUTCOME-RESOLVE: 21 0-21 1 "FLUID IS GERM KILLER

[GOAL 2 26 0 "FIND WAY TO MAKE PENICILLIN

                    AFTER G1
                    COND G1

        [DESCRIPTION: 26 1 "MAKING PENICILLIN IS PRACTICAL

                    EVENT-ADOPT: 26 0-26 1 (NEG)

        [PROBLEM: 28 1 "FIND PRACTICAL WAY TO MAKE PENICILLIN

                        DESCRIPTION: 23 0-23 5 "GREAT GERM KILLER
                        DESCRIPTION: 24 0: 24 2 "LONG TIME TO MAKE
                        DESCTIPTION: 25 0-25 1 "VARIABLE
                        DESCRIPTION: 26 1 "NOT PRACTICAL

        [PROCEDURE: 27 2 "WORK

                        OUTCOME-BLOCK: 26 0-26 1 "DECIDE NOT PRACTICAL
                        OUTCOME-RESPONSE: 27 0-27 2 "GO ON WITH OTHER WORK

[GOAL 3 29 0 (PROPERTY OF GOAL 4) "HELP WOUNDED

        PROBLEM: 29 2 "HELP WOUNDED

                    DESCRIPTION: 29 3-29 4 "PEOPLE WOUNDED

GOAL 4 29 0 "FIND NEW MEDICINE

                    COND FOR G3 (SUBGOAL)
                    BEFORE G3

        DESCRIPTION: 29 1 "NEW MEDICINE

                    EVENT-ADOPT: 29 0

        [PROBLEM: 30 2 "FIND NEW MEDICINE (ANSWER)

        PROCEDURE: 29 0 "LOOK FOR NEW MEDICINE

                    EVENT-ENACT: 29 0

                        OUTCOME-RESOLVE: 30 0-30 2 "PENICILLIN SEEM LIKE ANSWER

        GOAL 5 31 0 "MAKE PENICILLIN
```

Figure 8.6   Summary of Problem Frame for "The Discovery of Penicillin"

tion of problems and texts describing their solution, the marking of problem frame information should become better specified.

APPLICATIONS OF COGNITIVE DISCOURSE ANALYSIS

In our research on cognitive processes in discourse communication, we have been using propositional and frame analysis as tools to study children's text comprehension and story production. This research is currently being extended to comprehension and knowledge acquisition in secondary level science, writing in secondary school, and problem solving in clinical case comprehension and diagnosis (Patel & Frederiksen, in press).

In the research on children's text comprehension, we are completing a series of experiments investigating elementary school children's comprehension of texts that reflect different types of frame structures. After listening to or reading an experimental text, children are asked to recall the content of the text in their own words. For larger or more complex expository texts, probes are used to stimulate recall of sections of the text. The experimental text is first segmented into clausal units and then a discourse analysis is carried out using the propositional and frame grammars. First, the text is analyzed in terms of propositions that represent the semantic content of all text segments. Then, frame analyses are carried out using this propositional structure as a semantic text base. A subject's recall is coded against the propositional structure, as a proposition recalled, the basis for an inference, or both. Detailed scoring procedures have been worked out for this coding.

The results are analyzed at several different levels. First, global measures of comprehension are obtained by computing the total number of propositions recalled, the total number of propositions that formed the basis for inferences, or both. The first measure reflects the amount of literal semantic information recalled by the subjects, the second reflects inferential processing of the text, and the third reflects inferences more closely associated with specifying meaning at the propositional level. Second, recall and inference measures are obtained for sets of propositions that reflect different frame-level semantic structures. By expressing measures of recall and inference for propositions associated with particular frame structures as percentages, it is possible to measure the conditional probability of recalling a proposition given that it reflects a particular frame structure. If frame structures are being generated by a reader to process text propositions selectively, these probabilities should vary as a function of frame structure, reflecting the processing of text propositions in terms of frame structures. Furthermore, if an experimental text reflects more than one frame structure, then we can investigate subjects' comprehension of the text in terms of one frame structure versus another.

These methods were applied first in two experiments investigating subjects' comprehension of stories that varied in their frame structures (Frederiksen & Frederiksen, 1982). One story consisted of a conversational structure in which characters confronted and solved a problem by means of dialogue over the telephone. This story reflects narrative, conversational, and problem frame structures. A second story studied was a Russian folktale that reflected a relatively complex problem frame enacted through narrative events. In this story, conversation was minimal and did not serve an important function in acting out characters' plans for resolving the story's problem. Children studied were at three grade levels (primary 2, 3, and 5) and differences in recall of frame structures in groups of children at different levels of global recall were also studied. The results for the conversational story indicated that while conversational frames are relatively well understood (as reflected in analysis of propositions recalled and inferences for conversation frame propositions), problem frame structures are much more difficult for these children. Comprehension of the story's problem structure was best in older children, while comprehension of the conversational structure was not better in older than younger children. Children at higher levels of recall of propositional content showed greater frame effects, that is, they structured the story more in terms of both conversational and problem frames. When results for the second story, the folktale, were analyzed, results confirmed the finding that problem frames were relatively difficult and are still developing during elementary school.

In our second series of studies of expository text comprehension, we have been investigating subjects' differential abilities in comprehending science texts that reflect different types of frame structures. The four experimental texts were all written by the same author and published in an elementary school supplementary science series. All texts were on the same subject (molds) and employed clause and propositional structures of about the same complexity.

The four texts differed in the types of frame-level information they expressed—a narrative (about the discovery of penicillin), a procedure (for growing a mold culture), a description (of mold spores as seen through a microscope), and an explanation (of the role of molds in the food cycle). Since the children had not studied these topics, it was presumed that the texts could not be understood in terms of prior knowledge by most students. Subjects in the study were students in primary grades 3 and 5.

Each of these texts was analyzed in terms of its propositional structure and frame analyses were carried out using grammars for narrative, problem, procedural, descriptive, and explanatory frames. Measures of global recall and inference, and of the likelihood of recall of particular frame structures, were analyzed. Since subjects read and recalled all four texts, it was possible to investigate comprehension abilities for different types of frame structures within subjects. In a global analysis of all four texts, we found that some frame structures are more easily understood than others, and that some exhibit developmental change during this period more than do others. The narrative text was better understood than any of the others, with the procedure a close second. However, the descriptions were relatively difficult for the children, and the explanation was not well understood by any of the subjects. Developmental differences were most prevalent for the descriptive and explanatory texts, and least for the narrative.

Results of analyses of subjects' comprehension of the narrative and problem frame structures for the narrative text (the one analyzed in this paper) were parallel to those obtained for the stories in the previous study. All subjects showed evidence of structuring text events in terms of a narrative frame. There was evidence as well that some subjects (particularly those at higher levels of propositional recall) also structured the events in terms of the problem frame structure. That is, they showed preferences for various types of problem frame information. There were few developmental differences, and those that occurred appeared in measures reflecting comprehension of the problem structure of the text. These results support the view that children understand these texts by applying rules associated with particular kinds of semantic frame structure, and that they differ in their facility with or knowledge of rules for different types of frame structures. Furthermore, children differ in how they understand the same text. One may understand "The Discovery of Penicillin" as a narrative, while another may understand it in terms of the problems that the scientists were trying to solve.

In a final set of experiments in this series, we have replicated the expository text study but with texts that are more complex and in a different content area (dinosaurs). Analyses of these data will enable us to test the hypothesis that the rules subjects use in comprehending expository texts are independent of specific content, providing important evidence for the generality of frame production rules.

A second area of discourse processing in which we have been applying the cognitive discourse analysis procedures described here is the study of children's oral story production. In a collaboration with Robert Bracewell and Janet Donin Frederiksen, we have recently completed a study of elementary school children's story production in English (Frederiksen et al., 1985) and French (Rahming, Frederiksen, & Frederiksen, 1985). In this study, children viewed a sequence of pictures depicting a series of related events, and afterwards were asked to tell a story to accompany the pictures as they viewed them a second time. Some children were asked to produce a conversational structure for their story, and others a narrative account of the events that took place. Story productions were analyzed in terms of production of narrative and conversational frame structures. When measures reflecting the production of these structures were analyzed, the results indicated that children were able to control their production of narrative and conversational structures. However, they were more successful in producing narrative than conversational frames. The former were quite elaborated, and the latter were relatively simple. Furthermore, detailed analysis of specific aspects of frame structures the children produced revealed different patterns for specific aspects of frame structure predicted by the grammars. For example, in the conversational frame, children were in general relatively successful in producing turn taking sequences, but only older children were able to produce sequences of conversational acts that showed illocutionary dependencies (such as request-response-acknowledgment sequences generated by the grammar). Furthermore, these results were replicated across languages when a similar sample of French-speaking children were tested using the same tasks.

Thus, we have evidence that children use specific frame-production rules, and that these rules are language independent (as they should be if they reflect semantic representations). We have also analyzed the topical structure of the children's stories, examining correspondences between topical structure (an aspect of "text surface structure") and frame structure (an aspect of "deep semantic structure"). Results indicate that topicalization of information appears to closely follow the underlying semantic frame structure, consistent with the view that topicalization operates to signal frame structure to a reader by establishing a perspective on the text content (Frederiksen et al., 1985; Bracewell & Frederiksen, 1985).

The results we have obtained thus far in our production studies are consistent with the rule-based model of text production outlined earlier. Because these children were also tested using a story comprehension task, it will be possible to compare their ability to apply frame-production rules in text comprehension and production tasks. The rule-based model of discourse processing predicts that there should be a close relationship of text production and comprehension abilities.

In current studies of text comprehension, writing, and problem solving, the discourse analysis tools outlined in this chapter are being applied to more advanced comprehension and production in secondary and postsecondary students. We have found the discourse analysis methods to be applicable to the analysis of more complex texts, and to the experimental study of advanced discourse-processing skills.

APPENDIX A
Syntax for Propositions (BNF Notation)

The following are meta-symbols: ::=   <> | {}   @

P1   <proposition> ::= <proposition number> <content>
                     {<tense and aspect>,} {<modality>,}
                     <truth value> {,<truth value>};

P2   <proposition number> ::= . <integer>

P3   <content> ::= <state> | <event> | <algebraic relation> |
                  <dependency relation> | <identity relation> |
                  <propositional relation>

P4   <modality> ::= MOD: <modal>

P5   <modal> ::= QUAL | ROOT | CAN | COND

P6   <truth value> ::= POS | NEG | INT

STATES

P7   <state> ::= {<object>} <state argument>

P8   <state argument> ::= <identifying relation> |
                         <determination & quantification>

P9   <object> ::= <determined object> | <pronoun identifier>

P10 <determined object> ::= <object identifier> (<determiner>)

P11 <determiner> ::= <nongeneric> | <generic>

P12 <nongeneric> ::= <nongeneric determiner> ,
                      <nongeneric quantifier> ,

P13 <nongeneric determiner> ::= DEF | TOK

P14 <nongeneric quantifier> ::= NUM: <number>
                                      {,<degree relation>}

P15 <generic> ::= GEN , <generic quantifier> ,

P16 <generic quantifier> ::= <universal quantifier> |
                             <null quantifier>

P17 <universal quantifier> ::= UNIV: {<universal identifier>}

P18 <null quantifier> ::= NULL: {<null identifier>}

P19 <identifying relation> ::=
                  <category relation> | <part relation> |
                  <theme relation> | <attribute relation> |
                  <locative relation> | <temporal relation> |

(continued)

APPENDIX A (Continued)

```
                    <durative relation>  |  <number relation>

P20   <category relation> ::= CAT: {<category>}  ,

P21   <part relation> ::= PRT: {<part>}  ,

P22   <theme relation> ::= THM: <theme>  ,

P23   <theme> ::= {<concept>}  | {<proposition label>}

P24   <attribute relation> ::= ATT: {<attribute>}  ,

P25   <attribute> ::= <attribute identifier> {,<degree relation>}
                      {(<attribute relation>)}         .

P26   <locative relation> ::= LOC: {<locative>}  ,

P27   <locative> ::= <location> {,<degree relation>}
                                {(<locative relation>)}

P28   <temporal relation> ::= TEM: {<time>
                                   {,<degree relation>}}  ,

P29   <durative relation> ::= DUR: {<duration>
                                   {, <degree relation>}}  ,

P30   <number relation> ::= NUM: {<number>
                                 {,<degree relation>}}  ,

P31   <degree relation> ::= DEG: <degree>   {,<degree relation>}

P32   <determination & quantification> ::=
            <nongeneric determination & quantification> | <generic>

P33   <nongeneric determination and quantification> ::=
                  <nongeneric> {<determination & quantification>}

P34   <tense & aspect> ::= <tense>  {,<aspect>}

P35   <tense> ::= PAST | PRES | FUT

P36   <aspect> ::= ASPCT: <aspect value>

P37   <aspect value> ::= CONT | COMP | INCPT | CESS | ITER


                              EVENTS

P38   <event> ::= @<act identifier>  <case frame> %
                                     {<identifying relation>}

P39   <case frame> ::=
            <processive case frame> | <resultive case frame>

P40   <processive case frame> ::=
                  @<patient relation>  @<object relation>
                  @<instrument relation>  @<act relation>
                  @<recipient relation>  @<goal relation>
```

APPENDIX A (Continued)

```
                        @<theme relation>

P41   <patient relation> ::= PAT:  {<object>}  ,

P42   <object relation> ::= OBJ:  {<object>}  ,

P43   <instrument relation> ::= INST:  {<object>}  ,

P44   <act relation> ::= ACT:  <related act>  ,

P45   <related act> ::= {<act identifier>}  |  {<proposition label>}

P46   <recipient relation> ::= REC:  {<object>}  ,

P47   <goal relation> ::= GOAL:  <goal>  ,

P48   <goal> ::= {<concept>}  |  {<proposition label>}

P49   <theme relation> ::= THM:  <theme>  ,

P50   <resultive case frame> ::=
                        @<agent relation>  @<object relation>
                        @<instrument relation>  @<act relation>
                        @<recipient relation>  @<source relation>
                        @<result relation>  @<goal relation>
                        @<theme relation>

P51   <agent relation> ::= AGT:  {<object>}  ,

P52   <source relation> ::= SOURCE:  <source>  ,

P53   <source> ::= {<object>}  |  {<proposition label>}

P54   <result relation> ::= RSLT:  <result>  ,

P55   <result> ::= {<object>}  |  {<proposition label>}


                        ALGEBRAIC RELATIONS

P56   <algebraic relation> ::= <relation name> @<type>
                                       [ <variable> ]   ,
                                       [ <variable> ]   ,

P57   <relation name> ::= EQUIV:  | <order> | PROX:  | P-ORD:  |
                                <operation sequence>

P58   <order> ::= ORD:  | ORD:SUP:

P59   <operation sequence> ::= <operation>  {,<operation>}   :

P60   <operation> ::= <operation type>  =  {<operation value>}

P61   <operation type> ::= DIST | DIFF | SUM | MULT | DIV |
                                <function identifier>

P62   <operation value> ::= <measure>  | <real number>  | <integer>  |
                                <interval>  | <function value identifier>
```

(continued)

APPENDIX A (Continued)

```
P63   <type> ::= ATT: | LOC: | TEM: | DUR: | NUM: | DEG: |
                          <operation type>

P64   <variable> ::= {<proposition label>} | {<concept>}
```

DEPENDENCY RELATIONS

```
P65   <dependency relation> ::=
                  <binary dependency> | <conjoint dependency>

P66   <binary dependency> ::= <binary dependency relation>
                          [ {<proposition label>} | ]  ,
                          [ {<proposition label>} | ]

P67   <binary dependency relation> ::= CAU: | COND: | IF: | IFF:

P68   <conjoint dependency> ::= <conjoint dependency relation>
                          [ <conjoint dependency argument> ]  ,
                          [ <conjoint dependency argument> ]
                      {, [ <conjoint dependency argument> ]  }

P69   <conjoint dependency relation> ::= AND: | OR-EXCL: | OR-ALT:

P70   <conjoint dependency argument> ::=
                      {<concept>} | {<proposition label>}
```

IDENTITY RELATIONS

```
P71   <identity relation> ::= IDENT: [ <identity argument> ]  ,
                                     [ <identity argument> ]
                                 {, [ <identity argument> ]  }

P72   <identity argument> ::= {<concept>} | {<proposition label>}
```

PROPOSITIONAL RELATIONS

```
P73   <propositional relation> ::=
                      {<proposition label>} <identifying relation>
```

CONCEPTS

```
P74   <concept> ::=
          <act identifier> | <object> | <attribute identifier> |
          <location> | <time> | <duration> | <degree> | <number>

P75   <location> ::=
          <location identifier> | <object> | <act identifier> |

P76   <coordinates> ::= COORD: <measure> {, <measure>}

P77   <measure> ::= <real number> <unit identifier>
                      <coordinates>

P78   <time> ::=
```

APPENDIX A (Continued)

<measure> | <time identifier> | <measure pair>

P79   <duration> ::=
          <measure> | <duration identifier> | <measure pair>

P80   <degree> ::=<measure> | <degree identifier> | <measure pair>

P81   <number> ::= <integer> | <number identifier> | <integer pair>

P82   <integer pair> ::= <integer> , <integer>

P83   <interval> ::=
          <measure pair> | <integer pair> | <real number pair>

P84   <measure pair> ::= <measure> , <measure>

P85   <real number pair> ::= <real number> , <real number>

P86   <category> ::=
          <object> | <act identifier> | <proposition label>

P87   <part> ::= <object> | <act identifier> | <proposition label>

P88   <proposition label> ::=
          <proposition identifier> | <proposition number>

Notes on BNF Metasymbols:

::= denotes replacement of a symbol with the symbols that follow

< > enclose symbols (terminal symbols are identifiers, pronouns,
          integers or real numbers)

| denotes selection

{ } denotes optional repetition of the enclosed symbols

@   denotes optional symbol

Capital letters, square brackets, parantheses, %, =, and
          punctuation are literals.

APPENDIX B
Propositional Analysis of "The Discovery of Penicillin"

No.	Predicate	Arguments
1.0	WORK	PAT: ALEXANDER FLEMING, % LOC:LABORATORY, PAST, ASPCT: CONT;
1.1	POSSESS	PAT: HIS, OBJ: LABORATORY;
1.2	LABORATORY	LOC: *AT* ST.MARY'S HOSPITAL, % ;
1.3	ST.MARY'S HOSP.	LOC: *IN* LONDON, ENGLAND;
2.0	DAY	ATT: WARM, PAST;
3.0	WINDOWS	ATT: OPEN, PAST;
4.0	LEAVE	OBJ: DISH, RSLT: 4.1, % PAST, ASPCT: COMP;
4.1	DISH	ATT: UNCOVERED;
4.2	GERMS	LOC: DISH;
4.3	GERMS	ATT: DISEASE;
4.4	NEED	OBJ: GERMS, GOAL: EXPERIMENTATION, % ;
5.0	LOOK LIKE	OBJ: IT, THEME: 5.1, % PAST;
5.1	PROX:	[IT], [SOUP];
5.2	SOUP	ATT: CLOUDY;
6.0	WALK BY	PAT: FLEMING, % TEM: *AS*, PAST;
7.0	GLANCE AT	PAT: HE, OBJ: DISH, % TEM: , PAST;
7.1	EQUIV:TEM:	[6.0], [7.0];
8.0	CATCH EYE	PAT: HIS, OBJ: SOMETHING, % PAST;
9.0	LOOK	PAT: HE, % PAST, ASPCT:ITER *AGAIN*;
10.0	GROW	PAT: PATCH, % LOC: DISH, PAST, ASPCT:CONT;
10.1	MOLD	CAT: PATCH;
10.2	MOLD	ATT: BLUE-GREEN;
10.3	MOLD	CAT: PENICILLIUM;
11.0	SOUP	ATT: CLOUDY;
11.1	SOUP	ATT: THICK;
11.2	CAU:*WITH*	[GERMS], [11.1];

APPENDIX B (Continued)

11.3	CIRCLE	LOC: *ALL AROUND* MOLD, PAST;
11.4	CIRCLE	ATT: CLEAR, PAST;
12.0	GERMS	LOC: NEAR;
12.1	MOLD	LOC: ;
12.2	PROX:LOC:	[12.0], [12.1];
12.3	GERMS	ATT: DEAD, PAST;
13.0	KNOW	PAT: FLEMING, THM: 13.1, 13.2, % PAST;
13.1	IDENT:	[THIS], [SOMETHING];
13.2	SOMETHINC	ATT: IMPORTANT;
14.0	SCRAPE OFF	ACT: HE, OBJ: BIT, % PAST;
14.1	MOLD	PRT: BIT;
15.0	PUT	AGT: AND, OBJ: IT, RSLT: 15.1, 15.2, 15.3, 15.4, 15.5, % PAST;
15.1	IT	LOC: *IN* DISH;
15.2	FOOD	DEG: SOME;
15.3	FOOD	LOC: ;
15.4	PROX:*WITH*	[15.1], [15.3];
15.5	OWN	PAT: ITS, OBJ: DISH, % ;
16.0	SPREAD	PAT: MOLD, % PAST;
16.1	PLANT	CAT: MOLD;
17.0	GROW	AGT: PATCH, RSLT: 17.1, % PAST;
17.1	ORD:ATT:	[17.2], [ ];
17.2	PATCH	ATT: LARGER, DEG: ;
17.3	PATCH	ATT: BLUE-GREEN;
18.0	IT	ATT: BIG, DEG:*ENOUGH*, TEM: WHEN, PAST;
19.0	SET TO WORK	PAT: FLEMING, GOAL: 19.1, % TEM: , PAST;
19.1	FIND OUT	THM: 19.2, % ;
19.2	CAU:	[WHY], [19.3];
19.3	KILL	AGT: MOLD, OBJ: GERMS, % PAST, ASPCT:COMP;
19.4	EQUIV:TEM:	[18.0], [19.0];

(continued)

APPENDIX B (Continued)

20.0	EXPERIMENTS	DUR: MANY WEEKS, ATT: DIFFICULT, TEM: AFTER;
20.1	ORD:TEM:	[20.0], [20.2];
20.2	MANAGE	PAT: HE, ACT: 20.3, % ATT: FINALLY, TEM: , PAST;
20.3	SQUEEZE	SOURCE: MOLD, RSLT: 20.4, 20.5, 20.6;
20.4	DROPS	NUM: FEW;
20.5	FLUID	ATT: BROWNISH;
20.6	FLUID	PRT: DROPS;
21.0	IDENT:	[FLUID], [GERM-KILLER];
21.1	FLUID	ATT: REMARKABLE;
22.0	NAME	AGT: FLEMING, OBJ: IT, RSLT: 22.1, % PAST;
22.1	EQUIV:	[IT], [PENICILLIN];
23.0	TURN OUT	OBJ: PENICILLIN, RSLT: 23.1, 23.2, 23.3, 23.4, 23.5, % PAST;
23.1	GERM-KILLER	CAT: PENICILLIN;
23.2	GERM-KILLER	ATT: GREATER, DEG: FAR, DEG: ;
23.3	ORD:DEG:	[23.2], [23.4];
23.4	ANYTHING	ATT:*GREATER*, DEG: ;
23.5	KNOW	OBJ: ANYTHING, % TEM:BEFORE, PAST;
24.0	TAKE	ACT: 24.1, % DUR: SO LONG, PAST;
24.1	MAKE	RSLT: DROP, % ;
24.2	IT	PRT: DROP;
25.0	DRUG	CAT: IT, PAST;
25.1	DRUG	ATT: VALUABLE, QUAL:*SURELY*;
26.0	DECIDE	AGT: FLEMING, THM: 26.1, % PAST;
26.1	MAKE	RSLT: PENICILLIN, % ATT: PRACTICAL, PAST, NEG;
27.0	GO ON	PAT: HE, ACT:*WITH*27.1, 27.2, % TEM: , PAST;
27.1	OTHER	PAT: HIS, % ;
27.2	WORK	CAT: OTHER;

REFERENCES

Anderson, J., & Bower, G. H. (1973). *Human associative memory.* Washington, DC: Winston.

Anderson, J., & Ortony, A. (1975). On putting apples into bottles—a problem of polysemy. *Cognitive Psychology, 7,* 167-180.

Bartlett, F. (1932). *Remembering.* Cambridge: Cambridge University Press.

Bobrow, D. G., & Norman, D. A. (1975). Some principles of memory schemata. In D. G. Bobrow & A. M. Collins (Eds.), *Representation and understanding: Studies in cognitive science.* New York: Academic Press.

Bracewell, R. J., & Frederiksen, C. H. (1985, March). *Children's story production: Signalling frame structure with text structure.* Paper presented at the annual meeting of the American Educational Research Association, Chicago.

Bransford, Q., & Franks, J. J. (1971). The abstraction of linguistic ideas. *Cognitive Psychology, 3,* 193-209.

Bruce, B. (1980). Plans and social actions. In R. J. Spiro, B. C. Bruce, & W. F. Brewer (Eds.), *Theoretical issues in reading comprehension.* Hillsdale, NJ: Lawrence Erlbaum.

Bruce, B. (1983). Plans and discourse. *Text, 3,* 253-259.

Bruce, B., & Newman, D. (1978). Interacting plans. *Cognitive Science, 2,* 195-233.

Charolles, M. (1983). Coherence as a principle in the interpretation of discourse. *Text, 3,* 71-97.

Clements, P. (1976). The effects of staging on recall from prose. In R. Freedle (Ed.), *Advances in discourse processing* (Vol. 2). Norwood, NJ: Ablex.

Collins, A., Brown, J. S., & Larkin, K. M. (1980). Inference in text understanding. In R. Spiro, B. Bruce, & W. Brewer (Eds.), *Theoretical issues in reading comprehension.* Hillsdale, NJ: Lawrence Erlbaum.

Dijk, T. van, & Kintsch, W. (1984). *Strategies of discourse comprehension.* New York: Academic Press.

Dixon, P. (1982). Plans and written directions for complex tasks. *Journal of Verbal Learning and Verbal Behavior, 21,* 70-84.

Ericsson, K. A., & Simon, H. A. (1984). *Protocol analysis: Verbal reports as data.* Cambridge: MIT Press.

Frederiksen, C. H. (1975). Representing logical and semantic structure of knowledge acquired from discourse. *Cognitive Psychology, 7,* 371-485.

Frederiksen, C. H. (1977). Semantic processing units in understanding text. In R. Freedle (Ed.), *Discourse processes: Advances in theory and research* (Vol. 1). Norwood, NJ: Ablex.

Frederiksen, C. H. (1981). Inference in preschool children's conversations: A cognitive perspective. In J. Greene & C. Wallat (Eds.), *Language and ethnography in educational settings.* Norwood, NJ: Ablex.

Frederiksen, C. H. (1984, August). *Frame construction in children's discourse communication.* Paper presented at the meeting of the American Psychological Association, Toronto.

Frederiksen, C. H., & Frederiksen, J. D. (1982, March). The relationship of frame construction and comprehension of school-type text. In *Multidisciplinary perspectives on cognition and language.* Symposium conducted at the meeting of the American Educational Research Association, New York.

Frederiksen, C. H., Frederiksen, J. D., & Bracewell, R. J. (1985). Discourse analysis of children's text production. In A. Matsuhashi (Ed.), *Writing in real time*. New York: Longmans.

Graesser, A. C., Hoffman, N. L., & Clark, L. F. (1980). Structural components of reading time. *Journal of Verbal Learning and Verbal Behavior, 19,* 135-151.

Grimes, J. (1975). *The thread of discourse.* The Hague: Mouton.

Groen, G., Frederiksen, C. H., & Dillinger, M. (1984). A propositional analyst's assistant. *Behavior Research Methods, Instruments & Computers, 16,* 154-157.

Halliday, M.A.K., & Hasan, R. (1976). *Cohesion in English.* New York: Longmans.

Hobbs, J. R. (1979). Coherence and coreference. *Cognitive Science, 3,* 67-90.

Kieras, D. E. (1981). Component processes in the comprehension of simple prose. *Journal of Verbal Learning and Verbal Behavior, 20,* 1-23.

Kintsch, W. (1974). *The representation of meaning in memory.* Hillsdale, NJ: Lawrence Erlbaum.

Kintsch, W., & van Dijk, T. (1978). Toward a model of text comprehension and production. *Psychological Review, 85,* 363-394.

Mandler, J. M., & Johnson, N. S. (1977). Remembrance of things parsed: Story structure and recall. *Cognitive Psychology, 9,* 111-151.

Meyer, B.J.F. (1975). *The organization of prose and its effects on memory.* Amsterdam: North Holland.

Minsky, M. (1975). Chapter in P. H. Winston (Ed.), *The psychology of computer vision.* New York: McGraw-Hill.

Newell, A., & Simon, H. A. (1972). *Human problem solving.* Englewood Cliffs, NJ: Prentice-Hall.

Palmer, S. (1978). Fundamental aspects of cognitive representation. In E. Rosch, (Ed.), *Cognition and categorization.* Hillsdale, NJ: Lawrence Erlbaum.

Patel, V., & Frederiksen, C. H. (1983). Cognitive processes in comprehension and knowledge acquisition by medical students and physicians. In M. C. Devolder & H. G. Schmidt (Eds.), *Tutorials in problem-based learning.* Assen, Holland: Gorcum.

Patel, V., & Frederiksen, C. H. (in press). Knowledge representation and interpretation by medical students and physicians. *Journal of Medical Education.*

Plante, P. (1985). *La structure des donnees et des algorithmes en DEREDEC.* Neuchatel, Switzerland: Travaux du Centre de Recherches Semiologiques.

Polanyi, L., & Scha, R.J.H. (1983). The syntax of discourse. *Text, 3,* 261-270.

Quillian, R. (1968). Semantic memory. In M. Minsky (Ed.), *Semantic information processing.* Cambridge: MIT Press.

Rumelhart, D. E. (1975). Notes on a schema for stories. In D. G. Bobrow & A. Collins (Eds.), *Representation and understanding: Studies in cognitive science.* New York: Academic Press.

Rumelhart, D. E. (1980). Schemata: the building blocks of cognition. In R. J. Spiro, B. C. Bruce & W. F. Brewer (Eds.), *Theoretical issues in reading comprehension.* Hillsdale, NJ: Lawrence Erlbaum.

Rumelhart, D.E., & Norman, D.A. (1975). The active structural network. In D. A. Norman, D. E. Rumelhart, & the LNR Research Group (Eds.), *Explorations in cognition.* San Francisco: W. H. Freeman.

Schank, R. (1972). Conceptual dependency: A theory of natural language understanding. *Cognitive Psychology, 3,* 552-631.

Schank, R., & Abelson, R. P. (1977). *Scripts, plans, goals, and understanding: An inquiry into human knowledge structures.* Hillsdale, NJ: Lawrence Erlbaum.

Spiro, R. (1980). Constructive processes in prose comprehension and recall. In R. J. Spiro, B. C. Bruce, & W. F. Brewer (Eds.), *Theoretical issues in reading comprehension.* Hillsdale, NJ: Lawrence Erlbaum.

Stein, N., & Glenn, C. G. (1979). An analysis of story comprehension. In R. O. Freedle (Ed.), *New directions in discourse processing* (Vol. 2). Norwood, NJ: Ablex.

Tierney, R. J., & Mosenthal, J. (1982). Discourse comprehension and production: Analyzing text structure and cohesion. In J. Langer & M. Smith-Burke (Eds.), *Reader meets author/bridging the gap: A psycholinguistic and sociolinguistic perspective.* Newark, DE: International Reading Association.

Trabasso, T., & Nichols, D. W. (1978). Memory and inferences in comprehending narratives. In J. Becker & F. Wilkins (Eds.), *Information integration by children.* Hillsdale, NJ: Lawrence Erlbaum.

Trabasso, T., & Sperry, L. (in press). Causal relatedness and importance of story events. *Journal of Memory and Language.*

van den Broek, P., & Trabasso, T. (in press). Causal networks vs. goal hierarchies in summarizing text. *Discourse Processes.*

Vilain, M. (1985). *An approach to hybrid knowledge representation.* Cambridge, MA: BBN Laboratories.

Winograd, T. (1983). *Language as a cognitive process: Syntax.* Reading, MA: Addison-Wesley.

Wirth, N. (1976). *Algorithms + data structures = programs.* Englewood Cliffs, NJ: Prentice-Hall.

About the Authors

Wallace Chafe is a linguist at the University of California at Berkeley. He has been particularly interested in the study of discourse and in cognitive factors underlying language production. Initially he focused these concerns on spoken language, with reference to both American Indian languages and English. He was the director of a well-known study comparing subjects' retellings of the events in a prepared film, the so-called pear stories project (*The Pear Stories: Cognitive, Cultural, and Linguistic Aspects of Narrative Production*, 1980). More recently he has been concerned with the special properties of written language. He has been investigating differences between spoken and written language since 1980, and is currently working on a book-length treatment of that subject.

Roger D. Cherry teaches in the English Department at New Mexico State University. He is a coauthor (with Lester L. Faigley, David Jolliffe, and Anna Skinner) of *Assessing Writer's Knowledge and Processes of Composing* (1985). His current research interests include the role of *ethos* in written discourse and the relationships among speech act theory, pragmatics, and rhetorical theory.

Charles R. Cooper conducts writing workshops and teaches courses in composition studies in the Department of Literature, University of California, San Diego. With Lee Odell, he has edited *Research on Composing* (1978) and *Evaluating Writing* (1977). He has recently edited *Research on Response to Literature and the Teaching of Literature* (1984) and written a college rhetoric, *The St. Martin's Guide to Writing* (1985, with Rise Axelrod). He is currently studying the development of writing ability from childhood through adulthood.

Jan Firbas is Director of Linguistic Studies, Department of English, University of Brno, Czechoslovakia, where he coedits *Brno Studies in English*. He has also taught at universities in Germany, Bulgaria, India, The Netherlands, England, and the United States. His writings mainly concern functional sentence perspective and have appeared mostly in *Brno Studies in English*.

Carl H. Frederiksen teaches in the Faculty of Education, McGill University, Montreal. He was trained in cognitive and mathematical psychology at Harvard University's Center for Cognitive Studies and the University of Illinois, where he received his doctorate in psychology. He spent three years at the National Institute of Education in the United States, where he was instrumental in establishing the Center for the Study of Reading and organizing the National Conference on Writing. He has published frequently on topics related to text comprehension and discourse processing. In 1975 he published a much-referenced paper introducing a model for the propositional representation of discourse. He coedited *Writing: Process, Development and Communication* (with J.F. Dominic) and is currently working on a book entitled *Knowledge and Inference in Discourse Communication,* which reports in detail on work described in his chapter in the present volume.

Sidney Greenbaum is Quain Professor of English Language and Literature at University College, London, and Director of the Survey of English Usage. His books include *Studies in English Adverbial Usage* (1969), *Elicitation Experiments in English: Linguistic Studies in Use and Attitude* (with Randolph Quirk, 1970), *A Grammar of Contemporary English* (with Randolph Quirk, Geoffrey Leech, and Jan Svartvik, 1972), *Acceptability in Language* (1977), *The English Language Today* (1985), and *A Comprehensive Grammar of the English Language* (with Randolph Quirk, Geoffrey Leech, and Jan Svartvik, 1985). He is currently working on books on English grammar, usage, and style.

Michael Hoey is a Lecturer in English Language Research at the University of Birmingham. He is the author of a book on written discourse, *On the Surface of Discourse* (1983), a monograph on ways of analyzing discourse, *Signalling in Discourse,* and many articles. He is currently writing a book on the organizing function of cohesion and a monograph on narrative matrices.

Chaim Rabin has been Cowley Lecturer in Post-Biblical Hebrew at
Oxford (1943-1956) and Professor of Hebrew Language at the Hebrew University of Jerusalem (1956-1985). He has written on Hebrew, Arabic, and Semitic linguistics, history of the Hebrew language, loanwords in Hebrew, and Afroasiatic (Hamito-Semitic)
etymology. In the field of general linguistics, he has written on
semantics, discourse analysis, sociolinguistics, language varieties and
normativism, problems of second-language learning, and the
sociology and linguistics of translation.

William J. Vande Kopple teaches composition and linguistics and
coordinates the Freshman English Program at Calvin College in
Grand Rapids, Michigan. He has published in *College Composition and
Communication* and *Research in the Teaching of English* on aspects of the
theory of functional sentence perspective, in the *Journal of Psycholinguistic Research* on the given-new strategy of comprehension, and
most recently in *College Composition and Communication* on metadiscourse. Currently he is studying topic continuity in kinds of written
English texts, and with Avon Crismore he is conducting a study of
how different readers read and react to kinds of metadiscourse.

Teun A. van Dijk is Professor of Discourse Studies at the University
of Amsterdam. His earlier research was in the fields of literary
scholarship, text grammar, and the psychology of text processing.
He is now primarily engaged in the social psychology of discourse,
with special applications in the study of news and ethnic prejudice.
His books include *Some Aspects of Text Grammars* (1972), *Text and
Context* (1977), *Macrostructures* (1980), *Issues in the Pragmatics of Discourse* (1981), *Strategies of Discourse Comprehension* (with Walter
Kintsch, 1983), *Prejudice in Discourse* (1984), and *News as Discourse* (in
press). He edited the *Handbook of Discourse Analysis* (4 vols., 1985),
and is editor of the journal *Text*.

Stephen P. Witte, until his recent resignation, taught in the English
Department at the University of Texas at Austin. He now works with
Information Transfer Services, a company that does contract work
on communication problems and evaluation for businesses, government agencies, and educational institutions. He is currently
coeditor (with John Daly) of *Written Communication: A Quarterly Journal of Research, Theory, and Application*. His essays have appeared in

College Composition and Communication and in *Research in the Teaching of English,* as well as in several edited volumes. His "Topical Structure and Revision: An Exploratory Study" was given the 1984 Richard Braddock Memorial Award by the Conference on College Composition and Communication. His *Evaluating College Writing Programs* (coauthored with Lester L. Faigley) appeared in 1983.